Toward a More Perfect Union

Toward a More Perfect Union

The Governance of Metropolitan America

RALPH W. CONANT
DANIEL J. MYERS

Second Edition

Chandler & Sharp Publishers, Inc.
NOVATO, CALIFORNIA

Chandler & Sharp Publishers, Inc.
11 Commercial Boulevard, Ste. A
Novato, CA 94949

ISBN 0-88316-577-5
Library of Congress Cataloging-in-Publication Data

Conant, Ralph Wendell, 1926–
    Toward a more perfect union : the governance of metropolitan america / by Ralph W. Conant and Daniel J. Myers. 2nd ed.
        p. cm.

Includes bibliographical references (p.) and index.
  ISBN-13 978-0-88316-577-5
  ISBN 0-88316-577-5
1. Urban policy—United States.   2. Sociology, Urban—United States.   3. Municipal government—United States.   I. Myers, Daniel J.   II. Title.
HT123.C6185   2006
307.76'0973   dc22
                    2005020273

Copyeditor: Steven Hiatt
Text design and composition: Hiatt & Dragon
Cover design: Stewart Cauley, Pollendesign

Printed in the USA

When it shall be said in any country in the world, "My poor are happy; my jails are empty of prisoners, my streets of beggars; the aged are not in want, the taxes are not oppressive—" then may that country boast of its constitution and its government.
—Thomas Paine

This volume is dedicated to
Barry J. Carroll
Audrey K. Conant
Leonard and Shirley Myers

Contents

List of Figures and Tables

Foreword

"The City" seems almost to denote the modern society. Although cities have been with us since antiquity, in preindustrial times no more than 10 to 20 percent of a society's population lived in cities. Today, however, that situation has reversed—in the most advanced societies, from half to three-quarters of the population lives or works in cities. The health, the beauty, and the prosperity of cities are perhaps the central features in the well-being of modern societies.

London and Paris, New York and Los Angeles, Tokyo and Shanghai, Sydney and Delhi have come to symbolize Britain and France, the U.S., Japan, and China, Australia and India. Indeed, for many visitors and residents, their social experience revolves around these metropolitan areas. And beyond these world cities are hundreds of other major cities with a population of over a million: in the United States alone, Chicago, Houston, Philadelphia, Phoenix, San Diego, San Antonio, and Dallas.

But what is a city? You may be surprised that in terms of size (though not reputation), cities such as Boston, Seattle, New Orleans, Cleveland, Miami, Detroit, Minneapolis, and St. Louis are relatively small, with populations of just over 300,000 to under 600,000 inhabitants. What makes these cities important, however, is not the population that lives within the city limits. Rather, each of these cities, and many others, form the vital center of sprawling metropolitan areas. Often extending across a half-dozen or more counties, and sometimes including a dozen or so other smaller municipalities or towns, such metropolitan areas have become the meaningful unit of social and economic activity for modern urban populations.

Boston, for example, is the hub of a metropolitan area of almost 6 million inhabitants. The Washington, D.C./Baltimore and San Francisco-Oakland metropolitan areas have over 6 million each. The New York and Los Angeles metropolitan areas, with populations of 21 million and 16 million people, respectively, are larger than many European countries. Over one-quarter of the U.S. population, accounting for an even larger portion of the national GDP, resides in just nine metropolitan areas of over 5 million inhabitants each. Over half of the U.S. population lives in the largest fifty metropolitan areas.

Given the size and importance of our country's metropolitan areas, one might think there would be sound ways to manage their key needs, from transportation and public education to law enforcement, health care, and housing. Yet in fact, the growth of these massive metropolitan areas is a recent phenomenon, having occurred mainly in the last fifty years. Meanwhile, the patterns of governance of our major cities and metro areas remain archaic, the legacy of systems of local administration that in many cases are hundreds of years old.

Modern metropolitan areas are chopped up into a bewildering variety of boroughs, wards, counties, townships, and major and minor cities, each with their own local government. Some metro areas encompass dozens of distinct jurisdictions. Some areas span two or more states—the New York metro area includes portions of New Jersey; the Cincinnati metro area extends into Indiana and Kentucky as well as Ohio; the Washington/Baltimore metro area includes portions of Virginia and Maryland as well as the District of Columbia. Some even span national boundaries: San Diego, California, is part of an international metro area with Tijuana, Mexico; so too is Detroit, Michigan, with Windsor, Canada.

The result of this massive growth of metro areas, forming ever-more tightly linked networks of residence and commerce, learning and working, travel and trade, extending across multiple local political boundaries, is a crisis of governance. Put simply, no unit of local government has the capacity to manage affairs across the full range of most metropolitan areas, and no unit of government at all has the capacity to force the many competing units within most metropolitan areas to work together. That metropolitan areas continue to function at all is a tribute to politicians' ability to improvise and cooperate under challenging conditions.

Nonetheless, the critical units in which most Americans live, work, and play are not fully governed by anyone. This not only places limits on government's ability to make and implement sensible policies. It makes it difficult for citizens to know whom to press for needed changes, or how best to participate in political decisions affecting their lives. It results in considerable inequalities of opportunities, living standards, and power that derive from problems of multiple jurisdictions and have the effect of eroding citizen's rights.

In this book, Ralph Conant and Daniel Myers describe the growth of metropolitan areas, and their impact on American society. They examine the evolution of our urban society, and focus on the problems of inequality and governance that have developed as a result. But they are far more constructive than critical. Conant and Myers offer powerful suggestions for setting urban priorities, improving regional planning, and strengthening citizen participation in metropolitan governance. They examine the historical role of state and federal governments in creating urban policy, and they offer insights into future needs based on social and technological trends.

In addition, Conant and Myers are not merely commentators on governance. They also examine the city sociologically, as a *community*. The relationships among the people who live and work in metropolitan areas are thus at the center of their study. They point toward building and invigorating the communities within metro areas as the critical policy goal for all levels of government.

The problems of modern metro areas are complex. However, this book is remarkably straightforward and clear. It is a valuable starting point for understanding the changes in urban life and urban policy in American in the last fifty years, and the future that lies ahead. Even more important, Conant and Myers offer us tools to shape that future. Scholars and students will find here a rich understanding of a wide range of key issues in urban policy, and guidance toward policies and institutions that can provide a better match between the practice of urban governance and the realities of urban life.

Jack A. Goldstone
Hazel Professor of Public Policy
George Mason University

Acknowledgments

Toward a More Perfect Union, in its first edition, was four years in the making. The second edition has been updated to include the latest available U.S. Census data and to analyze the initiatives of the George W. Bush administration. It presents a perspective on urban problems that covers several decades of ideas and observations by seminal thinkers in the field of metropolitan studies. In its larger perspective, the analysis covers urban and regional development in the United States from its emergence in the latter half of the nineteenth century and projects its progression through the first quarter of the twenty-first century.

William N. Cassella, an old friend and colleague from National Municipal (now Civic) League days, made detailed comments on an early draft. Other friends and colleagues who read and commented on subsequent drafts of the first edition are John E. Bebout, Barry J. Carroll, Norman Elkin, Adrienne Goldberg, Clarence Goldberg, Robert Hoggard, Maxine Kurtz, Wilbert J. LeMelle, Tom Forrester Lord, Martin Meyerson, Robert Sack, Randhir Sahni, Alan Shank, Jonathan Sharp, Beverlie Conant Sloane, David Charles Sloane, Sheila M. Stevens, George Strong, Benjamin Terner, and Robert J. Waste. A special thanks to Jack Goldstone for his foreword of the second edition, which provides the book with a contemporary perspective. We want to thank all of these friends and colleagues for their encouragement and commentary. We also thank Michael Gibbons, Keely Jones, Eugene Walls, Jon Hill, and David Ortiz, graduate students at the University of Notre Dame, for their help tracking down and processing data presented in the book.

Finally, we thank and acknowledge the following colleagues whose earlier writings have contributed to the ideas in this book: Alan Altschuler, John E. Bebout, Norman Elkin, Lyle C. Fitch, Scott Greer, Royce Hanson, Maxine Kurtz, and Jack Meltzer. In particular, Chapter 4 benefits from the work of Norton E. Long, Chapter 5 from that of Lyle C. Fitch, Chapter 7 from that of Maxine Kurtz, and Chapter 8 from that of Royce Hanson. We are grateful to all of them.

Chapter 1

Introduction: The State of Metropolitan America

The period between 1955 and 1975 was one of intense intellectual, governmental, and civic activity focused on the problems brought on by rapid postwar population growth (the baby boomers), accelerating migration to cities, and the massive shift of whites from central cities to suburbs. The latter two demographic movements had been in progress since before the turn of the twentieth century, but the post–World War II baby boom and massive demographic shifts in urban areas were not foreseen by most experts in the 1930s.

The demographic trends revealed in the Census of 1950 showed burgeoning populations in metropolitan areas. These trends were unexpected and sounded an alarm among attentive sociologists, political scientists, and policymakers, some of whom joined Victor Jones's earlier call for local governmental reorganization and regional planning.[1] For their part, Edward C. Banfield and Charles M. Tiebout and a few like-minded colleagues were skeptical about the administrative efficacy[2] and political feasibility[3] of projects aimed at metropolitan reorganization and areawide planning. Conant's study of the Muskegon proposal under Banfield's tutelage reflected his skepticism. The fact that the Muskegon area never achieved reorganization underscored the political basis of the skepticism.[4]

1

In the decades since 1975, cities have continued to change, some for the better, others for the worse. Scholarly work in urban studies has become increasingly sophisticated, focusing on housing, education, employment, and public safety as the key problems of inner cities. Scholars have always believed that solutions to these problems would improve the lives of the urban poor, raise many of them out of poverty, and in the long run reduce crime and other conditions associated with poverty. Some scholarly studies have produced new solutions and others have been dead ends. Some governmental programs have worked; others have proved useless or dysfunctional. But efforts at problem solving—both public and private—have improved with every new experiment. Scholars and policymakers have learned as much from the failures as from the successes.

Notable recent studies that address solutions include *Urban Decline and the Future of American Cities* by Katherine L. Bradbury, Anthony Downs, and Kenneth A. Small (1982); *New Visions for Metropolitan America* by Anthony Downs (1994); *Building Foundations: Housing and Federal Policy,* edited by Denise DiPasquale and Langley C. Keyes (1990); *Cities Without Suburbs* (1993 and 1995) and *Inside Game, Outside Game: Winning Stakes for Urban America* (1999) by David Rusk; *The Fractured Metropolis* by Jonathan Barnett (1995); *Reconstructing City Politics* by David L. Imbroscio (1997); and *Independent Cities* by Robert J. Waste (1998). The comprehensive textbook *Urban Politics* by Bernard H. Ross and Myron A. Levine, in its seventh edition (2005), is a valuable compendium of fact and commentary addressed mainly to students and policymakers.

A collection of scholarly papers, *Interwoven Destinies,* edited by Henry Cisneros (1993), is a sampling of some of the best contemporary thought and analysis in the urban field. *The New City-State* by Tom McEnery (1994) provides rare insights from the experience of the former mayor of San Jose, the "capital city" of Silicon Valley in California. There are others, of course, but these particular studies address with remarkable cogency the persistent, some say intractable, problems that have plagued cities in America throughout the past six or seven decades. They are the studies we found most helpful, especially in the closing chapters, where we consider trends in the quarter-century ahead.

The first broad-based governmental efforts to address poverty in the inner cities of America were hatched during the short-lived Kennedy administration (1960–1963). The energy and imagination with which President Lyndon Johnson followed through still resonates in American politics: the Great Society anti-poverty initiatives, the radically revised structure of federal welfare programs, the Civil Rights legislation, and the affirmative-action programs for higher education. In spite of these efforts and because some fell short of their goal of eliminating poverty, the problems of cities associated with poverty have persisted, as have American attitudes about social class, ethnicity, and race.

To his credit, Banfield foresaw and attempted to explain the persistence of problems of poverty in his classic *The Unheavenly City* (1968, 1970), and in other writings, including *The Unheavenly City Revisited* (1974). His work set off a storm of criticism that resulted in subsequent and clarifying studies of the culture of poverty more in keeping with the realities of life in America as seen by these authors. Such studies include Jack L. Roach and O.R. Gursslin, "An Evaluation of the Concept 'Culture of Poverty,'" *Social Forces* 45 (March 1967): 383–392; E. Leacock, *The Culture of Poverty: A Critique* (New York: Simon and Schuster, 1971); Frances Fox Piven and Richard A. Cloward, *Poor Peoples' Movements* (New York: Pantheon, 1977); W. Ryan, *Equality* (New York: Pantheon); D.T. Ellwood and M.J. Bane, *From Rhetoric to Reform,* (Cambridge, Mass.: Harvard University Press, 1994); P. Gottschalk, S. McLanahan, and G. Sandefur, *The Dynamics and Intergenerational Transmission of Poverty and Welfare Participation in Confronting Poverty: Prescriptions for Change* (Cambridge, Mass.: Harvard University Press, 1994; M. Shea, "Dynamics of Economic Well-Being," in *Poverty: Current Populations Reports* (Washington, D.C.: U.S. Department of Commerce, 1995).

Alice O'Connor has done a masterly job of analyzing and summing up the research on poverty all the way back to the Progressive Era of the early twentieth century in her *Poverty Knowledge: Social Science, Social Policy, and the Poor in Twentieth-Century U.S. History* (Princeton, N.J.: Princeton University Press, 2001).

Some interesting recent books on poverty in the United States that are among those we cite in our book *The Future of Poverty in American Cities* include William Julius Wilson, *The Truly Disadvantaged: The Inner City, the Underclass, and Public Policy* (Chicago: University of Chicago Press, 1987); and *When Work Disappears: The World of the New Urban Poor* (New York: Knopf, 1996); Michael B. Katz, *In the Shadow of the Poorhouse: A Social History of Welfare in America* (New York: Basic Books, 1986, 1996); Fred R. Harris and Lynn A. Curtis, eds., *Locked in the Poorhouse: Cities, Race, and Poverty in the United States* (Lanham, Md.: Rowman & Littlefield, 1998); Herbert J. Rubin, *Renewing Hope within Neighborhoods of Dispair* (Albany: State University of New York Press, 2000); and Barbara Ehrenreich, *Nickeled and Dimed: On (Not) Getting By in America* (New York: Henry Holt, 2001).

The years since 1975 have also witnessed a steady reduction of federal support for cities as well as waning of support for scholarly research in urban studies. After 1970, the Joint Center for Urban Studies became the Joint Center for Housing Studies, and the Lemberg Center for the Study of Violence and the Southwest Center for Urban Research in Houston both closed, to mention only three prominent urban research centers. Of course, urban policy centers have been established at universities across the country, but funds to support them have been hard to sustain. Robert Waste noted in his reply to a reviewer that a key motivation in writing *Independent Cities* was the difficulty in finding a good summary of national urban policy from World War II through the 1990s. One of the purposes of this book is to provide a perspective on that period and additional detail on federal and state initiatives to address urban problems.

Intergovernmental Coordination

A fundamental problem policymakers and scholars have always had in addressing the problems of urban areas is that the American governmental system has been characterized for most of its history by piecemeal cooperation and intervention reflected in inter-level ad hoc alliances and accommodations among federal, state, and local bureaucracies. In spite of Herculean efforts over the past half-century, we have not succeeded in developing effective, much less authoritative, territorial planning and coordination of public programs and activities at the local, metropolitan, or regional levels.

Some policymakers and urban scholars were still hopeful in 1975 that local governmental reorganization—consolidation, annexation, and so forth—would overcome political obstacles and provide administrative solutions to urban ills; that busing to achieve school integration would lay the basis for resolving racial problems in education; that urban renewal would, in the end, contribute to the stock of affordable housing for the poor; that superhighways would facilitate the movement of people in urban regions; that mass transportation would get the working class and poor to jobs in suburbs; that mass transportation would become an acceptable option for middle-class and upper-class commuters to relieve traffic congestion and air pollution. These solutions did work up to a point, but the realities of urban life have always outrun their long-run effectiveness.

The supposition of the 1960s and 1970s was that, because metropolitan regions (the Census Bureau's Metropolitan Statistical Areas—MSAs) were logical planning areas, they should also become self-governing municipalities, but the political resistance to governmental consolidation in most metropolitan areas has usually been sufficient to kill that idea. People have still preferred commuting in their automobiles, whether to the central city or to another suburb. They have routinely segregated themselves in city and suburban communities whose values and life styles seemed compatible. As a consequence, reorganization of local governments has not generally been successful, nor has school integration, especially where busing of children between city and suburb was involved. The Supreme Court of the United States in *Brown v. Board of Education* in 1954[5] overturned the "separate but equal" doctrine of *Plessy v. Ferguson* (1896)[6] but then pulled back from enforcing integration between city and suburb in *Milliken v. Bradley* in 1974,[7] where no public law or policy imposed public-school segregation.

Urban renewal and redevelopment programs, established by the federal Housing Act of 1949,[8] have mainly benefited business interests and middle-income and better-paid blue-collar workers, but rarely the poor.[9] Nor have mass transportation improvements lured enough suburbanites from their automobiles to relieve urban traffic congestion. Regional planning programs have helped upgrade the physical condition of urban areas but have done little to counter the social fragmentation that characterizes metropolitan areas.

This represents America's great paradox: that the nation has been populated with people from every part of the globe and is therefore socially diverse. Few other countries have so determinedly resisted a rigid class structure based on deliberate public policy.

Scholars who spend their professional lives analyzing problems and thinking through solutions have traditionally inspired much of the work of improving our cities. Policymakers depend on scholars for solutions to problems. But of course only the policymakers are in a position to adopt and implement solutions. Most of the problems discussed in this book are ones that have persisted in cities from their very beginnings. Some of the solutions have come with new technologies. Much of the analysis of problems is recycled and "repackaged" by new generations of scholars because the basic problems do not change very much. Some are mitigated, and others worsen: and mostly they worsen, as Banfield observed, and as Waste, Rusk, Downs, and others have documented. If urban renewal and slum clearance are to move ahead with the momentum they had in the 1950s and 1960s, new ideas and new programs are needed to make relocation of families in blighted areas an opportunity for rehousing of poor families in more desirable environments. Planned new towns and large-scale in-city urban renewal can serve this purpose, provided they are conceived as open communities available to the displaced and others as well. The upgrading of housing for displaced families would thus be part of a larger program to provide better housing and more housing for the expanding general population.

These problems need not worsen as our nation enters the twenty-first century. Indeed, for the first time in our history hope for betterment is supported by what appears to be permanent and expanding prosperity linked to an emerging global economy. A few years into the new century will tell the story. In Chapter 10—the concluding chapter—we address the prospects for the future.

Local, Regional, State, and Federal Roles

This book is about the American federal system and how it adapted to the changing conditions of urban society in the second half of the twentieth century and how it can adapt in the years ahead—how it can become a more perfect union in its capacity to create infrastructure and deliver services and maintain public morale. "Morale" in this context means a belief in the ability of democratic institutions to solve the problems of people fairly and efficiently.

While the subject is the federal system, the focus is on local and regional governance and the ways it can be improved in the service of its citizens. Although the work is grounded in the facts about structure and process, the book is primarily a critique of how the American governmental system carries out its responsibilities to its citizens, as these responsibilities are established in the laws and policies of the federal and state governments.

We believe the American system successfully links the purposes of government to the rights of its citizens and provides the conditions in which individual liberty and social creativity can flourish—for most people, most of the time. We believe, therefore, that our system of government is worth improving, and thus we suggest specific ways in which the structure and process can be improved. Our focus on local governance indicates our conviction that government of the people, by the people, and for the people must have vigorous roots in the cities, towns, and metropolitan regions where people live their daily lives. The alternative to vigorous local governance is unresponsive bureaucracies beholden to special-interest groups and political manipulators.

We prefer, with Socrates and Jean-Jacques Rousseau, a messy, contradictory, sometimes volatile democracy in which everyone who wants a say can have one. Democratic governance functions best in local communities and, for some purposes, in combinations of local communities—at the county or regional level. In our complex, fast-moving society, some functions are also carried out by "communities of interest" that relate to professions rather than to geographical or political communities. More than two centuries ago Rousseau gave us the philosophical basis for a working, practical democracy in *Du Contrat Social* (*The Social Contract*).[10] The Frenchman Alexis de Tocqueville called attention to the phenomenon of "communities of interest" in his *Democracy in America* more than a century and a half ago.[11] In Chapter 6 we explain with Rousseau's help why citizen participation is crucial to our system of government.

Our society, moving at an ever-quickening pace, is continually outrunning the structures that serve its needs. These structures, in the public and private sectors alike, require flexibility and must be reinvented periodically to adapt to change. Chapter 9 explores ways in which the states can take the lead in such beneficial structural change.

The subtitle of this book, *The Governance of Metropolitan America,* indicates its orientation and the scope of its concern with urban government and politics. The term "governance" is intended to cover the formal and the informal processes of government as well as public and private influences on those governing structures. The term is used to avoid emphasis on any single entity with the authority to allocate the scarce resources of the metropolitan community. In our federal system, even a metropolitan government is subject to the authority of the state and national governments. Furthermore, local government in most metropolitan areas is vested in a *multiplicity* of governments—cities, counties, and special authorities. Most local governments, even in the largest metropolitan areas, are small. Many overlap the boundaries of other units of local governments, thus increasing the number of governmental agencies with jurisdiction over people living in the region.

Some observers have defined the metropolitan problem as the "fragmentation" of local government. Our view is not so drastic, for we consider the fragmentation to be a consequence of the nation's philosophy of local government and of efforts to preserve diversity in an ever-changing society. The fragmentation is also a consequence of persistent racial discrimination in the housing markets of our communities. In our analysis, the negative consequences of fragmentation can be overcome by reinvigorating state-sponsored cooperative planning and decision-making arrangements designed to address metropolitanwide and regional public service needs. These are the substate districts that we propose in Chapter 9.

Whether all-inclusive metropolitan governments are desirable for our large metropolitan areas was debated for most of the twentieth century, and we will consider the pros and cons of that debate in subsequent chapters. The experience so far indicates that even where local governments have been consolidated into a single metropolitan government, as for example, New York City in 1898, the problems such arrangements were intended to solve always reappeared as populations expanded, diversified, and spilled over the new boundaries.

The most far-reaching change in the federal system in the last half of the twentieth century was the emergence and then partial withdrawal of the federal government as the leader in inducing cooperation among local governments. The Clinton administration in the 1990s partly succeeded in reversing this trend. While revenue sharing, as introduced by the Nixon administration in the 1970s, was de-emphasized by the Reagan administration and not reauthorized by Congress in 1986, that important program was retained in the Community Development Block Grant Program established by Congress in 1974.[12] The program has survived over the years as the primary urban-aid program. The George W. Bush administration, elected in 2000 and reelected in 2004, has focused mainly on wars in the Middle East and seems destined to leave a mixed legacy in domestic programs. Bush administration policies such as "faith-based initiatives" have further encouraged the decentralization within the federal system that was a hallmark of the Nixon and Reagan administrations.

In revenue-sharing programs since 1970, local government has gradually become a full partner in the federal system, a development not anticipated by the Founding Fathers or by early scholars. As a result, patterns now irreversible are operating through the formal and informal relationships that have developed among federal, state, and local governments. These relationships were consummated during the 1970s by local officials spending time in Washington and reciprocally by representatives of national agencies spending time in local communities. The intermingling is supported—often demanded—by private-interest groups, both national and local, that have a stake in programs under negotiation. In consequence, metropolitan areas have become the principal points of contact between national and local constituencies in the implementation of solutions to problems affecting every citizen.

Our national history records that Americans have always turned from one level of government to another or from one agency to another to get what they wanted or to prevent some undesired action. There are interests in our local communities—organized labor, racial and ethnic groups, business and professional groups, and nongovernmental organizations—with national orientations who routinely look for help from state and federal government to gain their ends at the community level. In such cases, local government may have lacked the resources or the will or the political clout to produce the ends they sought.

These observations explain why the governance of metropolitan areas in America is a political mix of the actions of public and private groups and in the public sector a mix of interacting local, state, and federal governments. No consolidation of local governments within metropolitan areas will alter their political character, eliminate conflict and disagreement, or erase the need for cooperation and coordination among local governments.

We try to deal with these realities and to suggest solutions that take the realities into account. Thus, we recognize the political unfeasibility of governmental consolidation in most of our metropolitan areas—especially in the larger, more socially heterogeneous, multicounty, multistate, in some cases, international ones. The metropolitan areas that managed consolidation in the nineteenth and twentieth centuries—San Francisco, New York City, Denver, Honolulu, Indianapolis, and Toronto among them—were probably the last of the breed. Annexation has, of course, continued in the few states where such unilateral central-city action is legal. But the experience of the past half-century informs us that solutions to metropolitan problems are more likely to be worked out without altering the framework of existing local government structures.

We therefore focus on practical means by which urban life—and governance—can continue to be improved within existing local governmental frameworks. Fortunately, policymakers at the beginning of the twenty-first century have at hand sophisticated planning and management tools for the task that they lacked a half-century ago.

The focus here on local government reflects our belief that an effective democracy depends for its vitality on the existence of responsive local institutions through which citizens can exert control on government at all levels. Our emphasis on new and restructured state and local instrumentalities reflects our view that these governments should continue the ongoing process of relieving the federal government of much of the burden of implementing domestic programs.

This process appears to be accelerating as the federal government concentrates on uniquely national and international problems. The restructured federal welfare program legislated by Congress in 1996 is an example of responsibility for domestic programs devolving to the state and local levels.[13] The George W. Bush administration's initiative in local public education (the "No Child Left Behind Act") is another example of the federal government's effort to set standards for a state/local service and to leave implementation to state and local officials.[14]

The federal government will continue its involvement in metropolitan areas, though at reduced levels, largely through the distribution of federally amassed public resources, establishment of minimum standards for programs of national significance, promulgation of guidelines for planning and coordination of locally implemented programs, and administration of federally funded public works, such as federal highways and mass transit systems.

Some programs initiated on the national level are most effectively *implemented* on the local level, where they can be tailored to local needs and conditions. The federal housing and welfare programs and President Johnson's War on Poverty and Model Cities programs had to be "deregulated" and handed over to state and local control to make them work for their intended beneficiaries. In the decades since those programs were initiated, citizens of states and municipalities have gradually taken steps to strengthen the capacity of their governments to administer effectively and responsibly all sorts of federally initiated programs. Our metropolitan areas have prospered as a result.

Persistent Poverty

The downside is that millions of people, especially children, youth, and minorities, do not share in the country's prosperity. Their condition is fully documented in the poverty literature, and solutions have eluded national and local policymakers ever since Franklin Roosevelt tried to pull the nation back from economic disaster in the 1930s. The problems then embraced an entire nation, the competent, the educated, and the unemployed alike. In that period, it took a world war to jump-start the economy and open up opportunity for the majority.

Seven decades later, as the nation enjoys unprecedented wealth, unprecedented levels of employment, unprecedented global reach, and unprecedented confidence in the future, poverty, homelessness, and crime still plague some neighborhoods in more than a hundred of our cities. These neighborhoods are populated in disproportionate numbers by minorities, principally African Americans, Hispanics, and other, newer, immigrant groups. Their housing and schools are generally substandard, they have limited access to healthcare, their streets are crime-ridden, and proximate good-paying jobs are scarce. Poverty in our cities is made more intractable by racism. If there were no racism there would still be poverty, but poverty in the absence of racism might not be so hard to manage.

Federal programs to mitigate such problems, some initiated in Roosevelt's New Deal and others in the Kennedy and Johnson administrations in the 1960s, helped alleviate the symptoms but proved inadequate in dealing with the root causes of poverty. The question, of course, is how much is *worth* doing? We address this question in the concluding chapter.

The answer for Franklin Roosevelt was easy, politically speaking, because the Great Depression had put the entire nation at risk. John F. Kennedy and Lyndon Johnson saw political opportunity (votes) in the poor neighborhoods of the central cities. Jimmy Carter was sufficiently motivated by altruism to press upon a reluctant Congress a diluted revival of some of Johnson's Great Society programs. His Republican predecessor, Richard Nixon, working with a Democratic Congress, was impressed enough with the political gold to be mined in the cities to offer revenue sharing in the form of block grants to local governments. The other purpose was to push responsibility for allocation of resources closer to the people most affected.

Ronald Reagan, whose primary agenda was to bring the Soviet Union to its knees and to reduce taxes, chipped away at Nixon's revenue sharing. George Bush, elected in 1988, had no urban program of consequence. As Robert Waste observed in *Independent Cities,* virtually no explicit urban policy existed in the Reagan/Bush years, 1980 to 1992.[15] President Bill Clinton started out with an ambitious set of priorities—100,000 new teachers, 50,000 more local police, an omnibus cradle-to-grave health program, to mention a few—but most were blocked or watered down. During his eight-year administration, he had to settle for incremental progress in a long list of urban-help programs that became known as the "refrigerator list." President George W. Bush seems thus likely to leave a mixed legacy in domestic programs, at least based on the policies initiated and/or implemented during his first term. Major new funds were pumped into urban areas from the Homeland Security program, which was a response to terrorist attacks on the World Trade Center in New York and the Pentagon in Washington, D.C., on September 11, 2001, less than a year into Bush's first term. The specific funds to add police to local departments from the Clinton administration were reduced. The numbers of homeless people rose during Bush's first term due to cuts in federally sponsored housing for the poor. A variety of environmental policies were changed to favor industries over environmental quality.

A cautionary note: as American political leaders continue to seek a balance in the distribution of responsibility among levels of government, especially in shifting functions from the federal to the local level, they face voters who exert pressures to hold down local taxes and spending—the same voters who feel powerless to reduce spending by the federal government.

The Potential for Improvement

This book takes a hard look at American cities in the early years of the twenty-first century. We recognize that most of them have experienced improvement over the decades but that that improvement must continue if the people who live in them are to enjoy a good quality of life. Waste and others seem to take a less optimistic view, contending that twenty-four or thirty-four cities in the country are past a "point of no return" (David Rusk's lists in his 1993 and 1995 editions).[16] Waste added ten that he labeled "shooting gallery" cities and "urban reservation" cities.[17] Waste and Rusk have documented deplorable social conditions in the cities on their separate lists, but surely no American city is beyond improvement or beyond a "point of no return." Rusk and Waste suggest several ways to address the problems. Downs is emphatic about the prospects for improvement, although he hedges his case.[18]

What follows in this book is a restatement of the problems of American cities as well as an updating of "solutions." Fresh *new* approaches rarely come along, although Waste, Downs, Rusk, and Imbroscio each make a vigorous case for theirs. We try to demonstrate that the potential for improvement depends on new planning authority at the regional level, with intelligent application of emerging technologies and with a renewed and focused allocation of federal and state dollars. There is also much potential in the persistent application of federal and state programs that have demonstrated their effectiveness.

Our intent is to provide a perspective on contemporary problems of urban development; on trends in policies at the federal, state, and local levels aimed at dealing with those problems; and on the social, political, and historical context in which urban development has occurred. Toward this end, we summarize in Chapter 2 the principal features of urban society in America. In Chapter 3 we discuss the social problems that burden most American cities and the role of comprehensive planning in achieving solutions. In Chapter 4 we discuss the tensions and the conflicts that divide people and communities in metropolitan areas in the absence of effective regional governing mechanisms. In Chapter 5 we set forth in theoretical economic terms the pros and cons of centralized versus decentralized forms of local government. In Chapter 6 we reexamine the critical role of citizen participation in local governance. In Chapter 7 we review the development of urban planning and policy at the federal level and ways in which the federal and state governments have endeavored to provide policies and programs aimed at solving problems of urban development. In Chapter 8 we examine the history of the "New Communities" movement and the efficacy of reintroducing a federal program of new communities and new towns as an alternative strategy of urban development in the future. In Chapter 9, we suggest structurally improved substate planning and administrative districts to replace existing metropolitan and regional planning agencies and special-purpose districts. In Chapter 10, we explore future directions in federal and state urban policy and likely outcomes for the citizens of our urban areas in the first quarter of the twenty-first century.

The book takes the reader to the year 2025 as a vantage point from which to view the future. We try to look ahead because the policymakers and students to whom this book is primarily addressed need more than ever to focus on the longer-range future if efforts are to succeed in laying the groundwork for solutions to the common problems of our nation and our cities.

Notes

1. Victor Jones, *Metropolitan Government* (Chicago: The University of Chicago Press, 1942).
2. Charles M. Tiebout, "A Pure Theory of Local Expenditures," *Journal of Political Economy* (October 1964); and "An Economic Theory of Fiscal Decentralization," in National Bureau of Economic Research, *Public Finance: Needs, Sources, and Utilization* (Princeton, N.J.: Princeton University Press, 1961).
3. Edward C. Banfield, *The Unheavenly City* (Boston: Little, Brown & Company, 1970), Chapter 3.
4. Ralph W. Conant, "The Politics of Metropolitan Reorganization in a Michigan Area," unpublished doctoral dissertation, 1960.
5. *Brown v. Board of Education*, 347 U.S. 483 (1954).
6. *Plessy v. Ferguson*, 163 U.S. 537 (1896).
7. *Milliken v. Bradley*, 418 U.S. 717 (1974).
8. P.L. 81-171, Housing Act of 1949.
9. Herbert Gans, *The Urban Villagers: Group and Class in the Life of Italian-Americans* (New York: Free Press of Glencoe, 1962).
10. Jean-Jacques Rousseau, *The Social Contract*, trans. Maurice Cranston (Hammersmith, U.K.: Penguin, 1968 [1762]).
11. Alexis de Tocqueville, *Democracy in America*, ed. Harvey C. Mansfield, trans. Delba Winthrop (Chicago: University of Chicago Press, 2000 [1832].
12. P.L. 93-383, Housing and Community Development Act of 1974.
13. P.L. 104-193, The Personal Responsibility and Work Opportunity Reconciliation Act of 1996 (the Welfare Act of 1996).
14. P.L. 107-110, popularly known as the "No Child Left Behind Act."
15. Robert J. Waste, *Independent Cities* (New York: Oxford University Press, 1998), p. 74.
16. David Rusk, *Cities Without Suburbs* (Baltimore: Johns Hopkins University Press, 1993, 1995).
17. Waste, *Independent Cities*.
18. Anthony Downs, *New Visions for Metropolitan America* (Washington, D.C.: Brookings Institution, 1994).

Chapter 2

The Urban Society

Defining "Urban": A Focus on the MSA

Defining what is meant by "urban" has always been a troublesome task. The initial contrast was with rural areas that seemed a stark contrast to the cities that constituted the urban environment. Differences between the archetypes of these environments seemed so great that academic factions developed touting concern with one or the other environment. For example, early sociologists were so steeped in the problems of industrialization and urbanization that the field could have been called urban sociology. The neglect of nonurban areas led to a closely aligned, but clearly differentiable, field of rural sociology. Many present-day universities still maintain separate sociology and rural sociology departments.

The contrast between urban and rural, however, has become considerably less distinct over time. Although scholars and laypersons harbor an implicit distinction between the truly urban and the truly rural, considerable confusion arises when we specify a line between the two. Consider the repeated attempts of U.S. government agencies to delineate urban environments. Through 1940, the Census Bureau defined urban areas as incorporated places with populations of 2,500 or more. Unincorporated areas under "special rules" about population size and density supplemented this set of areas.

In 1950 the Census Bureau introduced a new way of distinguishing urban and rural residents: the urban population comprised all people in "urbanized areas" and all persons in places of 2,500 or more, whether incorporated or unincorporated. Urbanized areas contained a central city or twin cities and a surrounding area that met density requirements. Combined, the central city and its fringe had to contain at least 50,000 people. Since 1950, the core notion of "urban" has stabilized, but the managers of each census since have tinkered with modifications in the "special rules," introducing the notion of "extended cities" or changing the size requirements for central cities in urbanized areas.

Census Bureau data are also classified into Metropolitan Areas (MAs), previously called Metropolitan Statistical Areas (MSAs); Standard Metropolitan Statistical Areas (SMSAs); and originally Standard Metropolitan Areas. These distinctions were created for the purpose of collecting statistics in the urban areas of the country. In 2000, Metropolitan Areas were categorized as either MSAs or PMSAs (Primary Metropolitan Statistical Areas). To qualify as an MSA, an area must consist of "a large population nucleus together with adjacent communities which have a high degree of social and economic integration with that nucleus." The central city of the MSA must have a population of at least 50,000 or be part of a metropolitan region with a population of at least 100,000. PMSAs are MSAs that are part of a larger, extended urban area called a Consolidated Metropolitan Statistical Area (CMSA). In 1999, there were 258 MSAs and 73 PMSAs, for a total of 331 Metropolitan Areas, a substantial increase from the original 212 defined in 1960. The PMSAs also combine to make 18 CMSAs. For simplicity's sake, we will use "MSA" throughout the text, except where we discuss metropolitan areas in the earlier periods.[1]

Even in their present form, there are difficulties with these statistical definitions of rural, urban, and metropolitan areas. For example, the definitions of metropolitan areas and urban areas do not necessarily coincide and parts of MSAs that do not meet density criteria are classified as rural. For example, the San Bernardino-Riverside MSA in California includes vast areas of mountain and desert extending to the Arizona border, and the Utica-Rome area in New York includes hundreds of miles of forestland in Herkimer County. These outlying areas do not appear to contribute to the urban character of either metropolitan area. Likewise, some places exceeding 2,500 in population primarily serve agricultural hinterlands and are more rustic than urban in the attitudes of some of their citizens. But the number of those who are agriculturally oriented is usually small and their rural nature is more than offset by nonfarm people who are urban oriented. The continuing decline of agriculture as a way of life has reduced the numbers of rural people directly involved to less than 4% of the nation's population.

The sociological enterprise of identifying areas that are truly urban in character is complex and time-consuming, and by the time the task is complete, the situation will have changed enough to invalidate the results. On the other hand, utilizing the term "MSAs" (our strategy) provides a reasonable balance by combining both political boundaries and elements of sociological understandings of "urban." In the end, the shorthand for a broad-based inquiry about the urban condition produces a categorization system that is utilitarian in some respects and unsatisfactory in others. Inevitably, some areas are arbitrarily placed either inside or outside the "urban" category. These areas are especially interesting because they are on the fringes and represent the envelope of the urban frontier. As such, they call for special attention on the part of urban scholars.

The Growing Urban Character of the United States

No matter how urbanization is defined, it is a ubiquitous phenomenon, both in the United States and around the world. As of 2004, there were 294 million people living in the United States. Some 235 million of these (80%) lived in the 331 metropolitan areas defined at that time. More than 75% lived in "urban places," while less than 25% lived in rural areas. And although the rate at which we are becoming more urbanized is decreasing, urban growth in raw numbers remains steady (Figure 2.1). An additional trend since 1970 has been for urban-oriented people to relocate to rural areas while retaining their urban orientation and professional and social contacts.[2]

Urbanization has also reached into all sections of the country. In 1960, the Census Bureau listed only one region, designated East South Central, containing Kentucky, Tennessee, Alabama, and Mississippi, as "predominantly rural." Since then, even this region has become predominantly urban. The 1960 Cen-

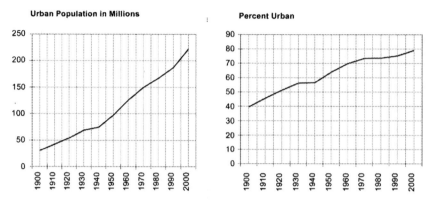

Figure 2.1 Population and Urban Orientation, 1900–2000
Source: U.S. Bureau of the Census

sus also identified eleven states that had rural majorities. By 1970, Arkansas, Idaho, and Kentucky had moved into the urban category, leaving only eight rural states: Vermont, North Dakota, South Dakota, West Virginia, North Carolina, South Carolina, Mississippi, and Alaska. By 2000, only Maine, Vermont, West Virginia, and Mississippi were predominantly rural. In 1960, there were only three states that did not contain all or part of an MSA—Vermont, Alaska, and Wyoming. By 2000, even these "rural" states had their MSAs—Burlington, Vermont; Anchorage, Alaska; and Casper and Cheyenne, Wyoming.

A Historical Perspective

The patterns of urbanization in the U.S. have been defined in great part by transportation systems. City building in the century before 1910 was defined first by the horse and buggy, and later by the trolley and intercity rail systems. A machine-made revolution led by the internal combustion engine profoundly altered those early city centers. As the automobile and the truck came to dominate transportation of goods and people, central cities became ringed by freeways and by suburbs supported in part by relocated or newly established industrial plants, shopping centers, and office buildings. Villages, towns, and some cities that were once isolated were absorbed in the larger economy of urban regions. Later, as the jet airplane began to dominate transportation, the connections within and between urban areas began to change. As a result, larger areas became urbanized and the urban character changed from simply reflecting an urban/rural difference to including a central city/suburban distinction and spreading the distribution of urban areas to regional and national levels. These patterns reflect contemporary urban America, and they affect the character of our urban problems as well as the means available for addressing them.

Other revolutions accompanied changes in transportation. The pace and magnitude of urban development would not have been so great if Americans had not learned to substitute capital and technology to produce food for more and more people on less and less land and with less and less manpower (due particularly to the use of the internal combustion engine to power farm machinery). This trend continues as the number of farms decreases and the average size of farms increases.[3] Genetic engineering is the scientific engine that is likely to continue the process.

The consequence is that, although we think of farming and "the country" as going together, less than 20% of Americans living in so-called rural areas live on farms. Furthermore, the increase in productivity of farm labor has been accompanied by an increase in corporate, as opposed to family, farming and the further narrowing of the economic, cultural, and social distance between the agricultural and other sectors of our society. As factories move into fields and farmlands come to be managed like factories, traditional notions about the distinction between urban and rural become less relevant to the realities of our lives. The computer is as much a part of today's farmstead as today's factory, and options and futures markets are as essential to agribusiness from the farm up as stock and bond markets are to the operation of industry. The "country" is not what it used to be.

To the changes in agriculture, we must add revolutions in communications and homemaking. Changes in these two fundamental elements of social life have also brought rural people closer to the city and urban amenities to people who live outside the city. In short, while American society is becoming quantitatively more urban, it has become qualitatively more urbane.

MSAs: *The* Key Urban Units

MSAs thus are more than statistical or political artifacts. They are, from an urbanist's perspective, emergent *social* communities—however fragmented—

that have evolved with economic and technological change. Yet these communities exist without a coherent government or direction from any authoritative source. They contain scores—in some places hundreds—of local governmental units that give residents control over a limited number of public functions important to them, to their lives, and to their aspirations. Among these functions are the use of their land, the level of local taxes, the education of their children, the character and quality of local protective services, and the privilege of living apart from people of different life styles, ethnic background, and skin color.

These functions speak to the sources of fragmentation in metropolitan areas. One important source has been the drive to maximize income via publicly provided goods obtained at bargain prices and minimal taxes. Contrast the current situation with the time before the Great Depression and the New Deal. Then, most consumption was in the private sector and rationing was by price. Public goods consisted mainly of essential and indivisible services: defense, foreign policy, highways, and the like. But in the present day, the middle class demands more public services, and they translate their unequal income into unequal consumption of public goods. Educational systems flourish in wealthy suburbs by spending more per student than in poor urban areas. We discuss these issues in Chapter 4.

In theory, unified metropolitan government makes possible a redistribution of advantages and income that reduces the inequities enjoyed by privileged enclaves. But what authority should govern? The state? The federal government? Special governmental agencies created by the state? Those who argue for authoritative direction at the level of the MSAs do so because they see political and administrative unification as a means of alleviating America's most challenging domestic problems. We deal with this question in Chapter 9.

Suburbanization: Urban Population Trends

While urban America has continued growing at a rapid rate since World War II, the gains have not come primarily from growth in established central cities. Only in cases where cities could add massive territory through annexation (as in Texas) or through merger or partial merger with surrounding areas (as in

Indianapolis and Jacksonville) has population growth been extensive. Instead, growth has come in the fringe areas surrounding the central cities of MSAs. The peak growth rate of SMSAs occurred in the 1950s—about double that of the rest of the country. During that decade, both central cities and fringe areas were growing, but the population increase within SMSAs *outside* central cities more than quadrupled that of the central city rate.

Since its peak, the population growth within MSAs has slowed but continues to grow faster than in the rest of the country. The overall population growth in MSAs from 1970 to 2000 was about 41.3%, and 90% of all MSAs grew during the period. As before, the bulk of the growth continues to be in the suburban areas, where an increase of 59.5% occurred from 1970 to 2000, compared to only 18.9% growth in the central cities during the same period. Many central cities have posted actual losses: of the current central cities, 166 (31%) lost population from 1970 to 2000. Of the 331 MSAs, only 75 had growth rates in central cities that kept up with growth rates in the suburbs. This pattern means that the urban character of America continually shifted from cities to suburban and fringe areas. Not all suburban areas are growing, but only 7% of suburban areas in MSAs posted declines from 1970 to 1996.

The Increasing Importance of the Urban/Suburban Distinction

Aside from ubiquitous social and economic distinctions, one of the oldest divisions in urban society is between city and suburb—between the older, more densely settled central cities and newer, more spacious outlying areas. Until the Great Depression, the city was the seat of prestige, the home of the rich, the powerful, and the highly cultured. Contrast this picture of affluence with the contemporary one between the old, decaying central city and well-ordered suburbs, the preferred abiding places of the wealthy and the upwardly mobile. A century ago people were proud to be city dwellers; now many deny an urban label and strive to escape the city. Many affluent urban families who live in the city have acquired second homes "in the country." Vermont has always been listed in the U.S. Census as "rural" but in recent decades has become inhabited by city people who have acquired Vermont farms as refuges. Today, Vermont has become virtually a suburb of Boston, New York, and Montreal.

The character of suburbia has come to dominate the lives of urbanites. To-day two-thirds of the metropolitan population lives in separately incorporated suburbs and in unincorporated places. And although almost all states are now predominantly urban (and all of them have urban developments that are of statewide or even interstate concern), these central cities account for decreasing shares of the population and thus have less influence on state government. For example, New York City contained a majority of the state's population through 1950, but by 1960 its share of the population had dropped to 46.4%. The trend continued. and by 2000 the city only accounted for 42.2% of New York State's population. Despite common interests, large cities from New York to Buffalo do not readily join hands to achieve political control of the state. The big-city component of the state is fractionated and has grown weaker, compared to the suburban component.

This trend holds for other states as well. In New Jersey, once the most densely populated state, six old central cities, Newark, Jersey City, Paterson, Camden, Elizabeth, and Trenton, each with a population over a 100,000, in 1970 contained only 15.3% of the state's people. The other 85% were scattered across the state. By 1970, only twenty-one states had a city with 15% or more of the state's total population. By 2000, only eleven states meeting this criterion remained (Portland, Ore.; Sioux Falls, S.D.; Providence, R.I.; Omaha, Neb.; Chicago, Ill.; Las Vegas, Nev.; Albuquerque, N.M.; Phoenix, Ariz.; Honolulu, Hawaii; Anchorage, Alaska; New York, N.Y.).

The growing dominance of diverse suburbs has important implications both for local and national governance. For local government, suburbs depend on the county, village, or township. A traditional acceptance of the "right" of community self-governance, together with an unclear definition of community, has allowed the separate incorporation of residential enclaves, industrial areas for tax shelters, and gambling centers as "villages," "towns," or "cities." Even homeowners' associations created in covenants in some residential developments afford a measure of local control at the submunicipal level. As a consequence, suburbs vary by social class, ethnicity, and life style. Thus, the governmental boundaries within metropolitan areas correspond roughly to the social fragmentation that occurred over the course of the twentieth century.

The increasing political power of the suburbs is apparent on a national level as well. In 1992, Clinton owed his victory to suburban voters and became the president of a nation that was for the first time more suburban than urban. Robert Waste emphasizes the shift of power from urban centers to suburban fringes.[4] He points out that the half of the U.S. Senate that comes from the 26 smallest states represents only 14% of the U.S. population. The result is that neither the majority of the Senate nor the president is elected by city voters.

The Complex Configuration of the Urban Landscape

The growing importance of the suburbs in urban America does not mean that there is a simple dichotomy between the cities and suburbs. In fact, the character of cities and suburbs, and the relationship between them, is dynamic and multifaceted.

To begin with, a single downtown node surrounded by its suburbs is becoming a less and less accurate image of urban arrangements. Rather than population, government, and commercial activity focusing on a nucleus, America has moved to a multinuclear metropolis in which several nodes of influence operate (see Figure 2.2). This change has mainly occurred since the 1950s, although a few cities like New York and Los Angeles began to develop scattered nodes in earlier decades. While urban nodes in outlying areas were rarely as strong as "downtown" a quarter-century ago, some have virtually replaced downtown as financial and business districts. Thus, a predominant volume of regional economic activity has become suburban in character and decentralized business is expanding further.

Second, some suburbs increasingly resemble central cities as their populations mature and become socially and economically heterogeneous. In fact, with the exception of racial characteristics, the gap has narrowed in some cities to the vanishing point. Older urban nodes are showing recognizable urban decay. The process begins as older housing of the inner suburban rings is gradually taken over by low-income people. In a few decades low-income and poor people outside the central city will outnumber those who live inside.

Third, it is important to recognize that a sociological understanding of suburbanites does not focus only on where they live, but also on social behavior and mores. Not all suburbanites live in outlying places. There is, for example,

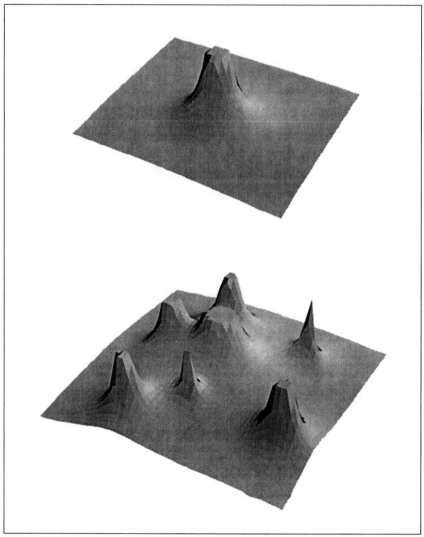

Figure 2.2   Past Single-Node Cities versus Present Multimode Model

little distinction between the populations of Chevy Chase in the District of Columbia and the adjacent Chevy Chase, Maryland. Spring Valley within the District is just as suburban as adjoining places in next-door Montgomery County. Such examples are to be found in every city and metropolitan area in the nation.

Urban areas are also becoming considerably less distinct from one another. One crucial element of our national pattern of urban settlement is the way it has developed in ribbons, or strips, in some areas extending hundreds of miles across several states. The Northeast Corridor can be traced on the map from Portland, Maine, to Norfolk, Virginia. In this case, the Interstate Highway System allows automobile travel that entire distance without encountering a single traffic light. Other massive urban developments are in the Los Angeles and San Francisco Bay areas of California. There are urbanized strips along the Great Lakes, on the West Coast, and in Texas, and others are rapidly developing even in formerly rural states.

Urban development along the Gulf Coast from Florida to Texas, though not yet continuous, will become so in a few years. One can imagine such developments eventually running into each other from New York State to Wisconsin, across northwestern Pennsylvania, northern Ohio, southern Michigan, and northern Indiana and Illinois. Still others are occurring in central North Carolina, central and southwestern Ohio, northern Kentucky, and the Northwest around Portland and Seattle.

The complex fragments, layers, and connections in the metropolitan environment defy centralized forms of governance. Though the political distinctions within and among metropolitan units are troublesome, the differences in conditions across them only serve to exacerbate the challenges of coordination. Centralized metropolitan government may not be politically feasible, but regional and state development planning is both feasible and necessary.

Urban Social Conditions and Problems

Minority Migration

The problems that existed in American urban environments at the end of the twentieth century were largely problems experienced by racial and ethnic minorities. The poor minorities and newcomers have usually congregated in urban environments and by doing so have been a principal source of urban growth. Immigration and internal migration of poor and nonwhite populations to cities has been driven by the search for better education and economic opportunities. These groups typically settled in older neighborhoods of central cities where housing is affordable and ethnic enclaves have been established.

The first massive waves of immigrants in the nineteenth and early twentieth centuries were mainly Europeans. They were accompanied by an internal migration of Blacks from the rural South into northern and southern cities after the Civil War. Black migration to industrial centers in the North intensified during World War II as a result of federal government attempts to round up manpower for industrial plants occupied with war production. The internal migration of Blacks continued on an increasing scale after World War II, until more Blacks than whites populated some urban industrial centers. By 1980, many of these cities, north and south, east and west, had elected Black mayors, councilmen, legislators, and members of Congress.

When Blacks moved in, whites tended to move out. For a time in the 1960s and 1970s a phenomenon identified by Morton Grodzins as the "tipping point" occurred in white neighborhoods and suburbs across the country. Once a few Black families had established themselves in a neighborhood (usually over strong and even violent resistance), it often turned into a Black neighborhood. Real estate operators sometimes deliberately orchestrated the process as pressures from Black homebuyers increased.

Hispanics from Mexico, the Caribbean, and elsewhere in Central and South America followed the African Americans[5] into cities in increasing numbers beginning in the 1950s. New York City, Chicago, Houston, San Antonio, all the Mexico–U.S. border cities, and most of California have been the destinations of choice. Some of these cities will probably have Hispanic majorities by 2020, several in the present decade.

By the 1980s, Asians were coming to the United States in larger numbers than ever before. Chinese and Japanese immigrants had been settling the West Coast states for 150 years, since the days of the gold rushes and railroad building. Other Asians have followed, especially in the decades since World War II, the Korean Conflict, and the Vietnam War. More recently, they have come in large numbers to take advantage of the economic opportunities and amenities of American life. Like other immigrants before them, Asians have tended to settle in central cities where others of their ethnic group have already established communities.

Racially and ethnically segregated neighborhoods, created through dis-criminatory practices and through choice, constitute some of the greatest challenges for urban managers. But the legacy of these neighborhoods is only one aspect of fragmentation in the modern metropolis.

Heterogeneity within and across Cities and Suburbs

What other kinds of diversity and fragmentation can be observed in metro-politan areas? In 1970, central cities were considerably more heterogeneous than suburbs. They included most of the segregated ethnic populations, the newcomers, and the very poor, as well as small numbers of the wealthy. In between, many central-city people were much like suburbanites in class and ethnicity.

This picture changed in important ways over the last quarter of the twenti-eth century. The 1970 Census showed that more Blacks than ever before lived in central cities; that the proportion living in suburbs was declining (although not in absolute numbers); and that in each metropolitan area the central cit-ies were less white. Since then, racial diversity has been on the rise in central cities, not because of changes in the numbers of Blacks but because of con-tinued white flight and increased numbers of Hispanics and other peoples. From 1980 to 2000, as Figure 2.3 indicates, the percentage of Blacks in central cities held steady, while the percentage of whites decreased and those of other peoples increased. (The absolute number in each minority group was increas-ing, however.)

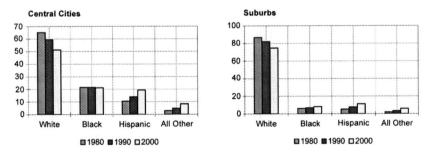

Figure 2.3   Racial Composition and Central Cities and Suburbs, 1980–2000

Because minorities are so overrepresented in central cites, it follows that they are underrepresented in the suburbs. Suburbs, however, are not uniformly white. There are Black enclaves in the suburbs, and there are some predominantly Black suburbs. On the whole, suburbs have become less white in character. From 1980 to 2000, for example, all racial groups increased their raw numbers in the suburbs, but minorities (particularly Hispanics and others) were gaining at faster rates than whites. The result, as shown in Figure 2.3, was that the percentage of whites in the suburbs actually decreased. Even so, central cities remained racially diverse as minority groups continued to be overrepresented in central cities and underrepresented in the suburbs. This stark segregation by race exacerbates all the normal frictions that affect relationships between central cities and suburbs.

Diversity of race is accompanied by diversity in wealth. Suburbs have never been the exclusive province of the rich nor are the central cities devoid of wealth. Not all suburban housing is expensive and much of it has come within the purchasing power of minority families. In most of the older metropolises, there are a substantial number of working-class suburbs in which house prices and rents are *lower* than those paid by minorities living in central cities. The white–minority division of developments in central cities and suburbs within the same price ranges that has traditionally been attributable to racial discrimination continues to be the major cause of housing deprivation. Other factors at work include access to public transportation, the hidden costs of owning automobiles, and the number of wage earners in the family.

The suburbs have become diversified in other ways as well. For example, all major religious groups have taken up residence there. Contrary to the WASP imagery associated with the suburbs, a substantial proportion of current residents are Catholic or Jewish. Likewise, the suburbs are not uniform in political behavior. Elite districts are juxtaposed with conservative and liberal districts. Suburbs that were formerly "bedroom" communities now house industrial and commercial establishments and the workforces that support them.

Despite this heterogeneity, there continue to be considerable differences between the suburbs and the central cities in economic health. At best, central cities could be described as economically stagnant. Most suburbs, on the other hand, have continued to increase in wealth. Table 2.1 shows that the median family income in central cities (when measured in constant dollars) has remained stable from 1969 to 1999, while income has grown nearly 18% in the suburbs. While these indicators of absolute income are discouraging, indicators of relative income are even more so. Inhabitants of central cities are more and more sliding out of the highest income bracket and more and more into the lowest bracket. The progression in the suburbs is just the opposite.

Table 2.1 Income in Central Cities and Suburbs, 1969–1999 (in 2004 Dollars)

	Median Family Income	
	Central Cities	Suburbs[*]
1969	$49,480	$55,361
1979	$48,790	$58,419
1989	$49,443	$62,236
1999	$50,580	$65,251
	Percent in Lowest (20%) Income Bracket	
	Central Cities	Suburbs
1969	20.2	14.5
1979	23.6	14.7
1989	24.5	14.0
1999	25.8	15.6
	Percent in Highest (20%) Income Bracket	
	Central Cities	Suburbs
1969	19.9	24.9
1979	18.4	24.9
1989	17.8	25.7
1999	17.3	24.8

Source: U.S. Census, Central Cities and MSAs as defined in 2000.
* Defined as all areas in the MSA but not in the central cities.

Other measures of well-being also favor the suburbs. As Table 2.2 shows, central cities lag behind suburbs in terms of poverty rates, unemployment, and housing status. Nor are the trends encouraging. Poverty has worsened in central cities since 1970 both in absolute terms and relative to suburbs. Unemployment rates increased in both cities and suburbs from 1970 to 2000, but the rates increased more rapidly in the central cities, thereby widening the economic gap between cities and suburbs. Housing indicators have remained fairly constant over time, with slight improvements in both areas during the 1990s.

Table 2.2 Central City and Suburb Conditons

	Percent with Incomes below Poverty Line*	
	Central Cities	Suburbs
1969	14.3	9.0
1979	16.2	8.2
1989	18.0	8.4
1999	17.6	8.4
	Percent Unemployed	
	Central Cities	Suburbs
1969	4.6	3.8
1979	7.1	5.6
1989	7.7	5.1
1999	7.4	4.6
	Percent of Housing Units Owner-Occupied	
	Central Cities	Suburbs
1969	49.1	71.3
1979	49.5	71.5
1989	49.0	71.0
1999	50.5	73.0

Source: U.S. Census Bureau
*Based on poverty definitions used by the U.S. Census Bureau.[6]

Thus, although there is growing heterogeneity within the suburbs, these changes are not relieving the strain produced by differential economic conditions across suburban borders. Political behavior in suburbs varies considerably as a reflection of economic and social composition, but a common feature of suburban governance is a stance against large central cities. Especially, suburbanites do not want to share social services—particularly those for which they would pay disproportionately more and receive disproportionately less. This "us-versus-them" mentality is common in suburbs and complicates efforts at regional planning.

Conditions of Life for Minorities

The concentration of minorities in central cities tends to exacerbate the "us-versus-them" dynamics, and minorities suffer most from the differences between the suburbs and the central cities. Blacks and Hispanics who live in large cities tend to have the highest rates of unemployment (especially among the youth), live in the worst housing, suffer the poorest education, and so forth. Whites who reside in central cities tend to be marginally better off, if for no other reason than that they are more likely to be employed. These factors all contribute to a marked difference in income distribution between urban African Americans and whites. Figure 2.4 plots the 1990 family-income distribution in central cities of metropolitan areas. While both races have strong representation in the middle ranges, the higher the bracket, the greater the ratio of white-to-Black representation. Nearly 17% of Blacks occupy the two lowest income brackets, compared to less than 2% of whites. On the other end of the spectrum, 38% of whites are in the top two brackets, compared to only 14% of Blacks. Furthermore, the situation is worsening, not improving.

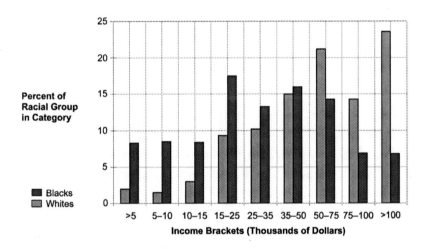

Figure 2.4 Income Distribution by Race, 2003

Further evidence of the relationship between the urban concentration of minorities and their economic difficulties is apparent when the racial composition of central cities is examined. Figure 2.5 illustrates this by plotting the percent nonwhite against the median family income for all central cities. This graph shows that there is a strong general tendency for income to be lower in cities with larger minority populations. In fact, as we move from cities that are virtually all white to cities that have virtually no whites, the median income is nearly cut in half, dropping by almost $20,000—a very potent point.

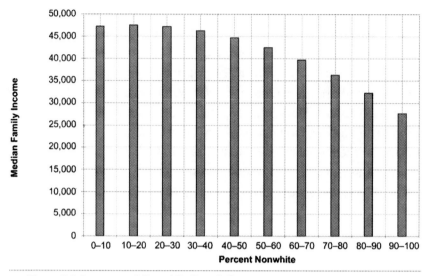

Figure 2.5 Income and Nonwhite Population

A similar relationship is revealed by the percentage of each population group living below the poverty line (Figure 2.6). As the nonwhite population increases, so does the extent of poverty in the city. When a city is nearly 100% white, less than 14% of its inhabitants live in poverty. By the time the nonwhite population reaches 80%, the proportion in poverty has just about doubled.[7]

Changes in income in recent decades indicate that both the advantaged and the disadvantaged are becoming relatively more so. The gap between the median incomes of Black and white families in central cities widened between 1980, when median Black income was 64% that of white families, and 1990, when it had dropped to 59% of white income. In this period, white family median income rose 93%, compared to a rise of only 77% for Blacks. The most important single fact is the large proportion of Black families that remain in the very-low-income brackets. In 2000, 24.9% of Blacks had incomes below the poverty level, compared to just 8.1% of whites. To a large extent, this situation reflects the disadvantages that Blacks continue to face in the job market.

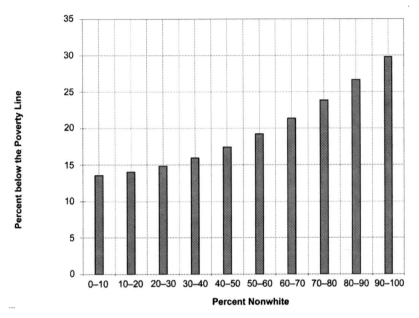

Figure 2.6 Poverty and the Nonwhite Population, 2000

The Need for Coordinated Planning

The difficulties faced within central cities and with respect to their relationships to suburbs and outlying areas can be classified as two sets of issues. The first set is made up of environmental and physical issues. These issues are concerned with the impact of cities and urban living on basic resources like land, air, water, and living organisms, as well as with the use of these resources to meet the needs of living and working space, transportation, and production of goods essential to urban society. The second set of issues are the somewhat less tangible social and human issues. What are the effects of the diverse and changing mixes of people and activities in different segments of the urban/ metropolitan scene?

The History of Environmental and Physical Issues

The impact of both sets of issues on the existing resource and institutional base made unavoidable the physical and social planning that was first developed during the Roosevelt administration and the Great Depression. The rapid urbanization that followed World War II gave further impetus to planning. Here we note a few of the specific problems that have been the subject of systematic planning to address environmental and physical issues. Generally, these concerns fall into the categories of water supply, pollution, transportation, and land-use controls.

Periodic water shortages over the past half-century in different parts of the country are an instructive example of crises created by urbanization. Water supply was once an individual or family matter. As cities developed in the eighteenth and nineteenth centuries, water supply became a municipal concern in areas where the population was too concentrated for individuals on their own to obtain water from a well, spring, or brook.

During the twentieth century as we moved from subsurface water to watersheds as sources, water supply became a regional and national concern. The concentration of people over vast spaces across municipal and even state boundary lines has created competition among cities for water flowing from common watersheds. What happens on one side of the river affects those on the other side, and what happens upstream affects those downstream. The problem of water supply can only be solved through the participation of all levels of government in regional planning and service authorities.

Neither the flow of water above or under the ground nor the sweep of winds across land or sea respects municipal, state, or national boundaries. An automobile, a brush fire, or an open hearth—no matter where it is—makes its contribution to the accumulated pall of carbon dioxide in the upper atmosphere. Atomic waste—wherever generated—may contribute to the radioactive component of the polar ice pack. It takes national and international strategies, not just local ones, to monitor and control such urban-generated alterations in the earth's environment. The similar and closely related problems of water supply and water and air pollution have in many urban areas yielded to regional planning and service authorities. A welter of special districts (discussed in later chapters) does the rest of the job.

When it comes to infrastructure deemed necessary for urban living, more and more of it cannot be built or maintained on a strictly local basis. Around the turn of the twentieth century, states began to enter seriously into the highway business, first with county and local roads and then with the beginnings of state highway systems. The first comprehensive federal highway system was developed between 1914 and World War II. In President Dwight D. Eisenhower's administration in the 1950s, the federal government commenced work on a second, greatly improved, national highway system. This was the Interstate Highway System, authorized by Congress in the National Defense Highway Construction Act of 1956.[8] This system, formally justified by defense and national security needs, was actually designed to meet the demands of automobile and truck traffic that had been building up since the 1930s. The emphasis of the interstate highway system was on national cross-country routes and on networks in and around cities. Ninety percent of the costs of the system are paid by the federal government and 10% are paid by the states.

Rail transportation systems also did not remain local or private. Whereas once the New York subway and elevated-rail system constituted an effective metropolitan transportation system, it became evident a half-century ago that a metropolitan system for the New York area could not be maintained without the collaboration of three states and the federal government. Amtrak has continually struggled to decouple itself from massive public subsidies, but by the end of the twentieth century little or no progress had been made. In the 1990s, the federal government began investing in experimental work to develop a high-speed ground transportation system to connect principal centers in the Northeast Corridor from Boston to Washington, D.C.

In much the same way, electronic communication by telegraph, telephone, radio, television, computers, and satellites long ago developed beyond the capability of local communities and local authorities to control. The same is true for the production and distribution of energy resources. A combination of public regulatory and private entrepreneurial activity has addressed these problems. As technology has advanced, these concerns have become even larger in scope. A global economy and communications system now carries information, energy, and pollution across international boundaries.

Land-use controls, traditionally left in local hands, had become ineffective by the 1950s, even within single municipalities. One of the reasons for the failure was the pressure of regional markets on municipalities that were in competition with one another for to increase their property-tax base. States that had not weakened their own powers through constitutional limitations were reluctant to use their powers to override local interests, except occasionally on the politically sensitive location of a highway or other critical public facility. All of these issues demanded, and continue to demand, coordination on a regional, statewide, and federal level.

Federal Involvement in Environmental and Physical Issues. As a result, the federal government became increasingly involved in the effort to introduce planning into urban development. Beginning with national support for local planning in the Housing Act of 1954,[9] the federal government moved toward requiring effective metropolitan planning as a prerequisite for the location of national, state, and local facilities. As we shall see in later chapters and especially in Chapters 7 and 9, policymakers have long since accepted that the federal government, either on its own or in collaboration with state and local government, is responsible for facilities and programs that, when planned and developed in harmony, can have a beneficial influence on the quality of life in urban areas.

Such programs include transportation by air, land, and sea; and control of air and water pollution, of strips of land along highways, and of other land that borders on federal facilities. They also include supervision of hospital and other health facilities, defense installations and contracts, housing and urban-renewal projects, and educational facilities. The planned management of such programs has become an essential tool for the development of new cities and towns.

History of Social and Human Issues

The social and human issues that gave rise to systematic planning in urban areas include health concerns, living conditions, welfare, education, and employment. The solutions to these issues are always affected by the way in which physical facilities are planned and deployed. The same conditions that made it necessary to deal with physical aspects of the city on a broader basis than the individual municipality made it equally necessary to deal with human-service needs on a regional scale.

The problem of meeting social and human needs in urban America has always been complicated by the ghettoization of race and poverty. It is a well-documented fact that poverty, inferior education, broken families, disease, mental illness, drug addiction, malnutrition, youth delinquency, unemployment (and underemployment), and other socially pathological conditions are concentrated in central cities and that the concentration is becoming more intense over time. Racial discrimination, still pervasive in our society, has kept poor African Americans and Hispanics, as well as certain other minorities, from escaping the poverty of the inner city that so many earlier immigrants experienced in the first generation or two after their arrival in this country.

African Americans have been subjected to the worst effects of racial discrimination throughout our national history. Whereas at the turn of the twentieth century most African Americans were rural southerners, by the end of World War II the great internal migration of African Americans to northern industrial centers was well under way and thereafter most became city people. Now African Americans constitute a large portion of the poorest and most economically depressed people in our country. Since the 1960s, Hispanics from Puerto Rico and Mexico, as well as other Caribbean Islands and Central and South American countries, have joined them. The darker the skin of the Hispanic person, the greater the barrier of discrimination he or she faces.

Despite efforts to counteract it, the urbanization of social problems continues in the early years of the twenty-first century and the conditions of the poor in the inner cities have a profound effect on the financing and delivery of public services. The experimental programs of the federal government, starting with President Lyndon Johnson's Great Society programs in the 1960s, have been aimed at finding solutions to the problem of adapting public services to the life style and needs of poor people. The task has not been easy and many failed programs have discouraged well-meaning political and civic leaders and undermined family unity.

In the end, the cities in which poverty conditions are concentrated have been largely incapable of dealing with them without direct or indirect help from adjacent, more affluent communities, from the states, and from the federal government. The concentration of these problems in cities, many of them originally exported from rural America, has not been offset by an increase in cities' fiscal resources for meeting them. The exclusiveness of suburbs, enforced in varying degrees by law, the market, and prejudice, has made it difficult for cities to export their problems or import the resources necessary to correct them. Suburban exclusiveness not only intensifies the plight of inner-city residents, but also reduces their responsiveness to efforts to open the road to upward mobility.

Federal Involvement in Social and Human Issues. For the same reason that states have not been able by themselves to deal with such physical problems as highway development or pollution control, the states have not been able by themselves to meet the human problems of the older cities and some of the older suburbs into which the social problems have spilled. The federal government began to address locally based social needs during the Great Depression and, as a result, we have a permanent social-security system, a public housing program, urban renewal, and employment security, each one effective and each one flawed in its own specific ways.

In the 1960s, the federal government added civil-rights protections, anti-poverty programs, health planning, library support, aid to public education, and other programs. These have provided national leadership and resources in collaborative efforts involving national, state, and local governments, as well as a variety of private agencies and interests. The Economic Opportunity Act of 1964,[10] the statutory basis for President Johnson's War on Poverty programs, typified the collaborative approach. These and other programs were concerned with rural as well as urban areas, but urban communities have benefited from successful attacks on rural poverty and deprivation, because rural problems, if untreated in their rural environs, tend to move to cities.

The main reason national urban programs developed more rapidly than the urban programs of states may be found in the composition of state legislatures prior to 1970. These legislatures were predominantly rural in their orientation before *Baker v. Carr*[11] and *Reynolds v. Sims*.[12] These decisions established the one-man, one-vote rule as the law of the land and forced the legislatures to reapportion seats at every census. By contrast, United States senators are elected at large in their states. Since a majority of the states were urban prior to 1970, U.S. senators had to pay serious attention to the urban needs and problems of their states. This was true even of states with urban minorities, because candidates for the U.S. Senate had to cater to urban as well as rural voters.

Even under reapportionment, urban legislators in state legislatures tend to represent small segments of large urban communities, an arrangement that has continued to emphasize narrow and fractionalized urban interests rather than broad ones. Reapportionment of state legislatures has helped states respond to urban problems, but only when the urban people who live outside the central cities send representatives who assume a generous attitude toward the needs of the whole urban society—or when they find it beneficial to trade support with city representatives.

Governing Urban Areas

The complex nature of the modern metropolis and its ever-changing character demand some level of coordinated governance. There have been past attempts to impose a governance structure over and across metropolitan areas, but these arrangements have been neither substantial enough or dynamic enough to meet the challenges produced by urban environments in the United States.

Consider, for example, the political and service implications of these diverse patterns of urbanization: the continuous urbanization between Connecticut and New York; the states with one dominant urban region such as Illinois and Colorado; the bipolar urban regions of Pennsylvania and California; the multinucleated urban developments of states like Florida, Ohio, and Texas.

One solution is to turn to the states for coordinated governance. In fact, the major metropolitan concentrations in several states (Illinois and California, for example) have a profound impact on the politics and governance of their respective states. A notable one is New York, where metropolitan development has led to the state assuming responsibility for a variety of regional functions through special authorities. But metropolitan regions are as a rule governmentally fractionated, and do not carry the political weight in the state equal to that of single cities of the same size.

In addition, the various ways in which urban and metropolitan populations are distributed within the states have different effects on politics and governance and on the ways in which citizens can be best served. Typically, when suburban areas or satellite cities have considerable power, they provide a major obstacle to metropolitan reorganization and governance. Those metropolitan consolidations that have occurred since World War II have involved cities and counties where municipal government outside the central cities was largely inconsequential. Moreover, many city consolidations were precipitated by such crises as the exposure of corruption in municipal government (Jacksonville-Duval County, where reorganization did not help), fear of takeover by Blacks (Atlanta-Fulton County), fear of loss of local control by conservatives (Indianapolis-Marion County). These are not circumstances that should or could drive a broad program of metropolitan reorganization.

As much as the configuration of metropolitan areas within states is important, their distribution and growth among states is also important because many metropolitan areas extend over state boundaries. As we have noted, there were thirty-four such MSAs in 2000. Even more important is that size and growth are indicators of the distributions of political power, economic resources, demand for public services, and the cause of changes in those distributions. During the last quarter of the twentieth century, the growth areas were in the South Atlantic, Mountain, and Pacific areas, followed after the mid-1980s by a strong resurgence in the Midwest and Upper Midwest. Particular states have also experienced high growth during the period since 1970: New Hampshire, Connecticut, New Jersey, and Texas. Meanwhile, scores of rural towns and counties in the vast central region between the Mississippi and the Rocky Mountains have thinned out. So have two states—North Dakota and South Dakota. A map showing growth rates by counties indicates that the concentration of population has increased since 1970 mainly around the outer edges of the country, including the northern edge around the Great Lakes.

The relative growth of cities and their suburbs is also cause for concern regarding state coordination. Since suburban populations are increasing and most central cities are not, the political power of suburbs has outrun that of central cities. This condition is reflected in state legislatures. One result is that state grants to suburbs tend to be larger than those to central cities in spite of the greater needs of the latter. Studies of state aid distribution patterns over the past quarter-century provide many examples of situations in which per-capita grants to suburbs are higher than those to central cities. These same studies have documented that central-city problems usually demand more dollars than comparable ones in suburbs.

Summary

What this all means is that substantial coordination is necessary from the federal level to meet the challenges presented by an urban environment that is continuing to grow in size, complexity, and interdependence. We are not saying that states and localities should be stripped of their responsibilities for their metropolitan areas. It is firm national policy, often reiterated, that federal programs be administered through state and local institutions. We have witnessed an increasing shift toward addressing state and local needs through national support of locally administered programs. The Welfare Reform Act of 1996 redirected the federal welfare program toward such a policy, with the states taking the lead in designing and administering welfare, and the federal government providing resources in block grants.[13]

Nevertheless, urban America expects to be served by a collaborative effort of national, state, and local governments. The facts regarding the distribution of urban settlement throughout the country make clear this necessity. As we show in Chapter 9, the key is regional and metropolitan planning as well as the efficiency with which intergovernmental collaboration proceeds. The nature of local participation depends on the capacity of people in state and local communities to exercise initiative and set aside parochialism. Only a coordinated national, state, and regional effort can tap the necessary fiscal and intellectual resources on a sufficient scale to deploy them over large enough areas to cope with the problems highlighted here and in Chapter 4. Thus to address this need we propose (in Chapter 9) that all the states create wall-to-wall substate planning and administrative districts based on counties.

Notes

1. Metropolitan Areas are defined and identified by the United States Office of Management and Budget on a continuing basis. Changes in the list of MAs occur each year when Census Bureau estimates indicate whether an area has met or lost its metropolitan status. When we report statistics using MAs, we also give the year and the number of MAs defined as of that year.
2. Eli Ginsberg, "The Changing Urban Scene: 1960–1990 and Beyond," in *Interwoven Destinies, Cities and the Nation,* ed. Henry G. Cisneros (New York: W.W. Norton, 1993), p. 36.
3. Source: U.S. Department of Agriculture Census of Agriculture 1997.

4. Robert J. Waste, *Independent Cities* (New York: Oxford University Press, 1998), p. 23.
5. In this book, we use the words "African American" and "Black" interchangeably to designate people in the United States of African ancestry. We use the term "Asian" to designate people in the United States whose origins are from a nation on the Pacific Rim and "Hispanic" for people in the United States whose origins are from Mexico, Puerto Rico, or another Latin American or Caribbean nation.
6. Joseph Dalaker and Mary Naifeh, U.S. Census Bureau, *Current Population Reports, Series P60-201, Poverty in the United States: 1997* (Washington, D.C.: U.S. Government Printing Office, 1998).
7. Technical Note: Figures 2.5 and 2.6 were derived from census data for all central cities in 2000. Curvilinear functions were fit to the data using ordinary least-squares, and values for each nonwhite population level were calculated from the regression equation using the midpoint of each level.
8. P.L. 84-627, National Defense Highway Construction Act of 1956 (embedded in the Federal-Aid Highway Act of 1956).
9. P.L. 560, Chapter 649, Housing Act of 1954.
10. P.L. 88-452, Equal Opportunity Act 1964.
11. 369 U.S. 186, 1962 (*Baker v. Carr*).
12. 377 U.S. 533, 1964 (*Reynolds v. Sims*).
13. P.L. 104-193, The Personal Responsibility and Work Opportunity Reconciliation Act of 1996 (the Welfare Act of 1996).

Chapter 3

Problems, Priorities, and Planning

A stable and prosperous economy is among the enduring priorities of the American people. They also want livable homes in safe, pleasant neighborhoods; availability of public education through college; access to affordable healthcare; reasonable security against crime, disorder, fire, natural disasters, and terrorism; wholesome air and water; access to cultural amenities and to nature; efficient air and ground transportation; and the alleviation of poverty, discrimination, and other forms of social deprivation. This chapter discusses these priorities, aspects of them that require areawide approaches, and the value of planning in bringing about solutions.

The strategies of improvement advocated by policymakers and social scientists of the 1960s and 1970s focused on public education, poverty, welfare, healthcare, housing, mass transportation, technological applications to urban problems, and, in the latter part of that period, environmental issues. Some urban scholars reasoned that several of these strategies, successfully implemented, might alleviate the conditions that had caused the social unrest and inner-city riots of the 1960s.

As urban areas developed in the first half of the twentieth century, the emerging problems that seemed to require areawide solutions included aspects of education, housing, employment, health, welfare, mass transportation and highway planning, water supply and sewage disposal, air and water pollution. Attentive policymakers could see that some aspects of all these problems required serious governmental attention on a regional level. Only areawide governing structures could effectively implement policies that would prudently manage resource redistribution, provide equal access to public goods and opportunity, and effect desegregation of housing and neighborhoods.

Absent a regional governmental authority to deal with these sensitive issues, the urban areas of America might never achieve a working consensus. There would be no authoritative mechanism for healing the schisms that are inherent in our socially diverse metropolitan communities. The consequences of a failure to achieve such a goal during the second half of the twentieth century should teach us that an areawide solution to metropolitan governance must be achieved. The stakes are high. The price of failure is at best rising crime rates; at worst, a decline in living conditions and periodic civil unrest in our inner cities.

The importance of achieving some form of regional governing authority is desirable (1) when coordination of a function over the whole area is essential to effective service throughout the area; (2) when the ability-to-pay theory of taxation should be applied to the area as a whole, instead of local units supporting public services at whatever level the economic base of each allows; (3) when services can be supplied more efficiently through large-scale operations; and (4) when citizens need assurance of a voice in decisions that affect them where they live and work.

From a historical perspective, the first urban area to recognize the need for metropolitanwide government was New York City and its adjacent counties, which became one city on January 1, 1898. Twenty-three city consolidations occurred in the decades that followed. But the earliest of these mergers came before the widespread availability of the automobile and the emergence of socially exclusive suburbs—and before the great migration of Blacks to cities. Once Blacks began to fill up city neighborhoods, resistance in suburbs slowed metropolitan reorganization. Annexations continued in states that permitted the cities to move without the consent of suburbs or where unincorporated vacant land was the target. In states where consolidation and annexation were not politically possible, special service districts were frequently used.

Urban Problems and Priorities

Poverty as a Lack of Money

A fashion among social scientists and policymakers of the 1960s and 1970s was to assert that poverty was largely a lack of money and that providing the poor with a guaranteed annual income could solve the age-old problem of poverty. In a stroke of legislation, poverty could be ended—except for dependency. Some people who were physically or psychologically incapacitated would be left for society to care for. They would get special services and supporting institutions. At least, it was argued, society would be down to a hard core having nothing to do with class or race.

One proposal called for a minimum annual payment to anyone whose income fell below a level necessary to maintain an acceptable standard of living. The law establishing the program would set the guidelines of an "acceptable standard of living" while the largesse of the nation would produce the required funds.

A minimum guaranteed income, already in place in some industrialized nations, would, it was reasoned, give poor people a new start, new hope, and the incentive to become productive citizens. The recipients of the largesse would become consumers in the national marketplace and thereby give the economy a boost. It was expected that recipients would use the guaranteed income largely as a base of family stability and as a foundation upon which to build toward new opportunities.

The chief argument was that if economic poverty were eliminated, the major social problems of the cities would be solved—crime, joblessness, and health issues. The frustration, bitterness, and loss of dignity that are part and parcel of destitution are the sources of crime, delinquency, and social unrest that are identified with slums and ethnic ghettos of our cities. Self-sufficient people with hope would readily join in the productive activities of society. Those who were physically or mentally incapacitated would be supported in any event. But theory was one thing, the political reality another.

None of the rationale for buying the nation's way out of the poverty problem prevailed. President Lyndon Johnson declared a war on poverty as part of his Great Society initiatives, but his long menu of projects did not include a guaranteed income. In 1970, President Richard Nixon surprised people in both political parties when he proposed the so-called negative income tax, wherein payments to the individual would be made if the individual's federal tax return showed income below a predetermined level. Instead of paying a tax, the individual whose income fell below the standard would receive a check to make up the difference between actual income and the income necessary to support a minimum standard of living.[1]

President Nixon's guaranteed income program got nowhere in Congress even though economists across the political spectrum supported the concept. However, Congress did authorize the Earned Income Tax Credit (EITC) in 1975, which was a form of the negative income tax but available only to families with earnings from employment. This program was expanded in 1986, 1990, and 1993. We discuss the EITC in greater detail in Chapter 10.

Welfare as a Safety Net

A New Deal–sponsored federal welfare program had for decades paid monthly cash benefits to parents with dependent children. In 1962, this program was renamed Aid to Families with Dependent Children (AFDC) and supplemented by food stamps in President Johnson's antipoverty program. Critics claimed that AFDC induced dependency, and in fact many families stayed in the program for generations.

By the 1990s, sufficient public resentment of "welfare as usual" had built up in the nation and provided the political leeway to promote new legislation that would require welfare recipients to move into the workforce with built-in deadlines.[2] The first such bill was the Welfare Reform Act of 1988,[3] authored by Daniel Patrick Moynihan. The act required each state to create demonstration projects that moved a fixed percentage of their AFDC population into job training, counseling, and work-requirement programs in exchange for receiving monthly AFDC monetary assistance.

Subsequently, the Welfare Reform Act of 1996 established training programs, and private business was provided with inducements to hire people from the welfare rolls. The act set five years as the maximum time a person could receive welfare benefits. States were required to set up their own programs with the aid of federal block grants.

Welfare rolls did drop dramatically in the 1990s: there was a nationwide drop of 58% in welfare cases from 1994 to 2001. But it is unclear how much of this drop was due to reform efforts and how much to an unprecedented period of national economic prosperity, low unemployment, negligible inflation, and high consumer confidence. Furthermore, the gains have been considerably less dramatic in major metropolitan areas. From 1994 to 1998, counties containing the nation's thirty largest cities saw a drop in welfare rolls of only about 30% (compared to 44% nationwide). As the economy slowed after 2000, some eighteen states experienced reversals and their welfare rolls began to grow again. By 2002, more than 20% of households in the U.S. were receiving some kind of means-tested welfare benefit.

Housing for the Poor

Urban scholars writing in the 1960s about the future of housing in central cities speculated that if public or private developers were to bring into the market moderately priced dwelling units that "felt" more like a house than an apartment, the postwar trend to suburban single-family homes might shift back to central-city locations. They observed that factors such as reduced air pollution, control of street crime, improved public education, and public transportation might also encourage the middle class to return to the city. Flight from central cities, they reasoned, was a flight from the tenements and life styles associated with poverty and low-status newcomers. Their speculations proved to be very far from the actual behavior of urban dwellers in the 1950s or in the years since.

Nevertheless, some housing developments in central cities lured middle-class and upwardly mobile professionals back into the central areas: the so-called gentrification process, which in the 1960s and 1970s targeted old neighborhoods like Back Bay in Boston.[4] In such neighborhoods, sound old mansions that had been originally built by the wealthy of another era were converted into upscale housing for a new generation of affluent professionals. The gentrification process became fashionable in many cities and provided attractive housing for successful professionals who preferred city living to suburbia, as well as "empty nest" older couples who no longer needed a suburban family home.

Urban Renewal: An Evolutionary Process

The civic objectives, the relationship between public and local government and between public and private involvement, and the sources of funding and operational characteristics of urban renewal have changed dramatically over the past five or six decades. Those changes can be described as (1) the "postwar" federal program era (which lasted roughly from the mid-1930s during the Great Depression to the mid-1970s); (2) the urban development action-grant (UDAG) era, which coincided with the expansion of the commercial real estate market in the 1970s and 1980s; and (3) the tax-increment financing (TIF) era of the 1990s.

The Postwar Era. The objective of urban renewal during this period was the creation of well-planned neighborhoods of new housing for working-class families. The federal government offered grants to local governments to pay 90% of the cost of acquiring and demolishing blighted and deteriorated properties so that the land could be made available at attractive "write-down" prices to various private and institutional investors. Success varied from city to city and from project to project, because many of the projects were located in undesirable areas at a time when population and capital were flowing to the suburbs.

The UDAG Era. The UDAG program was a response to changing market dynamics. By the mid-1970s, a trend toward major reinvestment in central cities, albeit on a very selective basis, became evident. Whereas the postwar program left selection of sites and the initiation of projects to local governments, UDAG grants were largely a response to projects initiated by private investors. Local agencies could offer grants (later expanded to grants and/or loans) to such projects, generally on the basis of at least six dollars of private investment for each UDAG dollar. In most cases, private investment was much greater than the six-to-one rule of thumb. The incentives for giving such grants ranged from cases where assistance was critical to financing the project that the city desired to situations where such aid enabled the city to impose requirements reflecting civic values, such as affirmative action programs, set-asides for low-income housing, and so forth.

The TIF Era. Although *tax-increment financing* has been around in some states for decades, the demise of the federal UDAG program made the TIFs an attractive alternative to relying on federal funds and programs to support local urban renewal. The fact that the 1990s witnessed an explosive reinvestment in retail, entertainment, cultural, educational, residential, and hotel properties in the central areas of major cities meant that an expanding local property-tax base could support TIFs. Operationally, TIFs give local governments the option of using such funds to initiate projects or to assist projects that have already been initiated by private or institutional investors. TIFs have been used to restore historic properties and to facilitate the adaptive reuse of obsolescent properties. This flexibility, locally funded, puts local government in a position to be a partner, a stimulator, or a benefactor—in short, to determine for itself what role, and to what extent, it wants to take in guiding renewal of the city. Of course, tax increment financing is practical only when the economy continues to generate increases in property values.

Bernard Frieden and Lynne Sagalyn explain tax-increment financing:

Tax-increment financing, a system for redeveloping blighted areas, dates back to 1952 in California; by the mid-1970s seventeen states had authorized this form of financing. It allows city redevelopment agencies to pay their expenses for a project by keeping the increase in property tax collections that normally results from new construction and rising assessments in a project area. Using this revenue stream as collateral, redevelopment agencies issue tax-exempt bonds and operate with much greater financial autonomy than the federal urban renewal program ever allowed. To start the process, a redevelopment agency draws boundaries for a tax-increment district, holds public hearings to establish that the area is in a blighted condition appropriate for redevelopment, and presents a project plan to the city council for approval. When the council approves the plan, the assessed valuation of property in the district, called the tax base, is frozen for the benefit of local governments that have been collecting taxes from it. Afterward any tax revenues that result from an increase in the tax flow from the county collection office go to the coffers of the redevelopment agency.

Politically, tax-increment financing is a redevelopment director's dream. Once committed, the money rolls in with a minimum of effort, exempt from the annual appropriation struggle over tax dollars. Since the bond issues based on this income are not direct obligations of the city, they do not have to go on the ballot for voter approval once the city council endorses them. In California the administrative machinery necessary to move this process is relatively simple, legal standards for establishing blight and drawing boundaries are liberal, and discretionary powers over the uses of the tax increments for redevelopment purposes are broad. As an instrument of public policy, tax-increment financing is controversial, but as a revenue raiser there is no question that it provides cities with a treasure chest for redevelopment.[5]

The federal urban renewal program was launched in the Housing Act of 1949 to clear city slums and to rehouse their occupants in "safe, sanitary, affordable housing."[6] The paradox of postwar federal housing and urban-renewal policies is that they were *conceived* during a period of economic and population stagnation (the Great Depression of the 1930s) but *initiated* during a period of tremendous pressure on scarce housing resources caused by demobilization of the armed forces and migration during the war of rural labor to defense industries in urban centers.

The conventional wisdom in the 1930s was that the American industrial system had reached "maturity." As part of its efforts to jump-start the Depression economy and to encourage a fairer distribution of resources to the one-third of the nation that was "ill-fed, ill-clothed and ill-housed," the federal government began to sponsor and fund systematic inventories of the nation's assets and liabilities (infrastructure, housing, and the like). For example, the federal government funded the 1939 Land-Use Survey of the city of Chicago. This survey, typical of others, found 76,000 units (nearly 8% of the city's total housing supply) in need of major repair or unfit for use. The Land-Use Survey produced two volumes of statistics and 150 others of maps, figures, and neighborhood detail that laid the factual basis for subsequent housing policy.

The immediate product of the Chicago inventory was a new city master plan, adopted by the Chicago Plan Commission in 1943, which classified the city's neighborhoods. One of the commission's recommendations called for total demolition of twenty-three square miles of blighted and near-blighted residential areas.[7]

The Illinois legislature, in its first general session after the war, passed into law the Blighted Areas Redevelopment Act of 1947, which served as a model for the U.S. Housing Act of 1949. The Illinois legislature created three parallel programs, all funded with state and local bonds and grants: a slum-clearance program; a middle-income program with a veterans' preference; and a public housing program for low-income families displaced by development programs.

These and similar programs were nurtured in an era when it seemed conceivable that the cities of America, hastily developed over the previous half-century or so, could be rebuilt in an orderly way. However, the severe housing shortages that developed after World War II made the dream a nightmare: elimination of blighted housing in one area exacerbated the competition for housing in adjoining areas, resulting in community friction and political controversy.

The urban housing market was hobbled by rent controls that stifled private-sector development; scarcity of large tracts of vacant land; and federal-mortgage-underwriting programs that facilitated rapid development of new suburbs. The duration of rent controls varied in different cities and states (for example, rent control in Chicago lasted until 1953). Their main problem was that they put *new* rental housing (generally not subject to rent control) at a severe price disadvantage and thus discouraged new construction. For example, if the spread between the highest rents at the top of the market was normally 20% less than new construction, under rent control that spread might be anywhere from 50% to 100%. Thus renters looking for housing would experience "price shock" when confronted with the rents for new construction.

What all this meant was that while the country seemed ready to deal with an inheritance of blight and slum clearance, conditions were not propitious for new in-city community building. In fact, the market conditions for new in-city building in many cities did not come into play until the mid-1970s.

The impact of postwar conditions as they played out against prewar assumptions and standards is evident in the evolution of public housing projects since the war. Most projects built in the 1930s and early 1940s were low-rise communities of townhouses and walk-up apartments on relatively large tracts of land with generous open spaces for playgrounds and landscaping. As Mayer and Wade reported in 1968 pertaining to the Chicago experience, "Over 5,000 units of public housing were constructed in various parts of the city before the end of World War II. The apartments did not go over four stories, and some row houses were also built. All had extensive open spaces for play areas, off-street parking and extensive landscaping. They remained for many decades among the most attractive low-income dwellings in Chicago."[8]

Beginning in 1993, the Department of Housing and Urban Development (HUD) allocated $4 billion to ninety cities to rehabilitate or demolish and reconstruct public housing projects. Chicago, with its decades of experience in public housing, opted for $1.5 billion to renovate or replace 25,000 units in fifty old public housing high-rises. Some of the replacement housing units were to be in mixed-income communities, while others harked back to the 1930s as new low-rise homes. Chicago also made available federal housing vouchers for qualified people to search for housing in the private rental market.

The construction of high-density, high-rise public housing was generally a postwar phenomenon in response to community opposition to public housing, often referred to by the acronym "NIMBY" (not in my backyard), which tended to result in development of fewer and higher-density projects. This all-too-common attitude was against a backdrop of a critical shortage of housing, particularly for low-income households. The high-rise construction style represented a shift away from building communities toward mass-produced housing, in effect to "warehouse" poverty with little regard for the social consequences.

Introduction of the Urban Development Action Grant program (UDAG) in the Carter administration was a reversal in federal funding strategy with respect to urban redevelopment. Whereas the 1949 and 1954 housing acts focused on eliminating blight by underwriting the costs of land acquisition and slum clearance in hopes of generating markets for reinvesting in central cities, the UDAG program let the private investor/developer make the initial moves of site selection and plan proposal and then brought UDAG assistance to bear to reduce the economic risks or to impose special conditions and requirements on the developer in the public interest. Whereas the federal program was bucking the market in the 1950s and 1960s, it was taking advantage of the market in the 1970s and 1980s.

The demise of the UDAG program in the Reagan administration created a gap in Chicago's and other cities' financial ability to stimulate and influence inner-city development, especially commercial and other nonresidential development. The gap has since been resolved by increased utilization of TIFs.

Through the 1950s and 1960s, large tracts of central-city land were cleared of deteriorated commercial and residential buildings. The redevelopment of most of these tracts turned out to be projects by private entrepreneurs for businesses and not-so-affordable high-rise apartments and condominiums. Herbert Gans's *Urban Villagers* documents the case of the redevelopment of Boston's West End under the federal urban renewal program.[9]

The residential market for central-city redevelopment, both from urban-renewal projects and private gentrification, was created largely by the postwar "baby boomers" when they hit the family housing market in the early 1970s. A few years earlier they had created a strong demand for apartment-style housing for young singles.

Like the gentrification movement, the process of urban redevelopment through the urban-renewal program made it possible for people whose work was in the city to live in the city. At the beginning of the twenty-first century, central cities are increasingly populated by the middle and upper classes in developments designed to ensure secure living with built-in amenities, including schools and day-care facilities. Moreover, changing family patterns involve smaller, often fragmented families. In the United Kingdom, where the government is expecting construction of 4 million new homes by 2020, fully 80 percent will be single-person dwellings located in cities.[10]

The gentrification movement resulted in pricing the poor out of selected near-in neighborhoods in central cities. That displacement, coupled with "de-institutionalization" of people with persistent mental illnesses and drastic reduction of federal-housing programs in the late 1970s and 1980s, produced a crisis of homelessness that has grown to alarming proportions.

In the United Kingdom, new towns were planned and built before old neighborhoods were torn down so that the displaced families would have housing into which they could move. By contrast, in the United States older neighborhoods were torn down and the displaced families were largely left to search for the own alternatives.

In the last two decades of the twentieth century the nation displaced more families than it housed, and so housing became a critical issue. Displaced homeowners often faced serious economic damage as a result of inequitable and obsolete public compensation practices. Such practices have not always provided a satisfactory level of compensation to assure replacement of lost housing. This is one reason why well-intentioned public programs of development/redevelopment were accused of aggravating rather than relieving the housing problem.

The reputed disparities between the prices paid displaced homeowners for their properties and asking prices for comparable nonsubstandard housing space in the urban market were so gross that even the U.S. Congress was compelled to take note. Eventually, legislation was passed permitting local public agencies to use federal funds to make relocation bonus payments to individual homeowners to close the gap between the prices paid by local public agencies for the homeowners' properties and prevailing market prices.

This was back-door relief. that did not address a system of compensation that produces inequitable results. Critics point out that homeowners were receiving standard housing to replace substandard and that the real issue is availability and affordability, not equity. Resolution of such questions is necessary to maintain public confidence in the basic fairness of public programs. Ad hoc temporary relief, exercised at the discretion of a local agency that may be responsible for the inequity, is not a sufficient protection of the urban homeowners' rights.

The Constitution requires that owners of private property taken by condemnation be given "just compensation." Most states follow suit in their eminent domain laws.[11] Statutory and case law define just compensation as "fair market value." Economic theory defines fair market value as that price which a free and willing buyer would offer and which a free and willing seller would accept for the property. Compulsion by either party—such as force, threat of legal action, enforceable deadlines, and the like—is anathema to this concept. It conjures up a vision of a transaction in which bargaining on the basis of self-interest is the only weapon permitted.

The fact is that compulsion is always present either implicitly or explicitly in condemnation proceedings. Whether the seller is willing or not, the outcome is never in doubt. Under this cloud, the "fairness" of the "fair market value" concept of just compensation is suspect.

The just compensation concept was developed in the early days of public acquisition. Just compensation needs to be redefined in terms that are relevant in a contemporary urban society and in a context that reflects the massive scale of present and proposed redevelopment plans. The states, through statutory clarification, should overturn the fair-market-value doctrine in favor of a "replacement-value" doctrine of compensation that would allow a displaced homeowner to replace the house lost. Then the residents of deteriorated urban areas would not be penalized for the historical accident of being there when society decides to redevelop an area. The relocation process upon which redevelopment programs are founded—at least in the eyes of public acceptance—is so critical that the concept of replacement value may restore public acceptance. As matters stand, the poor can contest government valuations in court but are often abused "in the public interest." Another approach is to establish an independent valuation tribunal to do the valuation—a tribunal with no stake or advantage in the acquisition of "cheap land."

The redevelopment process, although it involves the use of the eminent domain power, in practice revolves around the transference of land from one group of private owners to another group of private owners. As such, it raises a critical social issue: nonlocal private developers stand to benefit from future unearned increments in the value of the land that they have secured at public subsidy, while local citizens who suffered the inconvenience of displacement to make way for redevelopment do not stand to benefit. In fact, they sometimes pay serious economic and social penalties. The same is true in situations of private-to-public land transfers.

Thus, the charge is heard in our urban centers that public agencies are interested in residential redevelopment in order to gain control of attractive located urban land for use by a different economic class of citizens. At the same time, there has long been public interest in favor of local participation at the community level in the redevelopment process. A spate of "neighborhood housing corporations" has emerged across the country in response to this interest. These have been encouraged by governmental agencies, mainly at the state level. The main barriers to their successful participation are a lack of skills and influence with financing and political institutions and a lack of neighborhood capital.

In furtherance of such objectives and to mitigate the presumption of unfairness in the reuse of land, the states should enact legislation to permit homeowners whose properties are to be cleared the option of selling or retaining their interest in the land under their homes. If they chose to retain an interest in the land, their equity would be converted to liquid interests such as representative shares in a community land trust that would own and then lease the land to developers. In this fashion, displaced homeowners would participate in the future incremental increase in the value of the land. They could continue to retain their shares as part of their estates or sell them. This practice is common in the private sector, wherein property owners contribute the value of their land as their equity in a development project. The downside lies in the difficulty in creating a market for such interests. Real estate investment trusts (REITs), for example, lack access to good secondary markets. In America there is also a strong bias against home ownership in the form of land leaseholds. Yet such an approach would replace some of the unfairness of the city rebuilding/redevelopment programs, give local people a stake in their cities, and make land available for desirable reuse. It would further make neighborhood capital available in the form of equity in the land and leases as financing collateral.

Ever since the federal government scaled back its commitment to "safe and decent housing for every American," housing shortages have been severe. In contrast to the Reagan and Bush administrations, the Clinton administration in the 1990s attempted to reestablish public housing as a federal priority. The Clinton housing program envisioned several basic types of projects to address the housing needs of the poor and the homeless. These included outreach, intake, and assessment as well as emergency shelter to address the spectrum of needs of the homeless; transitional housing to provide scattered-site housing for individuals and families engaged in job training and job search activities; permanent and/or supportive housing for homeless individuals afflicted by problems of substance abuse, mental illness, and/or AIDS; and supportive services that ensure that individuals obtain and retain the skills to exit homelessness. This "continuum-of-care" program was intended to target the homeless and to serve the individual or family dependent on a low or fixed income due to disability or low-wage employment.[12]

The low-income tax credit (LITC), introduced as a temporary program in the Tax Reform Act of 1986,[13] was an obscure federal housing-subsidy program that some experts believe contributed substantially to the provision of affordable housing in urban areas in the 1980s and 1990s. Congress created the LITC to encourage investment in affordable rental housing and the program is an indirect subsidy of low-income housing. The program gained sufficient support among developers to become a permanent addition to the federal tax code in 1993. Eligible taxpayers, usually developers or corporations, receive the subsidy by claiming the tax credit on their federal income tax returns after they have made the investment. The credits are limited in quantity and are allocated to the states for administration. To qualify for the tax credit, an LITC building must satisfy specific low-income housing compliance rules for a fifteen-year period as well as satisfy certain other compliance rules for a minimum of thirty years.

Public Education

By the turn of the twentieth century, most social scientists and educators and many political leaders considered public education to be a national priority for reform and improvement, mainly because of the belated recognition that the poor, especially poor minorities, had been left behind in the nation's economy. For advocates of change, this meant that too many poor children deprived of educational opportunities would, as adults, be deprived of job and career opportunities. It became all too obvious that the consequence would be a permanent *dependent* underclass that would be a permanent cost to society and not a productive part of it. This was true throughout the twentieth century and it was true in the early years of the twenty-first century. While there is a permanent underclass, *individuals* will always be moving in and out of it. Therefore, social policy should keep the way open and maintain incentives for outward and upward mobility.

The Department of Education, proposed as a cabinet-level agency by President Jimmy Carter and established by Congress in 1979, symbolized a new commitment to the nation's public schools. That commitment was still in place in 2005, although the needs in some local districts have greatly outrun available federal resources. Some critics called the new department a payoff to the National Education Association for supporting Carter: "Everyone in the Office of Education in HEW got a promotion!"[14]

After World War II and Korea, the "baby-boom" generation forced expansion if not increases in the quality of American public schools. A succession of studies and reports on public education attempted to direct this highly decentralized expansion. The first one was in reaction to the successful launching in October 1957 of the Russian space satellite *Sputnik*, which pointed up shortcomings in American education, especially in the sciences and technology. The national concern that *Sputnik* engendered arrested the decline in public schools for a decade, after which public elementary and secondary schools suffered a further decline.[15]

Actually, most of the reform took place in districts populated by middle- and upper-class residents; there was very little in urban neighborhoods populated by the poor, the working poor, and minorities, except for partial funding of the Head Start program at the preschool level. Youth in these neighborhoods and in many rural communities are still deprived of educational opportunities matching those available in middle- and upper-class districts.

Elementary and Secondary Education. Americans think of public education as a local responsibility, yet they depend upon financial help from the state and federal governments. During the 1950s and 1960s, the federal government began to allocate major resources to public education. The Elementary and Secondary Education Act of 1965 (plus the 1978 amendments) has been the principal federal vehicle.[16] Most of the programs contained in it have survived.

Although the federal government continues to support public education, the level of commitment dropped from 5.8% of the federal budget in 1980 to 4.5% in 1999. There has been some recovery since 2000, and in 2002, 5.4% of the budget was spent on education. About half of federal funds are spent on primary and secondary education, the remainder on higher education and research in college and university settings. Support provided by the federal government for education accounts for about 6.3% of primary and secondary budgets, a drop of nearly one-third since 1980, when support accounted for 9.1%. Local taxes account for only about 44% of primary and secondary public school budgets; about 53% comes from state and federal sources.[17]

In spite of a strong tradition of local control, some policymakers and educators have recognized the need for metropolitan—even regionwide—administration and financial support of public schools. Two compelling problems of inequity in public education have suggested areawide solutions. First, in states where public schools are still financed by the property tax, the inability of that tax system to support adequate schools in depressed areas requires areawide or statewide adjustment.[18] Second, in urban areas where segregation by race and class exists, areawide solutions tending to encourage integration are required.

Some scholars and policymakers were hopeful in the 1960s and 1970s that the U.S. Supreme Court would eventually help to equalize educational opportunity by declaring the local property tax unconstitutional under the Equal Protection Clause of the Fourteenth Amendment. They were wrong. When the opportunity came in the *Rodriquez* case in 1973, the Court ruled 5–4 that the Texas school-finance system based on the local property tax (producing grossly unequal revenues among local school districts) served a legitimate state purpose; that public education was not among the constitutionally guaranteed rights; and that the Texas school-finance system did not violate the Equal Protection Clause of the Fourteenth Amendment because it did not put at a disadvantage any definable class of "poor" people or occasion discrimination because of the relative wealth of the families in any district.[19] An essay published in 1993 by the Phelps Stokes Fund makes the argument for reversing *Rodriquez*.[20]

In efforts to counter the *Rodriquez* decision, more than two dozen states had by 2000 amended their constitutions to declare education a basic right and have ruled out the local property tax as a constitutional source of support for public education. The first state to act was New Jersey, where the state Supreme Court ruled that the "thorough and efficient education" clause of the state constitution was violated by a state funding system that relied on municipal real estate taxes.[21] Then the California Supreme Court upheld, in the face of *Rodriquez*, a lower-court decision that the state funding program was invalid as a violation of state constitutional provisions that guaranteed equal protection of the law. The court said that, while education may not be a fundamental interest in the federal jurisdiction, the California constitution will not tolerate a system in which local wealth is the principal determinant of revenue for the schools.[22]

The second equity problem in public education that requires areawide solution is the recent resegregation of urban school systems. Official (*de jure*) segregation of public schools was declared unconstitutional in *Brown v. Board of Education* in 1954[23] and this decision was reaffirmed in subsequent cases. The segregation issue was revived in *Milliken v. Bradley* in 1974,[24] when the Supreme Court ruled that extraordinary measures such as busing were not required to achieve integration of schools in a metropolitan area as long as the segregation was not the result of a deliberate public policy.

The resegregation of school systems both in suburbs and in central cities addressed in *Milliken* stemmed directly from the social stratification that had developed in metropolitan areas from the development of suburban policies of exclusivity. Today the social stratification is largely the consequence of economics. Fair housing laws in most places have undercut its legal basis. In any case, the remedy for dysfunctional social stratification can only be effectively addressed on a regional basis and must be reversed or we risk producing a permanent class structure in violation of our democratic values. In 2001, 70% of minority students were attending predominantly minority schools.

For most parents access to education is the key to economic success: education determines access to jobs, jobs determine income, income absent discrimination determines access to housing, housing location in its turn determines access to schools and education. In the present-day organization of public education, contrary to the Jeffersonian schema of selection by merit, schools range all the way from the custodial institutions of the inner cities, where education of the poor is neglected, to institutions equipped to educate the children of the nation's elite, even those who are not meritorious. In the tradition of Jeffersonian meritocracy, education is for the purpose of providing an objective determination of the individual's future depending wholly upon his or her own natural endowments and effort, as determined by certain standardized tests. Ironically the tests, as administered by professional educators, sometimes reflect the culture of the dominant class and as a result can miss rough diamonds among the hard-core poor.[25] In some cases, the underachieving child of overachieving parents is saved from the fate of downward social or economic mobility by the differential educational opportunities of suburbanized public education.

Higher Education. In the 1950s and 1960s, only a few states offered a full range of higher-education facilities available to students at minimum cost. More states had done so by the turn of the twenty-first century, but some states—California, for example—that were pioneers in making higher education accessible to youth have backed away from free higher education and begun to charge tuition and other fees, thus limiting opportunities for many qualified students. California has also backed away from a policy of affirmative action that helped minority students from inadequate public schools catch up. One year after California's Proposition 209 (outlawing affirmative action) went into effect, the University of California at Berkeley admitted its least diversified class in two decades. In 1998, the number of Blacks and Latinos admitted was halved from the previous year, although more recent information indicated the possibility of a renewed increase in diversity.[26]

Some of the wealthier states have developed extensive community college and state university facilities that provide higher education for vast numbers of students who would otherwise have no practical access to college-level training. Forty years ago, teacher education was a long way from the levels of excellence set by a small handful of outstanding graduate schools of education. It remained so at the end of the century. At the same time, as opportunities throughout the economy opened up for individuals who would otherwise have gone into teaching, those who took up the slack were often not well prepared to replace them.

Healthcare as a Public Responsibility

Before 1932, public healthcare facilities were largely county hospitals for the care of poor people who could not afford private hospitals. There were also public tuberculosis sanitariums, built when the disease was rampant and there was no reliable cure. There were also nonprofit hospitals built by various Catholic, Protestant, Jewish, and other religious groups.

The decade of the Great Depression (1930–40) was a politically opportune time for public-health leaders to press for improved medical and health services for the poor. One major impetus was the work of the Committee on the Costs of Medical Care, a group set up in 1927 and financed by eight leading foundations. In a five-year period, the committee issued twenty-eight reports—the most comprehensive survey of medical economics up to that time. In 1932 the committee published a summary report that called for group practice for physicians and health insurance for patients. In 1935 President Roosevelt established the Interdepartmental Committee to Coordinate Health and Welfare Services. In 1938 the committee held a National Health Conference and issued a National Health Program. The National Health Program went to Congress as the Wagner Health Bill (Senate Bill 1620, 76th Congress).

Meanwhile, in Maryland a small group of health and medical leaders had developed a state medical-care program aimed primarily at serving the indigent and the medically indigent. (The term "medically indigent" referred to persons who were ordinarily self-sufficient but who could not pay the costs of an onset of illness or disability.) In the same period, members of the Johns Hopkins University medical faculty organized a discussion of the Wagner Health Bill. In 1939 the Maryland group, joined by other medical and health leaders in the state, organized the first all-Maryland Health Conference to discuss the state's responsibilities for health and medical needs. The majority of the conference was made up of nonprofessional groups from the cities and the counties and included representatives from the labor unions. Debate focused on the Wagner Health Bill and a national health program. At the close of the conference a resolution was passed expressing approval of the Wagner Bill provisions for a national health program. By 1945 Maryland had the nation's first comprehensive health program for the indigent. It succeeded because the state's medical profession had participated in the planning and endorsed the legislation.[27]

The work on a comprehensive health program for the indigent in Maryland encouraged the Roosevelt administration to press for passage of the Wagner Health Bill, but as with so many other New Deal initiatives, the opponents prevailed and then the war came along. But the groundwork had been laid for renewed effort by the Truman administration. In 1946 President Harry

Truman proposed a national healthcare program and federal-aid hospitals. The 1946 Hill-Burton Act provided federal aid for hospitals, but Truman's national healthcare program (eventually to become Medicare for the elderly and Medicaid for the poor) could not in those years prevail over the opposition of the medical profession.

Both programs were adopted by Congress in 1966—with the support of the American Medical Association and through the extraordinary legislative skill of President Lyndon Johnson. The doctors and other healthcare professionals came around when they were persuaded that the Medicare and Medicaid legislation could be written to favor the profession.

Medicare and Medicaid were targeted exclusively to help people eligible for Social Security benefits (those sixty-five years of age or older) and to assist the poor. Guaranteed healthcare coverage for everyone else was missing. When the Medicare/Medicaid program was signed into law, advocates rightly considered that the nation had taken a giant step forward in healthcare. Poor people were no longer denied care and ordinary, hardworking families would no longer be impoverished by extraordinary hospital and doctor expenses of the elderly or incapacitated members of the family.

By the 1990s, many Americans were demanding healthcare coverage that would protect them against rapidly accelerating rises in doctor and hospital bills—rises that greatly exceeded rates of inflation (Figure 3.1). President Bill Clinton, elected in 1992, responded with a national health-insurance proposal that would have made universal healthcare available to all Americans. Hillary Rodham Clinton, as first lady, guided the effort. The healthcare profession, as politically powerful as it had ever been, objected and the program did not survive in Congress.

Instead, Congress passed legislation initiated by President Clinton—the 1996 Health Insurance Portability Act—which protects people from the loss of health insurance in a change of job or relocation.[28] Over the next three years several additional elements of Clinton's healthcare program were implemented, starting with a program to raise child immunization rates to an all-time high. In 1997, Clinton signed into law the Children's Health Insurance Program—representing the largest single investment in healthcare for children since 1965. In 1998, Clinton proposed a major expansion of Medicare, offering coverage to early retirees at age sixty-two and the opportunity for displaced workers at age fifty-five and older to purchase coverage under Medicare. In his FY2000 budget, Clinton proposed long-term home-care services, as well as information and referral services to families caring for elderly relatives identified as chronically ill or disabled. That budget also proposed tax credits to encourage small businesses to provide healthcare benefits; earmarked funds for comprehensive healthcare delivery systems for the uninsured and for Medicare clinical trials to provide cutting-edge cancer treatments; and increased funding for HIV/AIDS treatment.

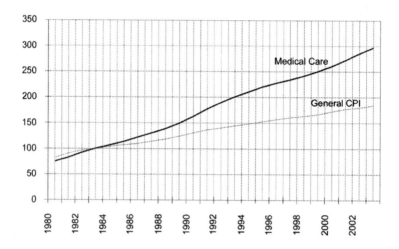

Figure 3.1 CPI for All Prices versus Medical Care Costs, 1981–2003

In 1999, Clinton endorsed a Senate proposal to help states allow disabled workers to buy insurance through Medicare and in 2000 reintroduced an earlier proposal to expand prescription drug coverage under Medicare. In 2003, Congress enacted and President George W. Bush signed into law the Medicare Prescription Drug Act (P.L. 108-173), which created a limited new drug benefit as Part D of Medicare to take effect in 2006. Low-income assistance was included in the program.

The U.S. Department of Health and Human Services (HHS) in 1998 considered methods to implement a mandate of the Health Insurance Portability Act to establish a patient identifier system that would ensure provision of seamless healthcare coverage as workers move from job to job. Such a patient identifier system would make possible the creation of a national database of individual medical histories from whatever healthcare provider they originate. Also in 1998, Congress began debate on legislation that would correct widespread abuses by the health management organizations. The HMOs have become the principal providers of health and medical services for people throughout the country.

New Technologies

Urbanologists in the 1960s and 1970s were generally optimistic about the application of new technologies in cities. Computers were then emerging as a tool of statistical analysis and planning. So, they thought, were new modes of public transit: high-speed, noiseless trains; battery-operated and hybrid automobiles; cheap, disposable family homes; new communities planned for working and living; vertical-takeoff air carriers that could operate near city centers on minimal acreage; telecommunications that combined the television and telephone to minimize business travel.

We already had telegraph, teletype, radio, telephones, television, answering machines, and, a few years later, the facsimile machine, wireless mobile and cell telephones, personal and laptop computers, the Internet, and e-mail. Early in the twentieth century, the elevator had made possible tall, compact buildings. Air-conditioning systems made it possible for cities like Houston to flourish as business and finance centers. With all these technologies, cities should have been easy places in which to live and work, and in many ways they were. They had improved and they continued to improve—for many people. But not all the technologies that could have contributed to better cities were actually implemented.

Urbanologists were aware that the application of new technologies in cities of the United States was likely to be slow, especially in housing and mass transportation. There was too much investment in obsolete infrastructure, in old techniques, old habits and routines, and familiar hardware to move rapidly to new modes. Yet the demand for improvements in cities pressed hard on policy leaders—in housing, transportation, communications, waste disposal, water supply, and other key facilities. The demand was there a half-century ago to make cities more comfortable, convenient, and economical, and gradually the improvements came, but not in all services and not in all cities.

Mass Transportation and Highways

Urbanologists fifty years ago reasoned that improved urban transportation would create market areas for the public and private institutions of the city several times greater than the existing ones. Moreover, they reasoned that the coverage, convenience, and economy of new modes of urban transportation would encourage business, industrial, cultural, and recreational organizations in a wide choice of locations within the urban region. As matters then stood, poor people were substantially cut off from expanding employment opportunities in industries that were then rapidly dispersing.

In the postwar period of rapid suburbanization, locational decisions for urban transport systems were made for the convenience of automobile and truck transportation rather than the traditional rail and bus transportation that would have been within the economic reach of low-income people in central-city neighborhoods. The new suburban industrial parks of the postwar period were located beyond the reach of existing mass transportation systems built during the late nineteenth and early twentieth centuries. While industry and jobs moved to suburbs, low-income people had no economic way of following them. The U.S. Census reported in 1970 that, for the first time in history, there were more industries and business establishments in the suburbs than in central cities.

Urban transportation systems could not be extended to many suburbs for lack of subsidies or sufficient demand. People who could afford to drive their private automobiles did so. The new suburbanites who worked in city centers made their homes in distant suburbs—and commuted in their automobiles, typically one person per automobile. The suburbanites who worked in the new suburban industrial locations also drove to work because they chose to do so or had no choice. The consequence was unrelieved traffic congestion in cities and often in suburbs.

In recent years, the situation has been exacerbated as the number of vehicles and the number of miles traveled on roadways have increased at astonishing rates. From 1980 to 2002, the number of vehicle miles traveled on U.S. highways increased 91%, from 1.5 trillion to 2.86 trillion. Likewise, the number of vehicles in the U.S. has continually been on the rise, with over 235 million vehicles on the road in 2001. At the same time, the miles of highway available to carry these vehicles increased at a very slow rate. From 1980 to 2002, miles of highway increased by only 2.8%. The number of vehicle miles traveled per highway mile increased by 87% in the same period. The transportation technologies that could have provided relief for this unabated congestion had too few customers.

The Intermodal Surface Transportation Efficiency Act of 1991 (ISTEA) offered hope that federal transportation funds would be used to encourage more efficient modes of transportation.[29] The legislation tied federal funding to regional plans that had to be in compliance with the Clean Air Amendments of 1990. ISTEA allowed states to use federal transportation funds with reasonable flexibility within the context of a regional plan. In 1998, Congress strengthened ISTEA in the Transportation Equity Act for the Twenty-first Century, with major funding and a broadened range of transportation-related programs. The new legislation left intact the core metropolitan and statewide transportation planning requirements of ISTEA.[30]

The Environment

Environmental activists celebrated the first "Earth Day" on April 22, 1970. The 1960s had been the decade of political activism in the United States and some European countries. The U.S. had launched the ill-fated Vietnam War and at about the same time had a long-overdue confrontation with the social consequences of slavery, the Civil War, and the aftermath of a hundred years of Jim Crow law and practice. During that decade, the country also went through a youth revolt and the sexual revolution.

The protest movements of the 1960s created the political conditions for the environmental activists to be heard and taken seriously. The "establishment" had been successfully challenged by the Vietnam War, by unsympathetic reaction to the antiwar movement of colleges and university administrations and trustees, and by grudging concessions to Blacks in inner cities. The issues of the 1960s and their advocates laid the political groundwork for the issues of the 1970s: a resurgence of the century-old feminist movement and the environmental movement, the latter given a strong impetus by Rachel Carson's influential book *Silent Spring*.[31] The environmental activists of the early 1970s found ready acceptance among youth, the civil rights advocates, and peace activists.

From the first Earth Day in 1970 to the late 1990s, the concerns of the environmentalists, from the need to ban of harmful pesticides (Rachel Carson's focus in *Silent Spring*) to smog and tobacco smoke, affected almost every aspect of urban life. A cabinet-level Environmental Protection Agency (EPA), established by the National Environmental Protection Act of 1970,[32] carried out the mandates of omnibus federal environmental legislation, including water and air quality standards, industrial pollution controls, and cleanup of toxic dump sites.

Water Supply and Sewerage Disposal

To meet the needs of water supply and sewage disposal in metropolitan areas, these essential services are usually managed by a combination of state and local action, often by means of special districts. Areawide authorities have in recent decades, under pressure from the federal government, undertaken regulation and control of air and water pollution.

Equity in Public Services

The local property tax affects equity in financing of public schools, and it can also affect equity in the distribution of other public services. A local government system financed primarily by the property tax unavoidably results in unequal public services if property values are distributed unequally among local political jurisdictions, which is almost always the case. As we have observed, unequal services in cities throughout the nation are to a large degree due to the nature of suburbanization. This unequal delivery of services affects whites as well as minorities, but minorities are the most severely hurt, especially African Americans and Hispanics.[33]

Comprehensive Planning: A Tool of Regional Governance

The trend toward large-scale enterprise, both public and private, has been with us at least since the Industrial Revolution and the development of urban areas, roughly since the last half of the nineteenth century. Large-scale enterprise follows population growth, concentration in cities, specialization in the labor force, and expansion of the industrial and service economy. These factors foster bigness in almost all forms of human activity. The bigger and wealthier we become, the more knowledge we acquire, the better technologies we develop, the more incentive we have to convert these advantages to profit via the economies of scale available to large organizations. There are exceptions, of course: many businesses that cannot take advantage of economies of scale, and the bigness typical of, say, steel mills may be an impediment to progress and new technologies.

Once the payoffs of centralization are realized and the wealth accumulated, we possess the technical and organizational wherewithal to *personalize* the services of the great institutions we have created through *concurrent* decentralization. Thus, with prudent management of population growth, we can arrive at a place where our expanding wealth, knowledge, and technical capacity allow us to enjoy the *qualitative* benefits of our achievements. The key is prudent management of population growth and intelligent management of physical development—which is where public planning comes into play.

Planning in our democracy must be simultaneously a state-local and a national activity, grounded in firm and carefully thought-out national, state, and local programs that are reciprocal and mutually reinforcing. One of the purposes of this book is to explain how cooperative national and local planning can productively guide the ongoing development of our cities and their environs. In the words of Charles L. Siemon,

> If we are serious about growth management, we need a vertically coordinated and consistent set of state, regional, and local physical plans for the future. What resources are of state significance and how they should be maintained are basic policy decisions that should be made at the state level and taken as "givens" by local programs. Similarly, regional resources

should be defined by a regional perspective as a given for local planning programs. It is only in this context of state and regional givens that local planning can make sense. This does not mean that state and regional givens need be identified in a didactic top-down manner, but it does mean that state and regional givens must be identified . . . as a predicate to local planning.[34]

In Chapter 9, we propose the reconstituted substate district as an appropriate planning and administrative mechanism for this purpose.

Consider an example from the private sector. The value in customer satisfaction and profit from the simultaneous development of centralized production and decentralized services has a long and successful tradition in our private economy. General Motors is in the business of manufacturing automobiles for a customer market. The company makes a profit by manufacturing automobiles in huge central facilities, but maximum profits are achieved in decentralized dealer facilities that personalize customer services. In the public sector, schools, libraries, and other public facilities in cities must be organized on the same principle if they are to take advantage of economies of scale and at the same time provide quality services.

The concept of simultaneous centralization and decentralization is the central issue in the ongoing development of urban regions. The complexities of life in urban communities, together with inadequacies of local governments, forced the states and the federal government in the 1960s and 1970s to undertake major initiatives for planning the physical and social development of growing metropolitan areas. As the roles of state and federal governments broadened, the need for multipurpose regional planning agencies was seen as necessary.

This need was documented in 1964 by a U.S. Senate subcommittee in the report *The Effectiveness of Metropolitan Planning*.[35] Legislation the following year funded metropolitan planning agencies in cities and authorized the Department of Housing and Urban Development.[36] By the mid-1970s, metropolitan planning agencies were operating in most of the larger and many of the smaller urban areas. As new federal programs were added to the list of programs that had to be referred to a regional or metropolitan planning agency, every metropolitan area had to have one.

The first metropolitan and regional planning agencies were citizen controlled, and so they lacked any real authority to get their plans implemented. Many of them by 1970 were converted to regional councils of governments (COGs) controlled by local officials. As official agencies of local government, the COGs could act on projects or scuttle them as local officials wished. The COGs had some authority but not the authority of a regional government. For this reason, some urban scholars and policymakers of the 1960s and 1970s urged that the councils of governments be developed as the skeletal structures of future metropolitan governments.

These proponents of regional government speculated that the councils of governments could be the means by which local communities would rid themselves of responsibility for services that required regional organization to administer. They speculated that the COGs might also form part of the apparatus through which federal and state governments would decentralize programs that required local and regional direction. Some scholars and policymakers argued that a network of regional planning agencies, including the COGs, would permit efficient and equitable distribution of public services and resources.

Civic leaders, especially chambers of commerce, supported the formation of COGs in hopes that improved distribution of government services and resources would boost the potential for economic growth. During the 1970s, some states supplemented the regional planning agencies with planning and development districts that included adjacent rural areas. The supposition was that such rural areas were destined for urbanization. Civic leaders and some urban scholars expected substate districts eventually to combine with the older metropolitan planning agencies to form a new layer of government in the federal system. "The Future of the Federal System," a paper Conant wrote in 1974, reflected this view.[37] The substate district proposal in Chapter 9 revisits this concept.

Some urban scholars of the period concluded that central cities were obsolescent and proposed that the decentralizing influences of emerging transportation and communications technology would produce a gradual dispersion of activities and services. Others suggested the contrary prognosis, that people would continue to value central cities for economic and aesthetic reasons. In the latter view, cities would always be magnets for people who needed face-to-face contacts—writers, artists, craftsmen—and for businesses requiring close and constant communication—high finance, management, large corporations, and advertising, to name a few.

It is hard to imagine that closed-circuit TV and other forms of remote communication will ever fully meet such needs. Cities have always specialized in social and business activities, and the cities of the twentieth century were increasingly specialized in these functions. In the 1990s, when advanced communications technologies were already ubiquitous—the computer in all its configurations, especially the Internet and e-mail, and the fax machine, interactive television, and digital telephone—when people were dispersing to rural communities and increasing numbers worked out of their homes, many of these same people continued to go to cities for face-to-face contacts. As Shira Boss has observed, "Despite all the high-tech ways to communicate, the not-so-secret weapon in the business world turns out to be a smile and a handshake. . . . Technology hasn't changed the fact that relationships are built on trust."[38] As Aristotle observed, "Man is by nature a political animal."

Paradoxically, the more technologies are used in business communications, the more time people are spending in face-to-face meetings: "Hotels report they are building more meeting space than ever, and corporate offices designed today include three times more conference rooms and collaborative space than 15 years ago, according to Facility Performance Group in Ann Arbor, Michigan."[39]

Cities also continued to function as depositories and showplaces of art, business and professional conventions, and more. Consider Nicholas Lemann's observation in an insightful *New Yorker* article: "In most cities, the tableau will be something quite similar to the one Philadelphia presents: General prosperity. Downtown transformed into an entertainment site operated by national leisure-time companies. Business growth, also of national firms, in the distant suburbs. The late-middle-aged and the uneducated made superfluous. The poor neighborhoods depopulating, and getting poorer. More people with money. Fewer people with power."[40]

As we have observed, some technological devices—the skyscraper, the high-speed elevator, mass transportation systems—were among the first agents of

centralization. Some urban design specialists of the 1960s and 1970s introduced cityscapes of "mixed-use" vertical complexes containing residential,
recreational, shopping, school, office, and other activities in arrangements
that permitted round-the-clock use of land. Chicago's Marina City, built in
the 1970s just north of the Loop, was a highly praised example of the innovation. Marina City, in the twenty-first century still a popular living facility, has
forty stories of apartments on top of twenty stories of parking on top of three
levels of shopping over a marina for two hundred pleasure boats. These facilities were originally integrated with sixteen floors of offices, theaters, bowling
alleys, tennis courts, and a swimming pool. Some of these latter uses have
been replaced by hotel facilities, a House of Blues nightclub, and a riverfront
steak house.

To reach their potential for integrated working and living, central cities
have to be made convenient and friendly. Efforts in this direction from the
1970s onward mainly followed the example of Chicago's Marina City, Boston's
Central Artery project, New York's Rockefeller Center, Hartford's Constitution Plaza, Philadelphia's Penn Center, Pittsburgh's Gateway Center, and, in
Europe, Berlin's Potsdamer Platz. Among the significant post-1970s projects
are Watertower Place in Chicago, Copley Plaza in Boston, the Bunker Hill
development in Los Angeles, and the Embarcadero in San Francisco. Some
of the features of these central-city developments include separation of traffic
levels, arcaded sidewalks, underground pedestrian passages lined with shops,
and outdoor play and recreation facilities on rooftops or on open floors, as
well as rail and bus access to the surrounding region and world at large.

Whole new cities have been built to accommodate relocated national capi-
tals—Abuja, Brazilia, Islamabad, and Belmopan in Belize are examples. New
towns were popular in the 1960s and 1970s in the U.S. (Reston, Virginia;
Columbia, Maryland); outside Helsinki (Tapiola); and several in the United
Kingdom. Most in the UK were created after World War II to relieve urban
congestion and to accommodate population growth and demand for spacious
living environments. Milton Keynes, fifty miles north of London on the M2,
built in 1968, is an outstanding example. New towns were also built in Sweden
and the Soviet Union for the same reasons and to diversify the urban landscape.

All of this suggests the need for a deliberate policy of extensive rebuilding. Constructing new towns-in-town, for example, would offer a variety of occupational opportunities, recreational facilities, and housing, along with a full range of educational and other urban amenities. We explore the potential of a revived "new-communities" strategy in Chapter 8 and other concepts for the future in Chapter 10. As we will show in those chapters, the key to making cities attractive requires providing premier public facilities and services: schools, hospitals, libraries, cultural centers, parks and recreational facilities, and decent housing ranging from high-density, self-contained projects to single-family homes. A drawback to such improvements: the price of an "affordable" home could soar unless government subsidies are included in the planning.

The job of revitalizing central cities involves people as well as structures. The effectiveness of cities in their traditional function of acculturation, where immigrants learn skills to live and succeed in an urban world, has been declining. Ever since the 1960s, that function has gradually shifted from the central city to the suburbs. But the poorest of the poor must still reside in the cheap, run-down housing of the inner city and the older suburbs.

One of the greatest obstacles to urban improvement is lack of information—and know-how—on the part of the poor to achieve behavioral and language skills that can lead to economic success and stability. There is little agreement among scholars and policymakers even on such fundamental matters as to whether living and working conditions in central cities are improving or not. Certainly the quality of life for the poor has continued to deteriorate in ways not readily offset by the fact that the real income of the majority of urban families has been rising.

The poor who live in urban centers seem incapable of supplying themselves with basic necessities of adequate shelter and transportation, let alone education, medical and health services, and recreation. There has been a perennial deterioration of urban life as evidenced by congestion, delinquency and crime, poor sanitation, water and air pollution, inadequate public transportation, slum conditions, and the number of dropouts from public schools. Such widespread deterioration, so contrary to the American ethic of progress, had not previously occurred except in periods of economic distress. In sum, drugs, crime, and single-parent families are still the core problems of urban poverty.

We return to the question of poverty in Chapter 10 and in our book *The Future of Poverty in American Cities* (2006). It is enough to say here that the presence of poverty in cities fosters an attitude in the polity that, as Barry Carroll put it, "Poor people make poor decisions . . . unless you want to give them the fruits of good decisions or take away their freedom, then perhaps all government can do is provide a system of incentives to help them make good decisions in their long-term best interest."[41] This widely shared attitude prevalent in the 1990s led to passage of the Welfare Reform Act of 1996.

The problems we cite here can best be met at the local and regional level by local and regional authorities who know what to do about them and how. Thus we urge that the planning and administrative measures required to halt deterioration and facilitate a healthier urban environment be primarily the responsibility of state and local governments with direction and support of a new structure at the regional level to be created by the state legislatures. Federal and state governments can help—must help—with financing, with revenue sharing, and with other measures to facilitate structural changes at the local and regional levels to provide the incentives and the planning authority for making such changes.

The prophets of doom and decay have predicted the end of productive and pleasurable life in cities unless drastic measures are taken to head off disaster. But it is not drastic measures that are required over the long run; only energetic and imaginative catching up—Tom McEnery's point in *The New City-State*.[42] McEnery was mayor of San Jose, California, from 1983 to 1990, during a period of crisis and remarkable recovery.

Viewed in perspective, traffic congestion can be seen as a sign of economic health in a community hard at work and determinedly at play. Likewise, urban sprawl is a sign of dynamic growth. Crime can be seen as a symptom of the personal frustration of people whose life situations require constructive attention. What critics of cities describe as symptoms of failure are in many cities the *neglected* problems of a self-regulating social system responding to growth and development. Some of these problems can be and are solved, given time, skill, and resources. Others are inherent to an expanding economy and may simply disappear with changing conditions. The intractable problems—the ones that do not disappear—are addressed in Chapter 10.

What is needed in addition to more responsive local-government structures are new tools of systems analysis—the heart of professional planning—to aid federal and local policymakers in improving understanding of the operation of the urban "system." Experts in systems analysis have developed models of urban systems that can reliably forecast the short-term and long-term effects of major public policies as well as their impact on actions in the private sector.

Such models make it possible for policymakers to influence urban development without the need to regulate it in detail. They can, for example, estimate the economic and social impacts of a proposed transit system before it is built and adjust plans to eliminate or minimize undesirable consequences. Systems analysis of urban areas does not require metropolitan reorganization, but it does require a sophisticated regional planning apparatus linked to and guided by local governments in the urban area to effect change.

A word of caution about systems analysis: experienced planners are aware of the limitations of this strategic tool. The data used in systems analysis always stop with the present, most recently available data and can look at the future only as a projection of the trends of the past. Furthermore, systems analysis depends upon the availability of data that are published and are reasonably uniform and consistent over time and space, making comparisons possible from one time period to another and from one place to another. This analytical approach lends itself to "big-picture" macro-style summaries and evaluation. In that context, systems analysis has been useful in measuring the distance between "what is" and "what ought to be" and therefore informs the review and formulation of broad public policies and programs designed to narrow the gap between reality (what is) and our professed ideals (what ought to be).

In periods of rapid change, however, the inherent limitations of the systems-analysis approach can obscure evidence of *incipient* change—change that can have significant beneficial consequences if recognized and properly exploited. Incipient change often is first discovered in small things happening in specific locales and usually calls for a fresh interpretation of what may at first glance seem mundane. Therefore, any public body that depends primarily on systems analysis as its primary intellectual tool without a periodic investigation of fresh field research and special studies to detect and gauge *incipient* change risks failing to recognize *emerging* events. Innovative development companies like Philip Klutznick's Urban Development Corporation of Chicago made successful use of incipient-change analysis in central-city projects, notably Copley Square in downtown Boston and Dearborn Park in downtown Chicago.

The key is planning—comprehensive regional planning—the central programmatic theme of this book. Metropolitan and regional planning is comprehensive in scope when it establishes guidelines for managing and coordinating the development of the facilities and services (public and private) necessary to the life, governance, welfare, and productivity of the community. Metropolitan planning is comprehensive when it takes into account the compatibility of specific developments with surrounding activities, provision of adequate services, and the prioritizing and programming of public investments based on fiscal capacity.

The concerns of metropolitan planning are typically those that require action beyond the local level, either by a number of local governments or by levels of government other than the local community alone. Others of concern require not only interlocal cooperation but joint action with higher levels of government. Highways, for example, are usually designed and built by state highway departments but must meet federal standards if they are to receive federal aid. Large parks and land reserves are generally acquired and managed by state agencies or special district commissions.

In practice, metropolitan planning focuses mainly on facilities that serve large segments of the metropolitan population: major highways, transit lines, airports, flood and pollution controls, regional water and sewerage systems, large parks, regional shopping centers, and large industrial centers. Metropolitan plans for such facilities are guided by considerations of efficiency, consistency between location of population and location of major service facilities, economy in the extension of utilities and services, and the adequacy of transportation and other facilities to meet regional demands, as well as reservation of sites to meet future regional needs.

Effective guidance of metropolitan development almost always depends on intricate coordination of action by local and state governments, often involving federal agencies. It also depends upon sensitive adjustments of government policies to meet the changing conditions of private development. Metropolitan planning can be an instrument for bringing about this kind of coordination within metropolitan areas.

For political reasons, metropolitan and regional planning have developed in the United States in response to the need for dealing comprehensively with areawide urban growth. Comprehensive regional planning was developed in this country in lieu of metropolitan government. Its task has been to identify problems associated with growth; assemble relevant information; project economic, social, and political trends; and translate the results for the use of federal, state, regional, and local governments in the formulation of their urban plans and programs. The task includes the assessment of regional needs and resources and programming resources so as to maximize the region's growth, thus enabling policymakers to isolate the critical ingredients for guiding growth. Identification of major points of intervention provides the tactical and strategic opportunities to shape the growth. The planning process requires taking into account population movement and change, the economic base, public fiscal policy and revenue structure, trends in land values and tax base, changes in transportation and land uses, and related factors.

A comprehensive planning approach recognizes that implementation, project operation, and administrative organization proceed within the framework of existing or proposed local political subdivisions and existing functional activity departments and agencies. The range of far-reaching issues, which must be understood as a prelude to coordinated local action, proceeds within a regional planning and programming framework.

Planning and program proposals are designed to achieve the optimal development program for the entire regional community. The planning process ultimately becomes a decision-making instrument in which the resulting plan constitutes a strategic blueprint that lends itself to implementation. Thus planning in a democratic polity is as much a "developmental-management" process as a planning process.

On a practical level, comprehensive planning anticipates infrastructure requirements, their engineering specifications, and the timing of installations. It further anticipates the impact of man-made development on the natural environment and determines areas of compatibility and limits of encroach-ment from the standpoint of common community values as well as natural conditions.

Comprehensive planning establishes criteria of good urban design and architecture derived from common community standards and from stan-dards having universal validity. It identifies and anticipates community so-cial problems through indicators that continually scan the economic, health, and welfare conditions of citizens. It suggests alternative courses of action for consideration by policymakers.

Another important function of metropolitan planning is dealing with con-flicts that arise in regional development. Competition by local communities to attract new industry is a case in point. A metropolitan area usually has a limited amount of land that is suitable for industrial development, with ad-equate access and utilities, proper drainage and soil conditions, reasonably priced and available in suitably sized large parcels. The metropolitan area as a whole has an interest in the best use of such land.

The familiar products of a comprehensive planning process are general plans that specify patterns and intensity of land use, provision of public facili-ties and other government services, and effective development of human and natural resources. These products include long-range programming of capital improvements and definitive plans for financing such expenditures. Compre-hensive planning is responsible for coordinating the plans and activities of state and local governments and agencies, as well as regulatory and adminis-trative measures.

The process and results of planning require a constituency that is likely to support implementation. Otherwise, as Siemon has pointed out, planning is little more than an abstraction.[43] The New Jersey State Planning Act[44] deals with this constituency issue in a process of "cross acceptance" that calls for collaboration among stakeholders in the preparation of the New Jersey State Development and Redevelopment Plan. The State Planning Commission drafted a statewide plan that it submitted to municipalities, counties, state agencies, and interested persons for the purpose of negotiating acceptance. At the conclusion of this process, the plan went back to the State Planning Commission for adoption. As Siemon observes, a consensus-based planning process does not guarantee a successful growth management program, but the absence of consensus can be fatal to the planning process.

An illustration of comprehensive planning is the planning efforts of public health services and facilities brought to fruition by the federal Partnership for Health Act of 1966.[45] The intent of this program was to bring together and make rational use of private and public resources (talent, money, goods, and services) in such a way as to meet all important health problems in the community, including the health problems of the socially and economically disadvantaged. The objective of community health planning was to leave no important gaps in services to individuals or in environmental health control, nor to tolerate any unnecessary or uneconomical duplication in the availability of facilities.[46] A drawback of the Partnership for Health program as it was developed in state-level and regional comprehensive health planning agencies was that these agencies were never closely articulated with the councils of governments or regional planning agencies. Also, membership in the state and regional health planning agencies was in most cases dominated by medical and health professionals who, over time, stifled effective comprehensive health facilities planning.[47]

The studies and recommendations of metropolitan planning agencies were addressed to local, state, and federal governments as well as to the citizens of the metropolitan area. These major "clients" of metropolitan planning used the planning services in different ways and derived different benefits from them.

Typically, individual communities have a narrow interest in industrial development because property-tax income goes to the community where the industry is located. Competition for new industry may lead to wasteful use of industrial land, as, for example, scarce in-town sites may by used for plants that could locate in the suburbs, or a suburb may discourage certain types of industries in hopes of attracting higher-tax-yield industries. Metropolitan planning can help competing localities coordinate their efforts and work for the advantages that result from regionwide economic growth.

Metropolitan planning offers local governments general technical assistance, regional studies, and projections as background for local decisions, as well as an opportunity to participate in decisions affecting both the region and the local community. Thus, metropolitan planning alerts local governments to the regional implications of their decisions and encourages informed decisionmaking in place of fragmented policies. The planning also helps to resolve conflicts between localities and the larger region when those conflicts prejudice the development of the region. Metropolitan planning can make an important contribution to these situations of conflict by clarifying the issues and analyzing alternative courses of action.

The states have a stake in metropolitan and regional planning in that they benefit from the technical studies and the interlocal cooperation that metropolitan planning fosters. Metropolitan planning agencies can also serve as staff extensions of state executive agencies and the state legislature, giving advice on the probable effects upon metropolitan development of such state actions as highway construction, park acquisition, housing programs, and tax policies involving local governments.

Aside from providing information to guide state decisionmakers, metropolitan planning agencies can assist in the informed resolution of conflicts between state and local points of view in matters relating to regional development. For example, the problem of arriving at a local consensus on the location of new highways can facilitate the work of the state highway department.

The federal government also has a stake in that it uses metropolitan planning in official review of local, federally supported projects, in establishing their practical and political feasibility and their usefulness to the regional community. Metropolitan planning agencies also serve as clearinghouses for coordination of federal programs within an area. Without such coordination, different federal agencies may work at cross-purposes in metropolitan development. For example, federal housing programs that promote suburban growth may also overload federally aided highways or, if badly located, may create premature demands for additional federal highway aid.

Metropolitan planning can help bring about the coordination of federally aided projects with local actions of many kinds. One aspect of this coordination is to be sure that locally sponsored projects are not at cross-purposes with federally aided undertakings. Improper planning of local streets, for example, can clog the interchanges of federally aided highways.

Local regulatory action may be desirable to protect investment in new facilities; special zoning may be required to keep tall structures out of approach zones to airports, or to regulate new development close to federal highway interchanges. In such cases, substate districts serving as metropolitan planning agencies could be the channels of communication between the federal agencies and local governments, assisting in the review of locally proposed projects and suggesting appropriate local action to accompany federal investment in community facilities.

The work of substate districts could and, where they exist, do play a coordinating role in bringing local policies affecting land development into harmony with one another within the metropolitan area, and in promoting agreement with federal policies affecting development of the same area. Effective coordination requires a consensus on the desired pattern of development and this consensus should ultimately be reflected in a regional plan.

In the absence of competent metropolitan and regional planning, consultation among local, state, and federal officials is likely to be haphazard and to deal mainly with single programs rather than the entire range of relevant policies. Both the comprehensiveness of metropolitan planning and the clear assignment of responsibility for initiating consultation to the metropolitan agencies provide the means of making federal policies more effective by relating them to the shared objectives of all levels of government in shaping the growth of metropolitan areas.

In sum, key functions of metropolitan planning are coordination of independent decisions affecting metropolitan growth and promotion of joint action to deal with metropolitan problems. One of metropolitan planning's most important functions is to present issues of metropolitan growth to governmental bodies, to stimulate public discussion of alternative patterns of development, and to bring the entire subject of urban growth within the scope of public policy decisions.

Achieving Planning Goals: A Basis for Inquiry and Action

A major goal of regional planning is to structure a set of policies, plans, and programs that establish a framework for municipal action—action designed to enhance the living circumstances of all residents in a given region. Achievement of this goal is realized through a course of action illustrated by the following broad lines of inquiry:

What are the consequences of changes occurring in the economic and service role of the region in terms of the area's capacity to support its present and projected population? What effects can be anticipated in regard to the need for additional land and housing to service the economy? What are the probable markets for new or improved housing as related to the anticipated level and distribution of consumer purchasing power?

How do prevailing public policies and practices influence the character of metropolitan growth and decay? To what extent do they tend to support or negate sound community development and renewal? How can they be structured to reinforce community- and housing-improvement programs?

What is the significance of decentralization and recentralization trends in the physical, economic, and social structure of the regional area and of the change in characteristics of the market for built-up and raw land? How can the location and timing of renewal and other development activities be related to these trends in order to maximize the benefits to be achieved through renewal investment?

What is the predictable range and variety of housing needs, and how do such needs correspond to the existing inventory of housing in terms of magnitudes, quality, location, and housing types? What impact will a proposed renewal planning effort have on meeting regionwide housing needs?

What are the generic causes and nature of blight when viewed in the regional framework? Is blight a form of obsolescence—a by-product of change in living standards—which in turn results in the redistribution of population, value, and land use? What refinements in renewal treatment, techniques, and tactics are required to cope with various forms of economic and functional obsolescence?

What are the "appropriate" roles of public and private action in the development and renewal of a regional area and how can these be coordinated to achieve optimum effectiveness? What is the impact of public facilities investment in renewal and other developmental activity—and private investment in property maintenance and in new growth?

How can urban renewal, public works, and privately financed developments and other development projects throughout a region be coordinated in terms of timing and program content?

What is the role of private industrial and commercial development in the establishment of housing needs?

The tasks of substate districts as regional-planning agencies include establishment of an index of the relative urgency of competing community needs, based on an examination of the adequacy of facilities to serve and support the regional area's population. Within this context, emphasis in the metropolitan and regional program should be placed on the achievement of economic growth as distinct from housing and residential goals and public services, including public and institutional facilities expansion that are derived from the latter examination. "Developmental management" proposals with respect to the development of vacant land, clearance or conservation of built-up areas, rehabilitation of existing facilities, or any combination of these are evaluated in the light of whether such proposals would substantially aid in the achievement of high-priority development goals.

Sound recommendations for closing housing gaps and providing for population displacement and relocation are largely dependent on reliable analysis of the housing market. Basic studies have been done in many states and regions, but such studies are seldom related to one another, nor have they provided the basis of a recommended program specific enough to be directed to the gaps in the regional housing supply.

Analysis of housing trends should be related to an analysis of commercial and industrial development, family size, family income, and geographic distribution. The purpose of the analysis would be to identify and measure existing and projected gaps between housing supply and housing need. In this context, the special housing needs of specific groups of consumers in the housing market can be determined. Needs of young married couples, migratory workers, single persons, out-of-town students, group households, the dependent, the aged, and the infirm can be assessed. Also, the nature and causes of existing housing gaps can be clarified.

The qualitative aspect of research regarding changing patterns of residential development determines the success of various governmental policies and practices that influence the growth, maintenance, and replacement of the area's housing stock. For this reason, social and economic changes resulting from housing trends can provide a springboard for shaping and influencing change. Policy need not always encourage current trends. Sometimes policy seeks to counterbalance trends in order to meet the requirements of all elements of the population or to improve the quality of life throughout the community.

As we suggested earlier, regional planning identifies and classifies the developmental opportunities of the region so as to establish general outlines for locational and phasing strategy. It also programs developmental activities and functions, including housing, education, health, welfare, water supply, and other activities which affect developmental activities.

The other important task of regional planning is to assess the extent and character of capital improvement programs, including an examination of the basis of tax assessments. Recommendations for changes in basic tax procedures follow. In order to influence physical growth and investment in desired directions, the impact of public facility investment is assessed for its influence on land values, and its effect on private investment in new and existing property. The assessment includes identification of specific types and scales of public facility investment germane to the maintenance and/or creation of land values.

Recommendations for optimal phasing of capital improvement programs in terms of stimulation of private investment or its growth directions are essential. Furthermore, opportunities for coordinating development and capital-improvement programs, including new techniques for such interrelationships, are identified and estimates made of deficiencies in available capital funding at the local and regional levels.

A detailed examination of the private and institutional patterns of development as they impact issues of environmental quality is required. In addition, the dynamic factors in the growth process are identified in order to develop criteria to guide public and private activity. It is apparent that public, private, and institutional spheres are interlocking components of the urban system. Actions cannot be undertaken in one sphere independent of the others or without consequences for the others. This accounts for the fact that public issues that surface as political controversies multiply and reflect intricate public and private entanglements. Competent planning ensures that such interdependencies are considered in local public decisionmaking.

Cost-benefit analysis for short- and long-term program purposes—a means of testing program alternatives—is part of regional planning. However, this method of analysis must be kept in perspective and judgments should be made in the light of achieving particular goals, such as decent housing for every family, ample job opportunities for employables, and cultural diversity.

Finally, regional planning is responsible for recommending deployment of available programs and financial resources. These recommendations are made from priorities based on identified needs, standards of action, and mechanisms for enhancing interrelationships among localities.

The Planning Function of Localities

Diversity of life style in any state depends largely on the capacity of localities to act independently in some aspects of local development. This position is sometimes in conflict with the need to reduce the influence of local exclusiveness, since diversity involves not only mixtures, but contrasts. Thus, if a state is to encourage diversity and at the same time reduce the amount of local exclusiveness, certain planning functions should remain with the local jurisdiction at the same time that their influence over regional, state, and national goals is being constrained.

Under these conditions, it is possible for localities to maintain control over their own development patterns, mixtures, and arrangements without the accompanying power to exclude certain commercial and industrial functions and residential types. They may also maintain variations in the pattern and style of school, recreation, and other public services beyond established regional goals and standards. Moreover, localities should shape the scale and form of developmental programs, including urban renewal. In short, localities should retain control of most of their current planning and operational functions, subject only to the constraints dictated by regional needs.

The result sought is a structure that recognizes the regional scale required for problem solving in which local variation and participation are encouraged without penalties resulting from unconstrained local autonomy. The substate districts proposed in Chapter 9 meet that structural requirement.

It is essential to note the necessity of dealing with planning and governance at the neighborhood, community, and small-unit level, for these levels represent an important component in any discussion of planning and governance, if administrative and management needs are to be fully met. In these cases, regional planning can obscure a set of planning considerations that can only be conceptualized at the smaller scale. Moreover, as Siemon has observed, establishment of a greater-than-local perspective does not necessarily mean that local governments give up their prerogatives in local matters. "A greater-than-local perspective can work without destroying the fabric of local autonomy . . . in truly local matters."[48] In the end, people always demand the governmental scale that enables them to influence the decisions that affect the quality of their daily lives.

We must take cities for what they are—the milieu in which most people live, prosper, and find self-fulfillment, and in which others shrivel and die. Cities are created by people, and so reflect the political and social life of the people who inhabit them. They reflect with remarkable and sometimes devastating accuracy the wants and demands of people, the endless variety of relations among them, and the extent to which the people in any particular city are public or private minded. American cities seem much the latter: individualistic, pleasure seeking, robust, exploitative, consumer oriented. To the extent that we judge our cities to be great or faulty, we judge ourselves and our way of life.

Notes

1. The negative income tax proposal was made in Milton Friedman, *Capitalism and Freedom* (Chicago: University of Chicago Press, 1962), Chapter 12. See also Christopher Green, *Negative Taxes and the Poverty Problem* (Washington, D.C.: The Brookings Institution, 1967); James Tobin, Joseph A. Pechman, and Peter M. Mieszkowski, "Is a Negative Income Tax Practical?" *Yale Law Journal* 77 (November 1967): 1–27; and James C. Vadakin, "A Critique of the Guaranteed Annual Income," *The Public Interest* 11 (Spring 1968): 53–66. One of the earliest proposals for a federal guarantee of annual income came from Louisiana Senator Huey Long's "Share the Wealth" movement in 1935, which proposed $5,000 per year to every family. See Basil Rauch, *The History of the New Deal* (New York: Creative Age Press, 1944), p. 172.

2. Daniel Patrick Moynihan, *The Politics of a Guaranteed Income: The Nixon Administration and the Family Assistance Plan* (New York: Random House, 1973).

3. P.L. 100-485, Welfare Reform Act of 1988 (the Family Support Act).

4. Five pioneering empirical studies cited by Legates and Hartman in their article "Gentrification-Caused Displacement," *Urban Lawyer* 14, no. 1 (1982): Black, "Private Market Housing in Central Cities: A Survey," *Urban Land* (November 1975); P. Clay, *Neighborhood Renewal* (Lexington, Mass.: Lexington Books, 1979); D. Gale, *The Back-to-the-City Movement . . . Or Is It? A Survey of Recent Homeowners in the Mount Pleasant Neighborhood of Washington, D.C.* (Washington, D.C.: George Washington University Press); G. Grier and E. Grier, *Urban Displacement: A Reconnaissance* (Washington, D.C., 1978); and National Urban Coalition, *Displacement: City Neighborhoods in Transition* (Washington, D.C., 1977). The Legates and Hartman article cited here summarizes their nationwide survey of available studies up to 1982. The literature on gentrification since then is extensive but generally reflects the finding of the early studies, which, taken together, suggested the need for effective public policies to deal with gentrification-caused displacement. The most valuable ones include Wilson, *The Truly Disadvantaged: The Inner City, the Underclass and Public Policy* (1987); Lehman, "The Origins of the Underclass," *Atlantic Monthly* (June 1986); Bryant and Lee, "Gentrification and the Law: Combating Urban Displacement," *Journal of Urban and Contemporary Law* 25 (1983).

5. Bernard J. Frieden and Lynne B. Sagalyn, *Downtown, Inc.: How America Builds Cities* (Cambridge, Mass.: MIT Press, 1989), pp. 97–98.

6. P.L. 81-171, Housing Act of 1949.

7. Harold M. Mayer and Richard C. Wade, *Chicago: Growth of a Metropolis* (Chicago: University of Chicago Press, 1969).

8. Mayer and Wade, *Chicago*, pp. 365–366.

9. Herbert J. Gans, *The Urban Villagers: Group and Class in the Life of Italian-Americans* (New York: Free Press, 1982).

10. United Kingdom Department of the Environment, Transport and the Regions: *Toward an Urban Renaissance*, The Report of the Urban Task Force. Chaired by Lord Rogers of Riverside, British Labor Government, 1999. Also see the story in the *Christian Science Monitor*, "Building People Places," April 20, 2000, pp. 15, 16.

11. Eminent domain, or the right of eminent domain, is the power of a government over all the property within its limits, by which it is entitled to appropriate, or to authorize the appropriation of, private property for public use, giving just compensation to the owner. *Webster's New Twentieth-Century Dictionary of the English Language Unabridged*, 2nd edn.

12. Tom Forrester Lord, "The Continuum of Care and Affordable Housing," Houston Housing and Management Corporation, 1998.

13. P.L. 99-514, Tax Reform Act of 1986.

14. Personal communication to Conant commenting on a draft of Chapter 3.

15. National Commission on Excellence in Education, *A Nation at Risk: The Imperative for Educational Reform, A Report to the Nation and the Secretary of Education* (Washington, D.C.: Government Printing Office, April 1983).

16. P.L. 89-10, Elementary and Secondary Education Act of 1965, as amended.

17. U.S. National Center for Educational Statistics, Digest of Education Statistics.

18. In 1993–94, districts with medium incomes of $35,000 or more spent at least $7,000 per student; districts with median incomes of less than $20,000 spent only about $5,600 per student. U.S. Department of Education, National Center for Education Statistics,

Common Core of Data, "School District Fiscal Data," 1993–94.

19. *San Antonio Independent School District et al., Appellants, v. Demetrio P. Rodriquez et al.*, No. 71-1332, 411 U.S. 1 (1973).

20. Ralph W. Conant, *Public School Finance: Toward a Level Playing Field for Our Youth.* Education Policy and School Reform Program, Phelps Stokes Fund. New York: Phelps Stokes Fund, 1993.

21. In *Robinson v. Cahill*, 62 N.J. 473, 303 A.2d 273 (1973), cert. denied, 414 U.S. 976, *reh'g*, 67 N.J. 333, 339 A.2D 193 (1975), the New Jersey Supreme Court ruled that to rely on municipal real estate taxes to fund public education was unconstitutional. Subsequently, the New Jersey legislature passed the Public School Education Act of 1975, N.J. Stat. Ann. 18A: 7A-1, which was declared constitutional in *Robinson v. Cahill*, 69 N.J. 449, 355 A.2d 129 (1976).

22. *Serrano v. Priest*, 18 Cal. 3d 728, 135 Cal. Rptr. 345, 557 P.2d 939 (1977). See J. Coons, W. Clunem and S. Sugarman, *Private Wealth and Public Education* (Cambridge: Harvard University Press, 1970), a seminal work that was the basis of the original (1971) *Serrano* decision.

23. *Brown v. Board of Education*, 37 U.S. 483, 494 (1954).

24. *Milliken v. Bradley*, 418 U.S. 717 (1974).

25. Ralph W. Conant, "Rough Diamonds among the Hard-Core Poor," *Dialogue* (April 1999). New York: Phelps-Stokes Fund.

26. "Challenging Race Sensitive Admissions Policies," *Frontline*, 1999.

27. Ralph W. Conant, *The Politics of Community Health* (Washington, D.C.: Public Affairs Press, 1968).

28. P.L. 104-191, Health Insurance Portability Act of 1996.

29. P.L. 102-240, Intermodal Surface Transportation Act of 1991 (ISTEA).

30. P.L. 105-178, Transportation Equity Act of 1998 (TEA).

31. Rachel Carson, *Silent Spring* (New York: Houghton Mifflin, 1962).

32. P.L. 91-190, National Environmental Protection Act of 1969.

33. Cf. *Hawkins v. Town of Shaw, Miss.*, 303 F. Supp. 1162 (1969). This case was a class-action suit on behalf of a Black citizen of Shaw, Mississippi, for an injunction restraining town officials from discriminating because of poverty and race in providing inhabitants with certain municipal services. The district court held that the defendants (the town officials) had not discriminated because of race and poverty in providing inhabitants of the town with street paving, street lighting, sanitary sewers, water mains, fire hydrants, and surface drainage. The complaint was dismissed.

34. Charles L. Siemon, "Successful Growth Management Techniques: Observations from the Monkey Cage," in *Urban Lawyer* 29, no. 2 (Spring 1997): 247.

35. *The Effectiveness of Metropolitan Planning*, prepared in cooperation with the Subcommittee on Intergovernmental Relations of the Committee on Government Operations, United States Senate by the Joint Center for Urban Studies of the Massachusetts Institute of Technology and Harvard University (Washington, D.C.: U.S. Government Printing Office, 1964). The contributors were Charles M. Haar, project director, and Frank C. Colcord, Jr., Ralph W. Conant, Alan L. Feld, Marcia M. Feld, Robert Fogelson, Bernard Frieden, Barbara G. Hering, Stephen Lefkowitz, William W. Nash, Francine E. Rabinowitz, Bradbury Seasholes, and Terry Steinhart.

36. P.L. 89-117, Housing and Urban Development Act of 1965.

37. Ralph W. Conant, "The Future of the Federal System," unpublished MS, 1974.

38. *Christian Science Monitor*, December 20, 1999.

39. Ibid.

40. Nicholas Lemann, "Letter from Philadelphia: No Man's Town," *New Yorker*, June 5, 2000.

41. Personal communication to Conant commenting on a draft of Chapter 3.

42. Tom McEnery, *The New City-State, Change and Renewal in America's Cities* (Niwot, Colo.: Roberts Rinehart, 1994).

43. Siemon, "Successful Growth Management Techniques," p. 235.

44. N.J. Stat. Ann. 52:18A-197 (West 1996).

45. P.L. 89-749, Comprehensive Health Planning and Public Health Services Amendments of 1966.

46. Ralph W. Conant, *The Politics of Community Health* (Washington, D.C.: Public Affairs Press, 1968), p. 99.

47. Ralph W. Conant, "The Natural Enemies of Health Planning," unpublished paper, 1975.

48. Siemon, "Successful Growth Management Techniques," p. 250.

Chapter 4

Schism and Consensus

There was a time when the poor lived in every town, mostly in one or two neighborhoods out of which they could climb if they had the wit and the will. Some of those who made it out of the old neighborhood believed that those left behind could have made it if they had stayed in school or worked harder. In those days, before the Great Depression, Social Darwinism was no distant philosophy. Few believed that the poor should be encouraged to stay poor by providing services, much less public money, for basic needs and comforts. Social Darwinism was the rationale of all public and private social programs that provided services to the poor. Redistribution of earned income was out of the question.

The Gap between the Rich and Poor

Historically, Social Darwinism has worked well for most Americans. The Industrial Revolution came at a time when the nation as a whole had the human and material resources to make the grade. Since the application of the steam engine, the effective beginning of the Industrial Age in America, the nation has created a productive wealth that had surpassed $10 trillion in GDP annually by 2000 and has enjoyed a sustained increase in the standard of living.

That increase is seen in rising family income adjusted for inflation from 1970 to 2001. Not all groups have benefited equally, of course. As is apparent in Table 4.1, African Americans and Hispanics have consistently lagged substantially behind whites.

Of course, the gap between the affluent and the poor continues to widen. Figure 4.1 shows income distribution by quintiles. As would be expected, those who are in the top 20% control much more income than those in the lowest quintile. The gap between those in the top and bottom quintiles continues to grow. In 1970, the top fifth controlled 41% of income, and that percentage grew to 48% in 2001. In 1970, the bottom fifth earned 5.4% of total income; that percentage had dropped to 4.2% by 2001.

Table 4.1: Median Family Income in 2004 Dollars

	All	White	African American	Hispanic
1970	45608	47314	29023	N/A
1975	46601	47249	29820	32443
1980	48764	50808	29398	34134
1985	49207	51721	29781	33757
1990	51637	53918	31290	34223
1995	50870	53419	32531	30776
2001	55413	58711	36216	37178

Source: U.S. Bureau of Census.

Further, Americans have maintained a system of government that maximizes the conditions of liberty for most of its citizens. Ingeniously, the system also provides for corrections of flaws because it is structured to withstand and assimilate criticism without lasting damage to its framework and foundations. In addition, the system has made it possible for most people to secure an education, to participate in political activities, and on merit to enter and rise in its economic and social structures.

Nevertheless, the barriers to geographic, occupational, and social mobility for Eastern and Southern European immigrants and their native-born children (Poles, Lithuanians, Ukrainians, Jews, and Italians, to name some of the principal ones) did not really start to disappear until well after World War II. The

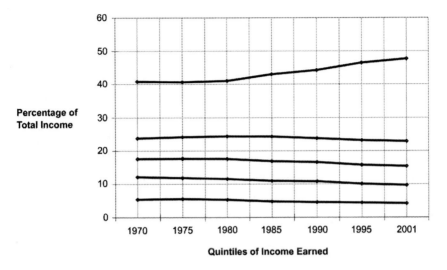

Figure 4.1 Percentage of Total Income by Quintiles of Income Earned, 1970–2001

1950s were a period when the old ethnic neighborhoods started to lose young families to the suburbs. The irony of the postwar era is that as the "minority ghettos" were swelling and solidifying for the descendants of the great European immigrations of the 1880–1912 period, it was an era of unparalleled mobility. The major contributing factors to this mobility were the service experience of 12 million draftees and the GI Bill of Rights. The latter program within a few short years between 1945 and 1952 created a college population of 9 to 10 million people and opened the professions to a new generation. African American, Hispanic, Asian American, and Native Americans continued for many more years to face those same social and economic barriers. For these and newer groups, those barriers have persisted into the twentieth-first century.

In the old days, in rural communities, towns, and small cities, the poor and the rich and everyone in between went to the same schools, and the schools provided the way to opportunity, American style. By 1940, the high school diploma was the ticket to a job and a career, and with that diploma bright young people could go to the top, even in companies that were still owned and dominated by the founding families. While 1940 was a depression year, it was not as bad as the early and mid-1930s. Ethnic and religious discrimination was still rampant, and good jobs were hard to find—and largely nonexistent in some categories. On the other hand, there were good opportunities for start-up family businesses (probably more so than today).

The political parties in the old central cities were the political power bases of the nation and an avenue of mobility (except for Blacks) for young men and women who preferred public service to a private career. The ward organizations provided the first step and lent support as the individual rose in the political system.[1] Cultural institutions were located in the central city and were accessible (except to Blacks) because they were local and central. In those institutions, people could partake of the dominant culture, learn its values and norms, and enter the mainstream. The institutions of economic activity—the factories, banks, and mercantile establishments—were also in the central cities and largely accessible.

The economic and cultural unity of metropolitan areas has traditionally been maintained by shared social, cultural, and recreational activities. Professional sports, drawing fans from a regional territory, provide a common loyalty among local audiences. Symphonies, museums, institutions of higher education, and other cultural attractions bring together the cultural elite. The metropolitan media, with viewers, listeners, and readers throughout the region, give residents a common definition of contemporary events and a focus on regional civic agendas.

The Urban/Suburban Shift

Until 1950, the physical scale of most American cities allowed easy, unplanned access of nearly everyone to nearly everything. Sometime after World War II, the scale of the local community began a dramatic expansion and social differentiation (a new class structure) and thus reversed the traditional American process of opportunity. The change accelerated in the wake of postwar population growth (the "baby boomers") and was accompanied by wholesale migration to cities from small towns and rural areas. The migration into cities was followed by social differentiation within the environs of cities and in their suburbs.

The differentiation was triggered by the massive arrival of Black and subsequently Hispanic migrants that the older city residents would not tolerate.

The differentiation took the form of whites moving away from the cities to autonomous suburbs. The movement was the beginning of the current fragmentation of metropolitan areas, which is a focus of this book. The differentiation was made feasible by new wealth created by the postwar economic recovery built upon the revival of American industry in war production and an educated labor and managerial pool created by the GI Bill of Rights. The new wealth created a new middle class, at first mostly of whites, including a lot of inner-city "ethnics" (Italians, Jews, the Irish, Poles, and others).

It was the people of this new middle class who began the "white flight" from the cities to the suburbs.[2] They were helped in important ways by federal subsidies for housing from the Veterans Administration and Federal Housing Administration through low-interest mortgage loans and by major highway construction on the outskirts of cities.[3] They were also helped by the structure of government in metropolitan areas, which allowed, or seemed to allow, high- and middle-income households to escape responsibility for the city's problems and permit discrimination in public services within metropolitan areas that would be unconstitutional within a single political jurisdiction. As Michael Harrington wrote more pointedly in the late 1960s, "Suburbia was Balkanized as a conscious strategy of a white middle class which wanted to flee big-city problems. This tactic allowed the suburbs to build comfortable, federally financed and lily-white Shangrilas."[4]

The migration of people and workplaces from city to suburb was still in full swing at the end of the century and, in the words of William Julius Wilson, "has caused an urban sprawl that is ecologically burdensome and expensive to maintain." The poor, he added, "who are disproportionately America's minorities, have been isolated in growing urban ghettos of despair and hopelessness."[5] Wilbert J. LeMelle, Sr., former ambassador, foundation executive, and college president, writes, "[W]hat a different society we might have today if the FHA had not been such a racist institution for over 40 years and contributed so profoundly to reinforcing the racial divide in American society. The effects of this tragic failure of a major government institution have been devastating, as we now know." LeMelle adds, "Not only did FHA discriminate against Blacks by limiting the number of loans to them, but its policy of not approving loans for them to move into white housing developments really established the racially segregated neighborhood patterns we are wrestling with today."[6]

Racial prejudice was only one of the reasons whites left the central cities, and for some not the principal one. Aging housing, dirt, noise, crime, and congestion were major repellents, quite apart from any issues involving minorities.[7] The phrase "white flight" can confuse cause and effect: availability and accessibility of housing in suburbs has always drawn the newly affluent out of the city. As the movement out accelerated, the housing left behind depreciated in value and became affordable to migrants from rural areas and abroad. Of course, welfare benefits available in cities were an attraction to unskilled migrants with families.

The rapid dispersion of the white population in the 1950s and 1960s was joined by a parallel dispersion of mercantile establishments, industrial units, and high-quality urban services that had been located in old central cities—especially public schools. The dispersion meant that whites, who still had access to the institutions that remained in the center, also had access to those that had moved out. The new migrants filled up the old central-city schools and used other leftover services and facilities. Whose fault was it that schools and other services deteriorated? The people who operated them? Or the newcomers who seemed to value them less?[28]

Jobs were close by in the central city, but not enough of them, and many of the jobs that were available were preempted by better-educated, urbanized, and more politically entrenched whites. For example, in 1950, 40% of whites held white-collar positions, compared to only 10% of Blacks. Conversely, 48% of Blacks held service and laborer positions, while only 14% of whites were employed in these sectors.[9] The color bar held in employment until the late 1960s and only then began gradually to give way. The color bar, which applied also to the newly arriving Spanish-speaking people, operated even more strictly in the housing market, blocking suburban movement and segregating even public housing projects.

To sum up the social consequences of metropolitan differentiation, middle-class and working-class whites who wished to relocate in an urban area in the 1950s and 1960s had a range of choices throughout the metropolitan area, limited only by their ability to buy into the housing market. The choice was great, for one of the advantages of decentralized government was that local governments offered different kinds and levels of services at different prices. Whites could literally choose, as in a supermarket, the combination and level of services they desired according to personal priorities—the market model of local government we discuss in Chapter 5. But discrimination limited the choices of urban migrants who were poor, Black, or Hispanic. Of course, people with good incomes always have more choices.

In effect, the middle class had it both ways. Imitating the rich, they found segregated suburban municipalities to be the most effective means for achieving the level of public services they desired. They kept taxes down with a few clean industries, a shopping mall, an office park or two, and they resisted any proposals to share their tax base with neighboring communities or with the central city. Thus they avoided the tax burdens associated with the high service costs in the aging central cities and near-in older suburbs. As a consequence, differentiation of services, once administered by neighborhoods in central cities, became securely available only in autonomous suburbs.

The demand of the middle class for exclusive patterns of suburban living laid the basis for the metropolitan status quo that is a primary focus of this book. One of the driving forces behind the structure of American metropolitan areas is the segregation of resources from needs. The result is that people of unequal income always receive an unequal share of public goods—both in quantity and quality—and in the long run unequal access to opportunity. Others by personal initiative recognize and seize opportunities to achieve equal income and gain access to improved living standards.

Indeed, the political foundation of metropolitan economies is the gross divergence of income levels and needs of people in different sections of the metropolis. It is not surprising that local governments should do their part by relating housing to individual incomes or that consumers of public goods should seek to enhance their purchasing power by choosing communities with similar or greater purchasing power and to avoid loss through association with the poor.

Segregation

In the process of the massive suburbanization of the last half of the twentieth century, poor neighborhoods in cities in many parts of the United States became walled-off ghettos of restricted opportunity for a growing segment of society, some of whom suffered poverty *because* of the restrictions.[10] Decades later in the early years of the twenty-first century, the minority neighborhoods in most large cities and in some of the smaller ones remained ghettoized for the same reasons: housing discrimination in the suburbs and lack of accessible jobs, especially for youth. Public schools in these communities were, with few exceptions, in worse condition physically and educationally than they were in the 1960s.[11] Suburbs eventually opened to Blacks and other minorities, but as minorities increased in numbers, especially in the near-in suburbs, many whites moved farther out into exurbia.[12]

Geographical ghettoization has had severe consequences for the political and social consensus in metropolitan societies. It has created a *psychological* ghettoization of fear, suspicion, antagonism, frustration, misunderstanding, and mutual ignorance of life styles and aspiration values. The psychological ghettoization is itself a barrier to opportunity and mainstream acculturation. It was externally imposed and reinforced by the dominant white community and was absorbed and internalized by the victimized community. The tragic result is that many African Americans resolved not to participate in the larger community, even when opportunities were available.

Middle-class African Americans have been profoundly reluctant to live in predominantly white neighborhoods even where they appear to be welcome. Many African American parents have not wanted their children bused to predominantly white schools. Ghetto residents have a strong preference for neighborhood stores and services, even when the prices are higher and even when white merchants outside the ghetto actively solicit their business.[13]

The schisms of social differentiation in metropolitan areas are likely to persist until racial barriers, especially in the housing market, in public education, and in differential delivery of municipal services, are eliminated. Eliminating these barriers will require an evolving consensus throughout metropolitan areas and of course cannot be confined to the public of the central city, for most new housing in urban areas is developed outside the boundaries of the central cities. The task of applying national norms of equality has sometimes required national actions overriding deeply rooted local law, customs, and traditions.

The norm of equal protection under the law was written into the Fourteenth Amendment to the Constitution following the Civil War in an attempt to overcome inequities of local and sectional law and custom, especially as they affected the former slave population. Thus the subsequent negation by national legislation and court decisions of the South's Jim Crow segregation laws as well as the customs and traditions upon which they were based. The Fourteenth Amendment was later interpreted by the Supreme Court to bring the states and localities under the Bill of Rights of the Constitution. In the century following the adoption of the Fourteenth Amendment, states' rights persisted as a major issue, especially in the states of the old Confederacy. Those calling loudest for states' rights were also seeking to maintain a status quo in their states for a legacy of slavery, racism, and discrimination. The irony is that the Founding Fathers envisioned federalism as a way to protect liberty and civil rights from an overbearing central government. But throughout much of U.S. history, it has been the national government that has played the key role of protector of liberty and civil rights in the face of oppressive action, or policies in some of the states.

Segregated neighborhoods continue to expand in older central areas and the white middle class continues to concentrate in separately governed suburban communities. Similarly, the ever-growing suburban job market is still partially closed to inner-city residents, largely because of limitations in public transportation between the inner cities and the suburbs.

In circumstances of geographical segregation, universal public education is made impotent as a means of healing social, racial, and ethnic class schisms. When segregation concentrates underprivileged citizens in certain school districts, the quality of education in those districts declines, resulting in alienated and functionally illiterate young adults. Free public education, which once produced a common urban culture, is producing a permanently differentiated underclass who are cut off from work, family, home ownership, and consumption. The under class, now a century or more in the making, shares in rising expectations and, diverted from normal self-sustaining work opportunities, traditionally looks to government for basic subsistence. The Welfare Reform Act of 1996 did, however, result in reductions in welfare rolls in most states.

Political Action for Equal Rights

Historically, the response of Americans to the denial of opportunities for social and economic advancement has been riot and rebellion. Acquiescence of the deprived has eventually given way to spontaneous action followed by an organized attack: farmers "raised less corn and more hell"; workmen organized strikes; veterans organized bonus marches on the nation's capital; poor people camped on the Capital Mall; antiwar groups demonstrated; urban Blacks rioted.

By the 1970s, leaders in central-city ghetto communities who had emerged in the wake of the riots of the 1960s were not willing to settle for a minor share in power and prestige. The old consensus of local communities, which rested partly upon policies of apartheid, fell apart. As the old constituencies were replaced, the legitimacy of local government came into question. In an atmosphere of dissension, young minority adults—unemployed, impoverished, and illiterate—became a dangerous force. They had learned about the potency of riot and insurrection from the 1960s and, before the riots, about the power of the street gang. At the very least, they constituted a veiled threat—a weapon in the hands of Black politicians who were moving into the governments of cities where minorities had become or approached a voting majority.[14]

Beginning in the 1970s, election of Black political activists to positions of power in city after city did not resolve the problem of a metropolitan consensus. The opposite situation developed in areas where social schisms were especially severe. In such areas, increasing Black political influence precipitated a new phase in metropolitan governance, a phase in which the struggle for public resources to meet urban problems moved from the local level to the regional, state, and national levels. At the local level, Blacks began to challenge unequal delivery of municipal services.

Thus in 1969, Black plaintiffs successfully sued for relief against town officials of Shaw, Mississippi, for discriminating because of race in providing certain municipal services. The United States Court of Appeals, Fifth Circuit, found that 98 percent of all homes fronting on unpaved streets in town were occupied by Blacks and 97 percent of homes not served by sewers were in Black neighborhoods, and that all new street lamps were installed in all-white neighborhoods. The court ruled that these disparities constituted a denial of equal protection of the law contrary to the Fourteenth Amendment. This case provided the basis for subsequent challenges to municipalities that denied some citizens the equality of public services.[15]

From the standpoint of minority groups who faced discrimination, such discriminatory actions appeared to be part of a strategy to bar them from opportunities in the housing market. Their leaders often saw metropolitan planning, scattering of central-city slums, and gerrymandering as inimitable to minority interests. They saw housing policy through urban renewal as a strategy that utilized the massive urban-renewal projects in the central cities, coupled with low-income and middle-income housing projects scattered in near suburbs, as a means to dilute their influence in the city. Indeed it would have, except that the near-in suburbs would eventually be taken over by minorities from inner-city relocation projects and new arrivals would find cheap housing in other parts of the central city, which then also became slums. In time, the political reasons for the reluctance of minorities and their political leaders to support metropolitan consolidation were eclipsed by a demand within minority communities to gain access to some of the wealth that had relocated to adjacent and outlying suburbs.

In former times, city politicians had to contend with overwhelming rural representation in the state and national legislatures. In the 1990s and into the twenty-first century, their plight was not eased by the one-man, one-vote rule in state legislatures, which favors suburbs, not central cities. The Black–white confrontation inevitably shifts to levels of government where resources are more plentiful than in local areas.

As the federal government assumed major responsibility for urban development policy in the 1960s and 1970s, three substantive issues demanded consideration as fundamental aspects of the policy structure to be shaped: redistribution of resources, primarily in the form of equalization of public services; fiscal equity throughout urban areas; and redevelopment of blighted areas.

The civil rights movement, ostensibly a drive for full citizenship, was ultimately a drive for redistribution of resources. The mere provision of equal services and facilities in a community where they had been traditionally unequal was in its practical effect a redistribution, for the taxes of deprived populations were seldom equal. Equalizing education between central city and suburbs in metropolitan areas where some school districts spend twice as much per child on education as the city provides a gross example.

There are practical as well as moral reasons for a policy of equalized services. The moral reason is written into the Constitution: simply that citizenship includes the right to equal opportunity. But it is a fine question as to whether the principle of equality of opportunity carries with it an implied floor or ceiling on such vital services as education. The practical reasons for the principle include the notion that unequal services lead to inefficiencies and waste: poorly educated children end up being a drag on society and lost as productive citizens; poorly treated sewage in one community ends up polluting the water available to adjacent ones. Yet in the face of this rationale, the Supreme Court rejected the claim of a right to equal support of public education in the *Rodriquez* case.[16]

In a larger perspective, the shared physical problems of residents of metropolitan areas should produce a common interest in finding solutions that cut across governmental jurisdictions, race, and class lines and other cleavages in metropolitan areas. Conversely, the conflicting demands of urban minorities for redistribution of resources and access to opportunity have given rise to their intense dissatisfaction with the metropolitan status quo. Their demands were justified by the fact that central cities historically shortchanged poor minorities, providing unequal public goods to poor and powerless citizens. Court cases have ruled out such practices, but they still persist in many central cities. The sticking point is resource redistribution and how it can be accomplished. Resource redistribution is a matter of equity, which is at the heart of the conflict over metropolitan reorganization.

A key to resource redistribution is a fiscal system that draws equitably upon the resources of the community and allocates revenues so as to benefit the community in overall goals and specific needs. Since metropolitan areas in the United States are composed of many autonomous governing jurisdictions with vastly different goals and needs, fiscal equity has rarely been politically attainable. Some metropolitan areas have special taxation districts, of course, but the lack of systems of fiscal equity in most urban areas has precluded application of the principle of equity in the provision of services.

It is important to note that the rundown character of the older centers is due largely to the fact that central cities provide many costly services to people who work in central business districts but pay their local taxes in outlying suburbs. The earnings tax is one solution but has not been widely adopted. In the long run, fiscal equity is practical only when the tax-paying and tax-benefiting population are approximately the same. Fiscal responsibility requires that those who decide the tax rate should also decide upon the uses to which the revenues are put and, in a democratic framework, are responsible to the constituency of taxpayers. When the political process can be grounded in such circumstances, it is possible to make decisions concerning minimal standards and redistribution of resources with a realistic claim to a just and responsible policy. Under these conditions, the legitimate interests in the constituency can have their day in court.

Only two metropolitan areas in the nation have a shared tax base for general government purposes—Minneapolis-St. Paul and Portland, Oregon. Minnesota established state-mandated revenue equalization formulas in 1974, covering 188 municipalities in the seven-county Minneapolis-St. Paul area. Forty percent of the annual increase in taxes on industrial and commercial property above the 1971 assessment base is paid into a fund that is then distributed among the 188 municipalities according to population and relative property values.

The Oregon state legislature in 1970 created the Portland Metropolitan Service District (MSD), an areawide governmental unit with responsibilities for areawide planning, regional solid waste disposal, a zoo, a convention center, and air- and water-quality programs. MSD's jurisdiction covers twenty-four municipalities in three counties. It is governed by a seven-member, directly elected, nonpartisan commission with taxing authority, a chief executive, 1,200 employees, and a $286 million annual budget (FY 2004/05). An initial fifty-year plan envisions a state-of-the-art mass transit system and vast green space reserves. The plan projects additional new suburbs for 1 million people.

In 1992, Portland-area voters adopted a home-rule charter for MSD, which then included three counties and twenty-four municipalities. MSD (popularly known as Metro) was at the end of the century the only directly elected regional government in the country and the areawide governmental jurisdiction with the broadest range of functions. Metro's functions included solid-waste collection, recycling and disposal; transportation planning and allocation of federal highway and road funds; regional air- and water-quality programs; operation of the regional zoo; and operation of the Oregon Convention Center. Metro's charter affirms that regional planning is its "primary function" and empowers the Metro Council to require local comprehensive plans and zoning regulations to comply with its Regional Framework Plan, to adjudicate inconsistencies between regional and local plans, and to change inconsistent local land-use standards and procedures.[17] Portland's Metro could be a model for the substate districts proposed in Chapter 9.

As matters stand in local politics, the stalemate between city and suburbs and among local jurisdictions is such that only a higher government authority with independent fiscal clout can produce a plan of fiscal equity in metropolitan areas. Federal revenue sharing could be designed to serve that end. As we shall see in Chapter 7, the federal revenue-sharing programs initiated by the Nixon administration did not go far enough toward achieving fiscal equity at the local and regional levels.

Suburban segregation reinforces the burden of poverty and segregation in the central city. Although growth at the peripheries and decay at the center are functionally linked, there is no governmental mechanism to develop a common policy framework. While long-run efforts have been made to revive central business districts, suburban governments benefit from rapid, unplanned commitment of land and services to shopping centers, industrial parks, tract housing, strip malls, and instant slums. The major structural commitment, the Interstate Highway System in urban areas, was laid out with almost no attention to its multiple effects on the social and economic landscape.

What are steps policy makers can take to mitigate the effects of

Government Responsibility for Reform

Whatever role the federal government plays in negotiating among the peoples of metropolitan areas to solve the problem of resource redistribution, fiscal equity, and redevelopment, governmental responsibility at all levels must be increased as new tasks of comprehensive planning are required. A consideration of reforms that address the central issues of local policymaking and consensus at the metropolitan level requires an explicit examination of the values that underlie conclusions pertaining to reform. This presumes of course that local units of government can be induced to act together with some consistency to avoid actions that are in conflict.

As a practical matter, local governments perform important functions in the national and regional political economy, since they reallocate the resources of a major part of the public sector. They have an inescapable role as regulators of private-sector decisions affecting the location and distribution of goods, activities, investments, and markets.

Local governments have consistently accounted for about one-quarter of total national public expenditures since 1950.[18] Local expenditures are an even more important economic activity on a regional scale. In their distinct economic role, local governments are producers of services and distributors of resources within their jurisdictions. Territorial jurisdictions, however, limit both their revenues and their distributive capabilities. The division of metropolitan areas into separate governments skews expenditure priorities as well as the tax base.

Local governments also function as administrative and distributive mechanisms for state and local programs, sometimes involving mandatory requirements by the state. In most cases, however, local governments select the programs in which they wish to participate. Such programs as urban renewal and public housing, therefore, exist where local jurisdictions have chosen to apply them. Thus, local governmental units provide the political bases for intergovernmental negotiation over the goods available in the national or regional economy.

Local priorities are influenced by what the state or the federal government will support in a metropolitan area. The size of funds and matching formulas for grants-in-aid influence local decisions. State revenue practices also restrict the sources that a locality may tap for revenue. The local economic base generally bears little resemblance to the tax base, and federal and state financial assistance in an urban area does not equalize economic and tax resources. Such assistance may produce a slightly more equitable distribution of expenditures among local governmental units, but it may also increase fiscal disparities that spring from differences in tax bases or eligibility for state and federal funds.

Regional Policy Planning

Local government has no choice but to be self-conscious about its role as raiser and spender of public funds, but not in its other economic functions. There is a regional economy but in most places no *public* regional economic policy. For the most part, local governments acquiesce in the decisions of the private market. Federal and state funds may impose a regional highway system; a special-purpose authority may deal with transportation terminals, a regional subway, sewerage systems, or a drainage basin. Moreover, in a few cases, states have established aggressive departments of development or community affairs with planning and coordinative responsibilities. But these are exceptional.

In addition to funding programs, several federal laws have attempted to promote coherent metropolitan spending of development funds. Sections 204 and 205 of the Demonstration Cities and Metropolitan Development Act of 1966[19] and the Intergovernmental Cooperation Act of 1968[20] were important federal efforts that contributed to organizing the metropolitan public economy. We discuss the Metropolitan Development Act in Chapter 7 in the context of federal planning policy.

The Intergovernmental Cooperation Act required that a regional review agency be composed of or responsible to the elected officials of the units of general local government within whose jurisdiction such an agency is authorized to engage in areawide planning. This requirement stimulated the establishment of councils of governments—voluntary associations of local governments—as the regional review agencies.

Two other pieces of federal legislation reinforced regional policy planning and therefore explicitly drew local attention to regional economies. The Coastal Zone Management Act of 1972 encouraged states to create state-level plans for control of coastal development.[21] So far, twenty-nine of thirty-four states with coastlines have adopted management policies that meet the standards of the act. In the Intermodal Surface Transportation Efficiency Act of 1991 (ISTEA),[22] Congress took an important step to facilitate regional approaches to metropolitan issues and to further strengthen the regional planning responsibilities of the councils of governments by requiring that governments in metropolitan areas designate a Metropolitan Planning Organization (MPO) to carry out highway and mass transportation planning functions. Funds were appropriated for these planning functions.

ISTEA mandated regional planning for transportation and *decentralized* transportation planning for states and local governments. Waste summarizes these mandates: "The Act requires that local governments in ... metropolitan areas develop an integrated transportation plan, provide for environmental protection ... and designate a Metropolitan Planning Organization ... as clearinghouse for federal transportation funding in the region, and to accomplish mass transit and highway goals specified in the Act."[23] In 1998, President Clinton signed into law the Transportation Equity Act for the Twenty-first Century (TEA-21), which contained funds for state and metropolitan area planning.[24]

As a result of the requirement for regional planning review of applications for federal loans or grants for open-space land projects, or for planning or construction of hospitals, airports, libraries, water supply and distribution facilities, waste treatment works, highways, transportation facilities, and water-development and land conservation projects, several hundred such agencies, referred to as Metropolitan Planning Organizations (MPOs) in ISTEA, are recognized by the U.S. Office of Management and Budget (OMB) under Section 204.

Many of the early regional agencies were metropolitan planning commissions consisting of appointed members rather than elected governmental officials. However, the National Association of Regional Councils (NARC) listed 675 councils of governments and regional councils in 2000.

There is no evidence that the regional review process produces substantial change in local or regional funding priorities or in the redistribution of federal funds among local governments in most urban areas. Although the review requirements of Section 205 of the Demonstration Cities and Metropolitan Development Act of 1966 resulted in the clearance and coordination of more aspects of federal urban expenditures than prior to its enactment, the councils of governments and other regional agencies generally accept local decisions as consonant with the regional interest.

Some councils of governments have forced the Interstate Highway System to reconcile differences with other local development policies; some have acquired other federal-regional programs such as comprehensive health planning not covered by OMB circulars, interpreting Section 204 of the Metropolitan Development Act. However, federal agencies have not made use of the leverage of Section 204 in influencing local spending patterns and metropolitan political structures, and so its impact upon local practices has been negligible. Under the facade of regional cooperation, each local government pursues its own fiscal interests.

Section 205, which provided financial incentives for regional coordination of development activities, never got federal guidelines for implementation by either OMB or the Department of Housing and Urban Development (HUD). It appears that the financial bonuses offered in Section 205 would be channeled directly to local governments for programs certified as regionally coordinated.

From the federal point of view, the likely road to regionalizing local government would have been further development of strategies explicit or implicit in federal grant legislation. In the federal view, the essence of good intergovernmental strategy was to be found in Sections 204 and 205. The two sections combined a conditional precedent to an application for a federal grant or loan under some thirty-nine programs of mandatory review with the possibility of a supplementary grant to urban applicants who demonstrated conformance to an established comprehensive planning process. Local officials understand the logic of conditional grants and the bonuses for meeting the conditions.

The Metropolitan Development Act came close to requiring the regional agency to prepare and adopt a capital budget for the region. Since priorities under Section 205 were never established by HUD, the working relationships between the federal and metropolitan planning regions or councils of governments could only have been strengthened by drawing the latter into the process of establishing the priorities that could have served as the basis of a national urban policy.

The Metropolitan Development Act instructed the secretary of HUD to "obtain and give full consideration to the comment of the body or bodies (state and local) responsible for comprehensive planning and programming for the metropolitan area" (Section 205d). The act also requires "programming of capital improvement based on a determination of relative urgency" (Section 208s). We return to the discussion of federal guidelines for regional planning in Chapter 7.

The statutory definition of comprehensive planning indicates that Congress considered short-term planning to be as important as long-term planning. In Section 208s comprehensive planning includes:

- Preparation, as a guide for long-range development, of general physical plans with respect to the pattern and intensity of land use and the provision of public facilities.
- Programming of capital improvements based on a determination of relative urgency.
- Long-range fiscal plans for implementing such plans and programs.
- Proposed regulatory and administrative measures that aid in achieving coordination of all related plans of the departments or subdivisions of the governments concerned and intergovernmental coordination of related planned activities among the states and local government concerned.

Regional agencies had to identify as regional priorities certain elements of the regional plan before a long-range plan was debated and adopted. It was not unusual for agencies to act before plans and policies were completed. In some ways the sequence is desirable because a continued interplay of planning, policymaking, and concrete action provides feedback for replanning and reformulation of policies and programs. The process was especially desirable when local, state, and federal governments were exploring uncharted ways of regional planning and regional action.

However marginal the success of these federal ventures into metropolitan economics, most categorical grant programs did not seek to upset administrative and policy practices of state and local governments. They were clientele programs that often resulted in federal subsidy of substandard services.

While intergovernmental programs have accumulated and expanded, the basic structure of local government has remained unchanged. There have been a handful of metropolitan consolidations, moderate annexation, a large and increasing number of special authorities, and facades of regional cooperation to meet federal requirements. Though economic considerations alone attest to the need for metropolitan governmental consolidation, they do not by themselves provide an adequate basis for institutional change in metropolitan governance. The political and sociological factors that created the structure of local government in metropolitan areas hold the structure in place. Creative solutions to areawide governance—such as those in Minneapolis-St. Paul, Portland, and Seattle Metro in Washington—are sound alternatives to further dysfunctional fragmentation based upon special districts.

In most metropolitan areas, the jurisdictional divisions forestall an integrated revenue system and comprehensive system of resource allocation. Part of the problem is the absence of any coherent federal or state policy toward management of the urban environment and economy. Only a center-left coalition in the U.S. Congress and between Congress and the White House nurtured over a long period of time has any chance of bringing about such a policy. The central difficulty is in the tradition and law surrounding state-local relationships and conflicting values that law and tradition perpetuate.

In a strict legal sense, local governments are creatures of the states. Their constitutional position is by no means comparable to that of states within the federal system. Local governments may exercise only those powers expressly granted by state constitutions and statutes. The practical effect of the express powers doctrine—"Dillon's Rule"—is that local governments are restricted from initiating programs in new areas of public concern or need. According to Dillon's Rule, the powers of municipalities are limited to those expressly delegated to them by the state.[25]

The constitutional status of local government is only partially explained by the rigidity of state-local law. The myth that local government is the foundation of popular government nourishes a "home rule" civic culture that jealously guards local boundaries and prerogatives. American civic culture sees each town and city as a miniature republic. Development of strong metropolitan institutions is often characterized as an invasion of the sacred right of home rule derived from Jeffersonian and Jacksonian ideologies.

The political viability of the home-rule myth is reflected in the long and largely unsuccessful battle for metropolitan consolidation in the United States. The fierce defensiveness of local units and the political power of their officials in state politics tend to reverse Dillon's Rule. State policy toward metropolitan affairs is often a creature of the parochial political interests of the counties and municipalities.

With few exceptions (notably Texas), incorporation of new local units is encouraged. Consolidation, merger, and annexation (except in Texas) are either discouraged or so encumbered by referenda that they are rendered unfeasible. Where suburban enclaves have incorporated to avoid city taxes and social problems or to have an independent school district, zoning board, and police department, there is an unwillingness to share in the problems and costs of the metropolis.

As the number of African American citizens in central cities increased in the 1960s and 1970s, metropolitan mergers were recognized as a potential dilution of their political power in the old city. Such attitudes reinforced the political inertia of existing constitutional and statutory arrangements of urban governance. They also reflected the great value that citizens and local officials place upon the political independence of local government.

The system is self-reinforcing. Structure and economic advantage interact with civic culture to resist institutional changes that might alter the existing balance of jurisdictions, finances, and power that have developed in metropolitan areas. It is hardly useful to condemn this arrangement or to assert that it is "inefficient," "unresponsive," or otherwise deficient. It may not meet the values and specifications of metropolitan reformers, but it serves the ends of citizens who perceive it as serving their interests.

The existing system of local governance performs sociopolitical functions that reflect values different from economic and constitutional ones. One is assimilation into the general political system. Though national and state politics play an important part in politicizing people, it is in *local* politics that most citizens obtain political experience. As we pointed out earlier in the chapter, the decline of the ward and spoils system removed two means through which electoral power was once translated into social status. With modifications, however, city politics remains an important aspect of cultural and political development, particularly for the lower middle class and deprived populations. The rise of African American, Hispanic, and more recent minority groups in the central cities is proof of this critical role of local politics.

Blacks have made extraordinary progress in the number of elected officials. In 1970, there were only 1,469 Black state and local elected officials. In 1980, there were 4,890. In 1990, there were 7,335. By 2000, there were 9,040. Likewise, Hispanics have made impressive gains in state and local elected offices, although data are not available as far back. In 1985, there were 3,147 Hispanic state and local elected officials. In 1990, there were 4,004. By 2000, there were 4,853.[26]

The grassroots ideology of local government had its 1960s manifestation in "participatory democracy." The wave of citizen participation in the 1960s and 1970s was consistent in urging people in local communities to assume control over public actions that affected their daily lives and environment. Such democratic fundamentalism illuminates the value placed upon the role of local political institutions in assimilating the population into the overall system of governance. City governments in recent times have been charged with being remote, and so officials have established neighborhood service centers, community school boards and special police precincts. Both the protests and the programs suggest strong belief in the cliché that government closest to the people governs best,[27] or, in Thomas Jefferson's words, "That government which governs least governs best." This popular theory of local government rests upon the assumption that a distinct local community of interest can be found and articulated politically. Since communities have always had a geographical identity in the past, this aspect has the power of an established tradition.

Basic to the theory that government closest to the people governs best is the idea that small-scale government is required in order to translate the local community of interest into programs for the community in city and regional politics. The idea of community in America traditionally has led to establishing a municipal corporation with jurisdictional boundary lines. In this arrangement, citizens experience intimate contact with communal government, learn the ropes of politics, and become full-fledged members of the larger body politic. Moreover, in this arrangement, the citizen can control the immediate environment and protect a common life style with neighbors.

However, the idea of so personal a community is in conflict with the economic, physical, and psychological realities of twenty-first-century urban life. That is because the geographical and socially contiguous community (the local municipality or neighborhood) is only one politically significant base for the organization of interest, citizen participation, and shared political experiences. Workplace, professional groupings, ethnic ties, ideology, and economic interests also importantly serve as organizational bases of community.

At the beginning of the twenty-first century, the technology of communications has also drastically reduced the traditional importance of urban settlements as the principal locations of communications flow. The urban place is being replaced by the nonplace realm, a concept consistent with Robert Ardrey's "territorial imperative," if humans are conceded to possess the capacity to relate in the abstract to nonspatial territories.[28]

Increasingly, fellow specialists locate globally, in communities of the mind. The cosmopolitan in the world of the twenty-first century relates to local, regional, national, and world realms, some aspects of which are territorially bound and others joined in various communities of interest. Some people relate in different aspects of their lives to communities of interest at several or all of these levels, others to more limited realms. The Internet and e-mail have added efficient communication technologies to our capacity for linking the infinite varieties of communities of interest locally, regionally, and around the world.[29]

In handling problems that must be resolved politically, leaders of a pluralistic society must take into account an endless variety of communities, neighborhoods, and ethnic and nationality groups—interest groups and associations that retain distinctive identities.

Although intergovernmental programs such as highways and housing require direction by national, state, and local governments, they must also listen to citizens of local communities and neighborhoods. But local communities may be so parochial in outlook that they are unable to act upon the political desires of their own residents. Housing and employment needs rarely can be satisfied by the governments of suburban enclaves or even those of cities, for these services are usually available in the regional market.

In local communities and sometimes in major cities, government has neither the territorial nor the legal jurisdiction to give it the capacity to resolve the practical problems for which urban citizens seek political help. This incapacity presents an acute dilemma for development of neighborhood institutions in the inner city: how to decentralize to allow citizens to play a significant role in neighborhood governance and at the same time cope with massive problems of unemployment, housing, and transportation. The latter class of problems requires solutions on a metropolitan and intergovernmental scale.

In larger urban areas, there are simultaneous demands to move toward areawide organization for some purposes and to community or neighborhood organizations for others. Both directions are essential. Centralized planning and operation of certain public and private functions are necessary to achieve economies of scale and efficiencies, while decentralization is a crucial aspect of citizen development and democratic control.

The boundaries of many suburban units, within which authority is exercised to regulate the use of land, function also as barriers to minority groups, poor people, the family with children, and other "undesirables." The economic restraints on the exercise of choice location within the metropolitan community are also present as exclusionary measures in the suburbs. The effect of both factors is to sharpen metropolitan social and economic disparities. The U.S. Advisory Commission on Intergovernmental Relations has documented the public policy implications of these disparities between central city and the suburbs.[30]

The success of local governments in integrating the population into the larger polity depends ultimately upon the political experience each local unit affords its citizens. If government is remote, impersonal, or unresponsive, no amount of ritualistic participation can overcome the sense of alienation citizens can feel.

The representative institutions of local government are the principal means through which citizens are able to participate in such matters of consequence as choosing officials and deciding public issues. The political organization of the metropolis, however, determines the official structure for representation as well as the aggregation of interests in the making of public policy.

Within any single jurisdiction, the organization of government reinforces the access of some groups to decisionmakers and inhibits that of others. The functional compartmentalization of most local governments, compounded by intergovernmental fiscal practices, makes it extremely difficult for them to deal with political pressures generated by special interests. An anti-freeway movement in a city with an at-large council may find it has no official arena in city government that might represent its point of view.

The geographical division of the metropolis into a variety of governmental units renders difficult the formation of metropolitan publics, since there are no metropolitanwide political processes through which such publics might function. Instead, groups organize around existing governmental units that, if jurisdictions divide classes or races, accentuate conflicts between them in metropolitan affairs. The existence of various governments, each with its own officials, also creates a system of institutional politics whose beneficiaries are reluctant to have the powers of their offices reduced.

There are no regional policies in most places because there is no regional political mechanism to resolve conflicts among jurisdictional interests. When a consensus can be achieved it is usually the lowest common denominator of action and often of little consequence in regional development. When controversial problems arise, such as the location of low-income housing or equitable distribution of revenue, they are usually ignored or brushed aside since there is no regional system of politics to influence subregional jurisdictions. The experiences with regional mechanisms in Minneapolis-St. Paul, Portland, and Seattle may be useful models for leadership in other metropolitan areas.

Edward Banfield and Morton Grodzins offered the view that such conflicts are best managed through barter and bargaining among jurisdictions, local leaders, and interest groups. In their judgment, metropolitan government is too hard to achieve to make the effort worthwhile and in any case does not solve such critical problems as housing and racial frictions. The Banfield-Grodzins model for conflict resolution involved the use of counterbalancing power, exercised through the leadership of big-city mayors and state governors. By intelligent use of power and negotiation, local government would move toward a form of metropolitan organization that could be capable of conflict resolution.[31] We expand upon this crucial point in Chapter 9, where we propose establishment (or restructuring) of substate planning and administrative districts.

The stalemate in metropolitan political systems, which goes back half a century or more, contributes to public disrespect and distrust for the officials and institutions of local government. As we point out in Chapter 6, legitimacy of local government depends upon acceptance, and acceptance depends upon both the historical and contemporary experience of citizens.

With all its social, economic, political, and legal diversities—and sheer numbers of people—there is a serious question as to whether the metropolis is governable in the democratic tradition. The fact is that many cities are too large for an intimate relationship to develop between the governors and the governed; other cities are too small to deal with such major economic questions as equitable use of revenues, location of industry, development of area-wide transportation facilities, water and air pollution, and equal opportunities for minorities in housing, employment, and education.

Many suburban jurisdictions are able to preserve a community political scale and therefore achieve a high sense of political identification, but with limited fiscal resources they are unable to control their physical environment or their safety. Evidence indicates that even in the administration of services, bigness does not necessarily result in either economies of scale or greater efficiency. Yet smallness does not assure a more desirable community.

The challenge, therefore, is to reconcile the desirability of scale economies and regional comprehension of problems with values emphasizing accountability and the political and social assimilation that might be obtained through decentralization. It may be necessary to draw upon the regional economic base to overcome the shift of income from central city to the periphery, to achieve regional public projects, and to take care of service deficiencies that develop in the central area. Such an arrangement would require well-organized and accessible political and bureaucratic systems, permit differential levels or types of services within subareas, and indulge local experimentation in some aspects of the political economy—or merely arrange for a shared revenue base, as in the Minneapolis-St. Paul plan. The substate district arrangement proposed in Chapter 9 would provide a sound and politically achievable solution.

Whatever the regional approach, identifiable and politically responsive local governments are required, but they must be achieved within a constitutional framework that provides not only interlocal methods of conflict resolution but also adequate authority to act upon politically sensed needs.

As we suggested earlier, the impetus for local reform must come from the states and from the federal government—where both the constitutional authority and the funds originate. Alternative routes to reform are discussed in later chapters. Suffice it to say here that a coherent national policy of urban development accompanied by inducements of shared revenue could accelerate change. So far in the past half-century Congress and the president have failed to develop such a policy and make it stick. The "permanent crisis," Waste insists, characterizes America's cities, and may or may not be permanent, but a crisis of extreme poverty is surely the condition in cities like the forty-four Waste and Rusk describe in their separate studies.

The importance of creating effective central institutions locally (substate districts) is that such institutions could expedite a decentralized political system and the delegation of administrative functions to the appropriate units of local government. In metropolitan areas where the primary planning and administrative unit encompasses a major portion of the urbanized population, it might be necessary to create subunits of government operating at the "community" level to preserve values associated with small-town government: intimate scale, direct responsibility and accountability, and an opportunity for broad citizen participation. Presently, individual jurisdictions within metropolitan areas have little or no organized relationship to each other and are usually products of a past era.

Should community governments vary in population from 50,000 to 150,000, they could have responsibility for conducting many activities directly, have authority for levying special assessments, and represent community interests at higher levels of government. The primary unit could reserve authority to override community government decisions and to reconcile periodically the boundaries of regional planning districts to reflect population changes or altered physical or political conditions.

Community governments in major urban areas would provide opportunities for citizens to obtain direct experience in government and to have elected officials close at hand. These governments would also offer important minorities a local power base in the overall pattern of urban politics. Similarly, they would afford a legitimate and workable basis of community control of institutions that intimately affect the daily lives and life opportunities of people.

Moreover, if community governments were also granted some general powers, many of the familiar difficulties in decentralizing urban government could be overcome. It would not be necessary to create separate community arrangements for public schools, neighborhood centers, health centers, youth programs, housing developments, police precincts, and other such elements, as they could be coordinated through a single community body.

Thus a community school committee, a public-safety committee, and a planning commission could function in an environment in which they truly represent the community as its elected representatives. Whatever the defects of elections in regard to representation, they are less severe than bureaucratic co-option by self-proclaimed spokespeople. Operating under such a system, a community district's jurisdiction could avoid many of the adverse consequences of uncertain bureaucratic participatory arrangements commonly employed by cities eager for federal funds but confused as to how to deal with the federal government's vague concept of citizen participation.

Legitimizing authority also could be served by a system of community governments, since they might be sufficient bases for administration of certain aspects of the legal system. Although reforms brought about by centralization of the courts and other aspects of the administration of justice have been of questionable benefit, there are advantages in using decentralized community government as a base for selecting petit and grand juries.

In addition, conducting trials at the community government level could broaden citizen interaction with the law and legal processes. In the zeal for uniform treatment and professionalization, the impetus of reform toward centralization has obscured the judicial system's civic function in educating citizens on the value of law in society.

Ironically, the arguments usually advanced against community government, which mainly concern the difficulties in altering massive institutions, in themselves make a strong case for reform. In many instances, cities have grown to a size beyond effective political control of local governments as they are presently organized. Expansion has stopped at boundaries that bear little relation to current realities of the political and social life of the city. In contrast, community governments could be politically and socially viable. The technique for success of such units is to weave them into a reconstituted arrangement of metropolitan areas that enhances rather than diminishes their economic, constitutional, and civic functions. That would be the function of the substate districts proposed in Chapter 9.

Notes

1. Robert K. Merton, "The Latent Functions of the Machine: A Sociologist's View," in *Social Theory and Social Structure* (New York: Free Press, 1957).
2. See Robert C. Wood, *Suburbia, Its People and Their Politics* (Boston: Houghton Mifflin, 1958); and Frederick M. Wirt, *On the City's Rim: Politics and Policy in Suburbia*, (Lexington, Mass.: D.C. Heath, 1972).
3. Raymond Vernon, "The Changing Economic Function of the Central City," Committee for Economic Development, New York, 1959.
4. Michael Harrington, *The Other America* (New York: Macmillan, 1962).
5. William Julius Wilson, *The Bridge over the Racial Divide: Rising Inequality and Coalition Politics* (Berkeley: University of California Press, 1999).
6. Wilbert J. LeMelle, Jr., in a private letter dated March 30, 2000.
7. John F. Kain, "Failure in Diagnosis: A Critique of the National Urban Policy," *Urban Lawyer* (Spring 1979): 261.
8. Mark Schneider and John R. Logan, "Fiscal Implications of Class Segregation: Inequalities in the Distribution of Public Goods and Services in Suburban Municipalities," *Urban Affairs Quarterly* 17 (September 1981).
9. U.S. Bureau of Labor Statistics.
10. Norton E. Long, *The Unwalled City: Reconstituting the Urban Community* (New York: Basic Books, 1972).
11. Jonathan Kozol, *Savage Inequalities* (New York: Crown, 1991).
12. Gary Orfield, "Minorities and Suburbanization," in *Critical Perspectives on Housing*, ed. Rachel G. Bratt, Chester Hartman, and Ann Myerson (Philadelphia: Temple University Press, 1986).
13. Elizabeth D. Huttman and Terry Jones, "American Suburbs: Desegregation and Resegregation," in *Urban Housing Segregation of Minorities in Western Europe and the United States,* ed. Elizabeth D. Huttman (Durham, N.C.: Duke University Press, 1991).
14. Ralph W. Conant, *The Prospects for Revolution: A Study of Riots, Civil Disobedience, and Insurrection in Contemporary America* (New York: Harper's Magazine Press, 1970).
15. *Hawkins v. Town of Shaw, Miss.,* 303 F. Supp. 1162 (1969).
16. *San Antonio Independent School District et al., Appellants, v. Demetrio P. Rodriquez et al.,* No. 71-1332, 411 U.S. 1. 1973.

17. David Rusk, *Cities Without Suburbs* (Washington, D.C.: Woodrow Wilson Center Press, 1993, 1995), p. 108.
18. U.S. Bureau of the Census.
19. P.L. 89-757, Demonstration Cities and Metropolitan Development Act of 1966.
20. P.L. 90-557, Intergovernmental Cooperation Act of 1968.
21. P.L. 92-583, Coastal Zone Management Act of 1972.
22. P.L. 102-240, Intermodal Surface Transportation Act of 1991 (ISTEA).
23. Robert J. Waste, *Independent Cities* (New York.: Oxford University Press, 1998), p. 73.
24. P.L. 105-178, Transportation Equity Act (TEA-21). The predecessor legislation, incorporated in TEA-21, was P.L. 102-240, the Transportation Restoration Act.
25. In its entirety, Dillon's Rule states: "It is a general and undisputed proposition of law that a municipal corporation possesses and can exercise the following powers, and no others: First, those granted in express words; second, those necessarily or fairly implied in or incident to the power expressly granted; third, those essential to the accomplishment of the declared objects and purposes of the corporation—not simply convenient, but indispensable. Any fair, reasonable, substantial doubt concerning the existence of the power is resolved by the courts against the corporation, and the power is denied." John F. Dillon, *Commentaries on the Law of Municipal Corporations,* 5th edn. (Boston: Little, Brown, 1911), vol. 1, sec. 237.
26. *Black Elected Officials: A National Roster,* Joint Center for Political and Economic Studies; *National Roster of Hispanic Elected Officials,* National Association of Latino Elected and Appointed Officials.
27. Robert F. Pecorella, *Community Power in a Post-Reform City* (Armonk, N.Y.: M.E. Sharpe, 1994).
28. Robert Ardrey, *The Territorial Imperative* (New York: Dell, 1966).
29. Reviewing this passage, the eminent geographer Robert Sack pointed out that even global communities of interest are place-oriented. For a more detailed discussion of how nonterritorial communities require place, see Robert Sack, *Homo Geographicus: A Framework for Action, Awareness, and Moral Concern* (Baltimore: Johns Hopkins University Press, 1997).
30. Advisory Commission on Intergovernmental Relations, *Improving Urban America: A Challenge to Federalism,* September 1976.
31. Edward C. Banfield and Morton Grodzins, *Government and Housing in Metropolitan Areas* (New York: McGraw-Hill, 1958).

Chapter 5

Models of Local Government Reorganization

This chapter focuses on proposals that policymakers and scholars have made for curing the troubles of our cities by restructuring their governments. Three types of proposals are considered: making urban governments smaller and their constituencies more homogeneous, making them larger and their constituencies more heterogeneous, or, simultaneously, both. The proposals ask whether the urban areas of America can be organized in ways to enhance the equitable and efficient production and delivery of public services.

The notion of metropolitan-scale government had its main run in the 1950s, when many people were exercised over the fact that urban growth was spilling over city boundaries more rapidly and in more places than ever before, creating unprecedented problems. Policymakers and scholars blamed the resulting problems on "fragmentation" of local governments in urban areas.

The contrary notion that "fragmentation" might be beneficial—to the extent of creating or preserving small-scale governments—came into vogue in the 1960s. It had two main roots: First, the concept of giving a larger piece of local political action to minorities—Blacks in particular—and the urban poor, who claimed to lack a political voice in the cities where they lived. The inner-city riots of the period served to underscore the demand. Second, the concept, widely associated with the political scientists Edward Banfield and Morton

Grodzins and the economist Charles Tiebout, that the existence of many jurisdictions in a metropolitan area, each able to control its own level and pattern of spending, would enable individual homeseekers to find jurisdictions congenial to their tastes, thereby approximating a market situation.[1]

The Tiebout thesis is that residential mobility and competition among local jurisdictions result in an efficient provision of local public goods approximating a market for private goods. In Kirk Stark's words, "The idea is that because consumers/voters can always 'vote with their feet,' local public officials must be sensitive to taxpayers' desired levels and types of services."[2]

The opposite concept—that of making urban governments larger and their constituencies more heterogeneous—was advocated by people associated with the city government reform movement ever since the middle of the nineteenth century. The city-county of Philadelphia was an early city-county consolidation, in 1854. Even earlier, the city of New Orleans was made coterminus with the parish of Orleans in 1804; Boston and Suffolk County were consolidated in 1821, as were Nantucket and Nantucket County; San Francisco and San Francisco County followed Philadelphia in 1856; present-day New York City was created in 1898 by consolidation of five contiguous boroughs. Twenty-two more city-county consolidations occurred in the decades that followed, through 1992. The best-known ones were Denver-Arapahoe County, Honolulu-Honolulu County, Nashville-Davidson County, Jacksonville-Duval County, and Indianapolis-Marion County (Unigov). Miami and Dade County were organized in 1957 as a two-tiered governmental system, called Metro Miami.

Public finance economists have traditionally been among the scholars who have supported the notion that all redistributive policies should be concentrated at the most centralized level of government.[3] The arguments are that local welfare assistance creates incentives for strategic migration, that both rich and poor will relocate to take advantage of redistribution, that relying on localities to provide welfare assistance will result in an underprovision of such assistance. Federal assumption of redistributive policies, Stark argues, would not only avoid such pitfalls but "foster a more efficient provision of local public goods, bringing local government policies more closely into line with the Tiebout model."[4]

From the 1960s forward, the most pressing needs for metropolitanwide jurisdictions were met, if at all, by establishing limited-function agencies, usually called special districts—a process in which the federal government took a prominent role. By 1990, there were more than 38,000 special districts in the U.S. Several heavily urbanized counties were given broad administrative and planning responsibilities, Baltimore and Montgomery counties in Maryland, and Fairfax and Arlington counties in Virginia among them.

A middle ground among the economic theorists helped to lay the philosophical groundwork for the citizen participation/decentralization movement of the 1960s (the Model Cities Program) and the 1970s (Nixon's general revenue-sharing program for all local governments). In 1973, economist Mark Pauly argued that local redistribution is not necessarily inconsistent with concerns for efficiency. Communities, Pauly said, want income redistribution in part for reasons of pure altruism (the impulse to help the poor where one lives), and the desire to minimize local crimes against property and person. Thus, through a combination of genuine concern for poverty close at hand and a dislike for its consequences, Pauly concludes, localities are likely to undertake redistributive outlays. "To the extent that people have different demands for such outlays, communities will sort themselves out according to their redistributive preferences." Stark adds that in such circumstances "at least some degree of local redistribution can continue without necessarily disrupting the efficiency properties of the Tiebout model."[5]

Pressures for decentralization were met both by continuing "fragmentation" and, in the larger cities, by various innovations such as the federal Model Cities and Concentrated Employment programs and moves to put public-service centers in neighborhoods. After initial enthusiasm, the Model Cities Program lost support among local officials, mostly because the novel requirement of "maximum feasible participation" of poor and minority citizens gave the latter too much say in the program. Thus, decentralization for the psychological purpose of giving poor communities greater voice and control over public services likewise proved futile; the power to allocate public funds lacks significance where funds are already meager.

Decentralization by radical reorganization was pushed hard in New York City in the 1970s. A Temporary Commission to Study Governmental Operations of the City of New York in 1972 recommended that various functions of city government be devolved to thirty to thirty-five "service delivery districts," with a central service delivery sector being retained for citywide aspects of services. The local service delivery districts were to be governed by councils and each would have an executive officer.[6]

Two Models of the Urban Governmental Process

To set the stage for considering the advantages and disadvantages of the small-scale governments typical of suburban areas versus the large-scale governments of central cities, we review two models of the urban governmental process: the market model, reflected in the plethora of jurisdictions of suburbs; and the games model, reflected in central-city government and politics.

Both models recognize that the main business of government is providing services and benefits not offered by the private sector and that government in urban areas has three main functions—social choice making, production and delivery of public goods, and income redistribution—plus an ancillary function—the financing of the public goods and services that government produces.

The Market Model

This model regards government as the analog of the producer firm in the private sector that arranges for production and delivery of public goods to voter-taxpayers. The latter are the analog of sovereign consumers in the private market. The market analogy suggests that public service arrangements should approximate market conditions. Those who advocate the market model as a guide to governmental organization are concerned primarily with economic efficiency. In this context, three aspects of efficiency are relevant: choice making, production, and equity.

Choice-Making Efficiency. Choice-making efficiency involves equating the marginal benefits of each public good with its marginal cost. Marginal cost is measured in terms of other goods and services that must be sacrificed to enjoy an additional unit of a particular good. The taxpayer has three variables to consider with respect to any public good: the personal value of the service, the cost, and the amount of tax people pay because the service is provided.

The first variable—service value—is largely subjective; community political and social processes mold it. It can change over time and can be managed to suit local taste in the small, homogeneous units of local government typical of suburbs.

The other two variables are largely independent of the taxpayer—in the short run at least. In an efficient market model, the values of the three variables tend to be equal for each taxpayer. A major difficulty in attaining efficiency lies in reconciling differences in individual preferences for various public and private goods. Some may prefer more police, some may prefer more parks, and others may prefer better roads or greater expenditure on education. Still others may prefer fewer public goods and lower taxes. Attempts to construct public welfare functions that yield fair allocations have proved futile.

Majority rule is no answer. For example, it is not difficult to show that fiscal inefficiency will result if a majority chooses a level of a public service that it prefers only mildly over alternatives, while the minority greatly prefers other alternatives: "Majority rule will be efficient only by accident."[7]

Production Efficiency. In the market model, government agencies are assumed to produce and deliver public goods with reasonable efficiency, meaning that production functions and output/input ratios cannot be improved in the short run. In this context, the main policy problems concern economies of scale and the size of the jurisdiction required for effective planning, decisionmaking, and production and delivery of goods. The problems may be simplified by the fact that the main elements of the administrative process—decisionmaking and policy implementation—may be performed by different organizational entities.

Income Redistribution. Fiscal equity, which aims at "fair" distribution of income after taxes, requires that equal taxes be imposed on individuals of equal economic capacity (as measured by wealth and income), and that tax rates be progressive—higher for individuals of greater economic capacity and lower for individuals of less economic capacity. Though fiscal equity is an accepted requirement of our governmental system, the hard fact is that most state and local tax structures are regressive.

The Games Model

The games model views governmental (and, more broadly, the communal) processes as a system of games in which various players strive for various prizes. In the games model, different individuals and groups want different, often conflicting, things from government, of which public goods are only one. Individuals and groups employ different tactics to get what they want. Appealing to voters is only one of the tactics that can be used. The prizes include positions of power and influence, jobs and contracts, wages and working conditions (of interest to labor unions), zoning and other regulations favorable to specific interests, the manner of enforcing statutes and regulations, and so forth.

In the games model, allocation of the "prizes" is much more complicated than the two-way bargaining process between taxpayers and producer governments of the market model. In the games model there are four sets of players whose conflicting interests must be resolved by the governmental process. They are public employees, elected officials, taxpayers, and the consumers of public goods.

The employees of local government are primarily interested in pay increases, reduced work time, and organizational status. Public employees protect themselves by a civil service and the merit system, as well as by manipulation of the political system through money and votes.

The protections are fortified by public employee unions whose purpose is to provide their members with leverage designed to enhance their working conditions. Government unions avoid most of the constraints affecting industrial unions, such as market fluctuations and profit, by utilizing laws defining unfair practices and a standard set of moves and countermoves that keep negotiations within bounds. Government unions often ignore antistrike laws. Also, government agencies lack the incentives for economic efficiency imposed on private firms by competition. They are in the position of monopolies that do not have to be concerned about consumer reaction to inefficiency or high prices.

Elected officials, in principle, perform their political function of reconciling conflicting interests, making decisions, and supervising the bureaucracy. Their interests are varied: power, prestige, financial reward, party success, and the desire to render public service.

Taxpayers comprise both those who are aware of the taxes they pay and those who are not. The aware group may make the connection between their taxes and the benefits received. Typically they would prefer to pay less and get more. They object particularly to paying taxes for income redistribution and avoid communities that offer generous welfare and other benefits to the poor. The unaware taxpayers are usually not aware of the taxes they pay because the taxes are hidden or indirect—for example, taxes on rented housing. Such taxes are popular with elected officials because they elicit few complaints.

Beneficiaries of government include the upper classes, middle classes, and working classes, which do not depend on government for much of their consumption. They look instead to the market, a habit that is bolstered by rising incomes and purchasing power. They depend on government only for basic housekeeping, transportation, protective services, and education. The latter is the largest public expenditure in most urban areas, accounting for about one-quarter of local government expenditures each year.

For the middle class, the personal experience of urban living is one of continuous, though in some cases gradual, improvement. The improvement is facilitated by the fact that middle- and upper-class groups can, if they choose, escape the stresses and strains of big-city life by moving out or by relocating to upscale enclaves inside the city.

The working-class groups do not have things so easy. Many of the working class in urban areas are trapped by rising taxes and at times by inflation, making progress difficult. In the past several decades, the working class in urban areas has not fully shared in the general prosperity and has joined in the revolt against the welfare system, convinced that their hard-earned tax dollars are being used to support the idle and the ne'er-do-well.

Among the middle and upper classes in urban areas there has been a growing impatience with congestion, pollution, crime and delinquency, restrictions on choice, and the ugliness of the landscape. In collective actions, they tend to be less creative than conservative; they lean toward preserving amenities and eliminating abominations. Most do not connect their discomfort with a need for systematic planning and improved urban design.

A second group of beneficiaries is the lower class, those who look to government for their most elementary needs: basic subsistence, improved housing, and neighborhoods free of violence, drug pushers, and vagrants. The relative deprivation pervasively experienced by this group is a source of active and sometimes violent protest against conditions in poor neighborhoods of central cities. This group bears the brunt of fiscal inequity in the production and delivery of public goods in America's urban areas.

Implicit Objectives of the Two Models

The market model and the games model differ in their objectives. The market model is value-oriented. Its most important feature is its emphasis on efficiency in both public choices and the production and delivery of public goods. The games model is value-free in that it does not entail ends such as efficiency. The model *does* depend on adherence to rules under which the community's games are played. Various players continually seek to change the rules to give themselves an advantage and, as part of the game, sometimes succeed. The game breaks up when any considerable number of players decide the rules are too heavily biased and decline to play under the "unfair" rules.

Collective Social Choice Making

A major function of government is to make collective choices respecting the kinds and amount of public goods to be purchased. There are two central issues of social choice making as a function of government in urban areas. The first is maximizing gratification of urban residents' demands for public services, demands expressed directly and ultimately in the voting booth. The second is fostering a sense of participation in processes whereby choices are made and service is provided.

Approaches Based on the Market Model

Market-based approaches to public services attempt to achieve results resembling those of consumers shopping in the market, each able to buy the items he/she wants within the limits of individual purchasing power. Of course, the market does not work perfectly. Purchases may be ill informed, regretted, harmful, or beyond the means of the people making them. It is not always possible to buy exactly what is needed because some items are "lumpy" in the sense that people have to buy more than they need, such as automobiles, lawn mowers, and other household implements. It is possible to attain economies of scale through formal arrangements, for example, by carpooling or sharing implements with friends and neighbors.

Also, preferences are to some degree transient, capable of being modified by various influences, notably advertising and the play of fashions and fads. Some of these influences have their counterparts in the public sector, but the imperfections of the private market narrow the advantage of precision that the private market is supposed to enjoy over the public sector.

A flaw in applying the market model to the public sector is that the majority of voters can coerce the minority into paying for the level of services desired by the majority. While overexploitation of the minority may be prevented by rules of uniform taxation, an incremental expenditure may be wasteful if the aggregate amount of the benefit to the majority exceeds the aggregate amount of excessive payments by the minority.

The market model leads toward two principles of government organization. The first is that voters of choice-making governmental jurisdictions should be as homogeneous as possible, with similar preferences as to the amounts and kinds of public services they desire. The second is that the number of voters should be small so as to reduce the costs of the interpersonal bargaining and negotiation necessary to arrive at mutually satisfactory public budgets.

The market model thus demands creation and *preservation* of numerous governments in urban areas so that the urban resident is afforded a variety of choices of tax and expenditure patterns. Thus the resident can choose the jurisdiction that accords with his/her social, economic, and political preferences.

The "smallness" principle depends on the assumption that small groups will be more homogeneous than large ones in tastes and preferences. Homogeneity is achieved as each household or business gravitates to the community that fits its preferences.

There is some evidence that this birds-of-a-feather principle tends to operate in the real world mainly according to wealth and income. Variances between residential incomes tend to be higher among suburban towns than within individual towns, indicating a tendency of income classes to flock together. Thus suburban towns tend to be rich or poor or middle income. Public services tend to be best in high-income communities. This is the reason expenditures on public goods and services are more closely correlated with income than with any other variable. This fact suggests that differences in preferences among persons of similar incomes are less important than the market analogy implies.

Yet there are differences. For example, older people and working-class families sometimes oppose expenditures on public schools; new residents may want improvements opposed by older residents. Whether such differences are sufficient to cause migration to other communities is another question. Considering the host of other factors that tie people to a community, many individuals would rather fight than switch.

The flight of the middle class from central cities and the reasons behind it afford little support to the Banfield/Tiebout principle that the justification for maintaining suburbs is the range and variety of public services and levels of taxation they offer. The fact is that the differences between central-city and suburban living that attract the middle class far transcend differences in public services.

Thus the Banfield/Tiebout argument applies mainly to households with high enough incomes to afford some choice as to how their incomes should be allocated between private and public—tax-financed—goods. Low-income groups, largely dependent on government services, have no such latitude of choice. Moreover, the latitude they might otherwise have is frustrated by a tendency of higher-income groups to resist incursions of lower-income residents, because the presence of the latter would raise taxes and otherwise "spoil" the community for the former. "Foot voting" is largely the prerogative of the higher-income groups, who play exclusionary politics to deny a similar foot vote to lower-income groups.

Experienced observers recognize three disadvantages of smallness and homogeneity: economies of scale, externalities, and income redistribution.

Economies of scale were discussed in a previous section on production efficiency in the market model. The problems of externalities refer to benefits conferred, or costs imposed, by the activities of one jurisdiction upon residents of other jurisdictions. In the case of external costs, the acting jurisdiction, not bearing the full costs of its activity, may produce more of a public good than is socially justified. The test is whether the resident-beneficiaries would be willing to compensate nonresidents who are damaged. To the extent they are not, the production is not justified. External costs may also be imposed upon a jurisdiction's own residents, who lack the political clout to stop the offending activity or to obtain restitution.

The same reasoning applies to external *benefits*, but in the obverse. Where part of the benefits from the activity of one jurisdiction accrue to the residents of other jurisdictions, the acting jurisdiction, if it has to pay all the costs, is likely to produce less than the optimal amount; other jurisdictions might be willing to pay it to produce the optimal amount.

A damaging example of such underproduction may accrue where the residents of a particular jurisdiction, who prefer private goods to public ones, desire to economize on public education. Though the amount spent on education is not necessarily a reliable indicator of quality, it is usually true that where education is less valued it is less good. Poor education is likely to result in ignorance, which adversely affects not only the local community but also society in general. This can be said similarly of recreational and other cultural opportunities for young people, and of law enforcement and health services.

In some cases, external benefits might be handled by voluntary intergovernmental cooperation, whereby other jurisdictions agree to pay the acting jurisdiction for increasing production of the externally beneficial good. But such arrangements are difficult to negotiate. External costs probably cannot be suppressed by intergovernmental arrangements. It is difficult to conceive of Jurisdiction B paying Jurisdiction A *not* to pollute the river or to upgrade A's educational program.

Income Redistribution

Income redistribution is the third problem, after economies of scale and externalities, recognized by advocates of smallness and homogeneity. The notion of efficiency and choice making presupposes an acceptable distribution of income. If taxes are imposed to finance income transfers to the poor, the total amount of taxes will exceed the total cost of public services delivered, thus complicating the mechanisms of collective choice.

To overcome this complication, political leaders may propose moving the income distribution function to a broader jurisdiction. The broadest jurisdiction is the federal government, which is in a better position than either the states or metropolitan areas to implement equitable redistribution, since both these jurisdictions vary greatly in per capita income and taxable resources.

Lack of Responsiveness to Consumer Demands and Needs

Social choices bear little resemblance to choices of informed consumers in the market. First, once we abandon the two-dimensional world of the market model for the games model, the community negotiation process goes beyond taxpayers and producer governments as other claimants appear. Legislators and elected public officials tend to be more interested in inputs and in the patronage they can confer than in outputs. Also, outputs are difficult to measure. This is the real world of urban governance.

Second, governmental bureaucracies are notoriously unresponsive to public demand. They tend to do what they like and persuade officials and legislators to come up with the funding. The experience of the last half-century confirms that increasing support of education or police or mass transportation has not always produced improved education, better protection, or more efficient transportation.

Third, few citizens have the time or the knowledge to evaluate services, except to recognize gross deficiencies. Putting together a package of desired services, with decisions as to how much one would like to spend for a preferred quality of each, is beyond the ordinary citizen. Increasing the number of jurisdictions that provide services does not improve matters. It only weakens the budgeting process, which attempts to weigh community needs and priorities and to balance them against each other, and complicates the task of understanding what is going on. This is also the real world.

One of the advantages of a general multifunction government is that it relieves constituents of the necessity of making many of the decisions they would have to make if public services were supplied through the private market. A disadvantage in general multifunction government is that voters have to take packages of services as a whole that they typically have had no role in putting together—except possibly as members of special-interest groups. In the process, voters are removed from their economic function as rational sovereign consumers and must settle for other "rationalities."

The mere fact that public-goods consumers may get more or less than they are willing to bid for is not an infallible indication of waste in public choice making. Individual preferences are themselves conditioned by the community decision-making process, debate over public issues, and the striking of compromises (the games model). It is common to find cases of people satisfied with the outcome of community decisions that they had opposed. Ex post facto judgments are likely to be more informed and hence better than judgments made before the fact.

The small-jurisdiction prescription, based on the notion that the costs of negotiation and cooperation rise with the number of people concerned, fails because its basic assumption is wrong: the smaller the constituency, the lower the level of voter participation. Insofar as it has any validity at all, the small-jurisdiction concept applies mainly to middle- and upper-income taxpayers and to services without major externalities. Smaller jurisdictions, particularly poor ones, do not meet a basic market-model condition, that is, constituents who are well enough informed about the public services they want, and about the costs and conditions under which public services are produced. Communication is typically deficient, participation is low, and self-interested manipulation by cliques and individuals can be easy. Also, political communication in small constituencies tends to be word of mouth, rumor and gossip, misinformation, and half-baked information.

Further, informed choice making in small jurisdictions tends to be impeded by poor political machinery, and such units often display unstable, highly factionalized and personalized politics or tight oligarchic control supported by consensual politics, both indicating low levels of political participation.

Another disadvantage to small-scale governments is their inability to bring countervailing power against powerful interest groups. Such countervailing power groups include business and labor, bureaucracies, and others seeking special consideration from government. Roscoe Martin once observed, "'Bring government back home' and 'Return government to the people' are battle cries equally familiar in the cause of local economy and in that of states' rights. . . . In point of fact it is quite clear that the goal sought is often not autonomy or states' rights as such but rather less government, and . . . government . . . immediately and . . . directly subject to control."[8]

The case for homogeneity is no better. It already exists to a large degree in suburbia, where groupings tend to be by income class rather than by finely differentiated preferences for public services. The impact of existing patterns is well known: the haves freeze out the have-nots, denying them access to housing and hence to jobs, to the better schools and hence to jobs, to recreational facilities, and to other advantages. It is unrealistic to imagine that these disadvantages will be overcome by anything the federal government does about income redistribution.

Differences over basic issues such as public education, environmental improvement, urban transportation, economic development, job training, health programs, and others cannot be resolved by small jurisdictions, homogeneous or not. To the extent that they cannot be resolved within the confines of metropolitan areas, they always move to the higher arenas of state or federal government.

Advantages of Larger Scale in Choice Making

In the twenty-first century's complicated urban society, informed decisions respecting expenditures and investment priorities require sophisticated planning and budgeting processes that lend themselves to economies of scale. Small jurisdictions cannot afford sophisticated planning and budgeting.

The production and delivery of services in most jurisdictions are the heart of the political-governmental process. They produce many "outputs," such as jobs and contracts, high offices, ego satisfaction, and the like, which tend to be regarded more highly than public goods delivered to beneficiaries.

Urban governments that ordinarily rate highest in efficiency and service delivery and tend to be medium-sized and smaller and to have constituencies that are predominantly middle class and interested mainly in adequate service. Most are run by professional city managers who concentrate on the technical aspects of administration instead of being obliged, as are so many large-city mayors, to devote time to conflict resolution.[9]

The smaller middle-class-dominated cities more nearly fit the market model, while the larger cities more nearly fit the games model. The fact that large-city governments take after the blind-to-efficiency games model does not mean that the larger cities are becoming unglued or in danger of collapse, or that things are worse than in earlier generations. Nor is there reason to suppose that a city like New York is governed worse than other jurisdictions.

One cannot conclude, either, that middle-sized and smaller units *as a class* are generally well governed, for good government depends on possessing both human and fiscal resources, and many smaller cities are not well endowed with either. There already exist many examples of the dubious benefits that self-determination may bestow on poor jurisdictions. In suburbia one finds many low-income enclaves even more economically bereft and worse governed than are the central cities. Where funds are scarce, the level of political sophistication low, the supply of professional, managerial, and technical manpower limited, and communications poor, community leadership is more likely to focus on jobs and handouts—the traditional concern of patronage—than on improving services.

The size of an agency required for efficient production and delivery of public goods depends in principle on several considerations, few of which lend themselves to quantitative analysis—the type of goods, for one. It has long been established that some goods can be efficiently planned and administered only by agencies of metropolitan or higher jurisdiction. Metropolitan-scale planning and administration may be more efficient for several reasons, including the following:

- Economies of scale in production; for example, maintenance, certain aspects of the police function, museums, and other cultural centers.
- Externalities that cannot adequately be handled by interjurisdictional agreements; for example, air and water pollution control.
- Interdependent elements of public service; for example, intra-urban transportation.

- Resolution of conflicts of interest among submetropolitan areas; for example, planning and zoning.

The list of functions that are candidates for metropolitan-scale administration has expanded over the past half-century. In the 1950s and 1960s, the principal candidates were water supply, air- and water-pollution control, and intra-urban transportation. In the period since, the list has lengthened to include health services, economic development, job-training programs, housing, and general environmental control.

In some cases where economies of scale or administrative efficiency require metropolitan-scale governmental institutions, these have been created for specific purposes. Mainly they have taken the form of limited-purpose jurisdictions designed for one or two services. For other types of services, economies of scale should be in principle a consideration in establishing the size of administrative jurisdictions. Other than for metropolitan-scale functions, where the scale of operations is dictated more by the need for comprehensive coverage than by production technology, there is little evidence of economies or diseconomies of scale in a broad population bracket of, say, between 40,000 and 4 million.

Even where economies of scale do exist, it is not necessary to tailor the size of jurisdictions to take advantage of them. Several jurisdictions may cooperate in functions requiring large productive units, such as incinerators or police academies, or services that can be obtained under contract with larger jurisdictions. Los Angeles County sells service packages to local municipal jurisdictions, the size and content of which are determined by the individual jurisdictions. Under these arrangements, the choice making is left to the individual jurisdictions.

Suburban areas around large cities need a rationalization of their governmental structures. With rapid growth and aging, the suburbs have developed many of the problems of the central cities—congestion, pollution, and inadequate water, sewage, and sanitary services. They also have increasing numbers of poverty-prone residents. Also, they must deal with rapid growth and development, maintain open space and environmental quality, and strive for economically efficient and aesthetically pleasing development.

Most suburban governments are not fully capable of coping with the development or the service needs of rapid growth. Structurally, there are two difficulties: many suburban jurisdictions are too small to achieve economies of scale, not only in production-delivery functions, but also in planning, management, and finance. Also, suburbs have numerous special districts that are not adequately supervised and have no built-in incentives to cooperate with other governmental units.

Concern about metropolitan-scale planning and jurisdiction over the past half-century has focused on decentralization-participation issues. Centralization and decentralization are usually construed in geographic terms. In fact, there are other bases of jurisdiction and representation, including the interest groups that are so numerous in large urban areas. Thus local political structures and patterns of control may not follow geographic boundaries. Political power may be highly diffused in single large urban jurisdictions (New York City) and highly concentrated in areas containing numerous jurisdictions (Chicago). Therefore, geographic decentralization for the purpose of increasing the power of particular groups may miss the main issues of representation and political power.

As we noted a few pages back, the notion that small jurisdictions make for better public choices rests on the market model of government and assumes that the constituencies of smaller jurisdictions are relatively more homogeneous than those of larger jurisdictions. It also assumes that taxpayer-consumers will locate in the jurisdictions whose tax and expenditure patterns meet their respective preferences.

Aside from better communication and information, there are certain economies of scale in social choice making that argue for larger rather than smaller jurisdictions, particularly where heterogeneous constituencies with different and conflicting preferences are involved.

With respect to the production and delivery of public goods, market models and games models produce different results. Market-model cities are mainly medium-sized and smaller cities dominated by middle-class constituencies that demand both quality and efficiency in public services. In game-model cities, which include larger, heterogeneous cities and poor smaller cities, the inputs, and who is in a position to supply and control them, become more important issues than the efficiency of services. In sum, there is no reason why geographic decentralization of city governments would improve production and delivery of services, even those that would lend themselves to smaller-scale production. In fact there is considerable experience to the contrary.

If control over production and delivery of public goods could be decentralized, leaders in poor communities might gain by acquiring a large stake in the inputs, even at the expense of quality of services. The possibility of deterioration does not worry advocates of decentralization, who claim that public services in poor neighborhoods could not be worse anyway.

Thinking about issues of decentralization, one must draw a firm line between decentralization (breaking up existing jurisdictions into smaller geographic ones) and participation, which implies integration of neglected areas into the social, economic, and political framework of the larger community.

The two concepts have very different implications. Decentralization implies further isolation of the constituency of each new jurisdiction—creation of a new game. Participation implies a larger measure of intercourse with, and absorption into, the larger community, with weaker players wielding more power and influence.

Decentralization inevitably encounters difficulties carving out territories that become "communities" that are meaningful for government and other social purposes. However the communities come about, drawing boundary lines seldom creates them. The notion of "community" is fundamental to the concept of government jurisdiction in a democratic society where government is presumed to derive its authority from the consent of the governed. While such governments derive from communities, it is also true that communities derive from the governments that serve them, and many communities may have as their main unifying force a stable local government.

There is a class of public goods and services, exemplified by intra-urban transportation and air- and water-pollution control, that can be provided effectively only by metropolitan-scale jurisdictions. The case for geographic centralization of governmental powers to provide such services is more persuasive than the case for decentralization of large-city governments.

The established suburbs and the developing areas in large urban concentrations are both confronted with governmental problems that have been neglected because of concentration on metropolitan areas as a whole. Suburban governments particularly are handicapped by jurisdictions that are too small, by a proliferation of overlapping jurisdictions, and by wide disparities in taxable capacity relative to need. Reorganization and rationalization of suburban governments deserve a priority at least equal to that of establishing metropolitan-scale jurisdictions and improving central-city government.

Income redistribution presents a greater problem than either social choice making or production and delivery of public goods. That is because the greatest social tensions arise from disparities of wealth and income among families and disparities in public services provided to rich and poor neighborhoods, even in the same governmental jurisdictions. No amount of urban government reorganization—either by means of consolidation schemes or decentralization ones—will do much to ease such tensions.

While metropolitan areas should in principle be able to pay for their own public services and income-redistribution measures, the conflicts between central cities and suburbs mitigate against their doing so. The greatest conflicts concern income-redistribution measures and special services required by the poor, the majority of whom still live in central cities. Also, there is great variation among metropolitan areas as to income and financial capacity.

These considerations argue that the responsibility for financing income redistribution and special services should be assumed by the federal government, even though redistribution conflicts rage at higher as well as lower levels. Since the main source of urban tension concerns the poor, federal funding for income maintenance, education, and special services should take precedence over unconditional grants.

Logic notwithstanding, it appears likely that the federal government, left to its own devices, may continue to back away from this crucial role, as evidenced in the welfare reform legislation of 1996. A major impediment lies in the fact that the substantial efforts of the 1960s and 1970s, particularly in the antipoverty and related programs, proved to have small effect. A large share of the equalization problem will for the foreseeable future continue to move to the states and metropolitan areas.

Another goal of federal policy should be to raise the level of competence of state and local governments in delivery of federally financed services and in comprehensive planning for growth management. One need is to continue to encourage the establishment of metropolitan-scale organizations to handle an increasing number of functions that require metropolitan-scale administration, especially planning. We propose in Chapter 9 the establishment of substate planning and administrative districts to fill this crucial role in the federal system.

Another need is to look specifically at the still-growing problems of suburban government and at the means of structuring and equipping suburban governments to cope more adequately with growth problems. There is also a need to continue to encourage participation of citizens in their local governments. *Unconditional* federal grants of the revenue-sharing kind are not well suited to meet any of these needs. Properly structured substate administrative and planning districts would meet these needs and could be designed to manage and allocate state and federal funds aimed at solving areawide urban problems.

Notes

1. Edward C. Banfield and Morton Grodzins, *Government and Housing in Metropolitan Areas* (New York: McGraw-Hill, 1958); Charles M. Tiebout, "A Pure Theory of Local Public Expenditures," *Journal of Political Economy* 64: 416–424; and "An Economic Theory of Decentralization," National Bureau of Economic Research, *Public Finance: Needs, Sources, and Utilization* (Princeton, N.J.: Princeton University Press, 1961). Tiebout's article was in response to Paul Samuelson and Richard Musgrave's proposition that there is no mechanism by which local government can accurately ascertain the amount of public goods that they should supply to satisfy the preferences of consumer-voters. Paul Samuelson, "The Pure Theory of Public Expenditures," *Review of Economics and Statistics* 36 (1954): 387; Richard Musgrave, "The Voluntary Exchange Theory of Public Economy," *Quarterly Journal of Economics* 52 (1939): 213.
2. Kirk J. Stark, "City Welfare: Views from Theory, History, and Practice, *Urban Lawyer* 27, no. 3 (1995): 498. Also see Wallace E. Oates, "On Local Finance and the Tiebout Model," *American Economic Review* 71 (1981): 93 (suggesting that the Tiebout model "involves a set of assumptions so patently unrealistic as to verge on the outrageous").
3. See, for example, Richard A. Musgrave and Peggie B. Musgrave, *Public Finance in Theory and Practice* (New York: McGraw-Hill, 1989), pp. 454–455; Wallace E. Oates, *Fiscal Federalism* (New York: Harcourt, Brace, Jovanovich, 1972), p. 8; Helen F. Ladd and Fred C. Doolittle, "Which Level of Government Should Assist the Poor?" *National Tax Journal* 35, no. 3 (1982): 323; Charles C. Brown and Wallace E. Oates, "Assistance to the Poor in the Federal System," *Journal of Public Economics* 32, no. 307 (1987): 328.
4. Kirk J. Stark, "City Welfare: Views from Theory, History, and Practice," *Urban Lawyer* 27, no. 3 (1995): 499.

5. Ibid., 502.
6. Temporary State Commission to Study Governmental Operations of the City of New York, Report of the Task Force on Jurisdiction and Structure, *Restructuring the Government of New York City*, March 15, 1972.
7. Richard E. Wagner, *The Fiscal Organization of American Federalism* (Chicago: Markham, 1971).
8. Arnold J. Meltsner and Aaron Waldavsky, "Leave City Budgeting Alone! A Survey, Case Study, and Recommendations for Reform," in *Financing the Metropolis*, ed. John P. Crecine (Beverly Hills, Calif.: Sage, 1970).
9. Richard S. Childs, *Civic Victories* (New York: Harper and Rowe, 1952).

Chapter 6

Citizen Participation in Metropolitan Governance

It is fundamental to the theory of democratic governance that the governed shall rule. The political philosopher Jean-Jacques Rousseau asserted in *Du Contrat Social* (*The Social Contract*, 1762)[1] that freedom could be fully achieved only in a society whose governing principle is the social contract, voluntarily entered into by all the citizens, who, nevertheless, retained their sovereignty in their collective rule of themselves. The practical application of the social contract is through a democratically elected legislature and executive, an independent judiciary, a balance of powers among the three branches through a system of checks and balances, and adherence to the rule of law. Citizen participation in governance at all levels is crucial to the expression of the *general will* of the people—which in Rousseau's theory is their means of guiding the governing institutions they have created.

Thus, in Rousseau's construct, the executive and the legislature are the people's agents to whom are delegated the responsibility for creating and administering the law that reflects the general will of the whole people. No part of the whole polity can dominate the rest and, short of treasonable force, no political leader can assume the mantle of sovereignty. Once a public officer or group of officers usurps power, that freedom of the citizenry is diminished and they become the subjects, not of their collective will, but of a dictator or oligarchy.

It may be unlikely that any modern polity can bring about a system of governance whose arrangements so assiduously preserve the civil liberties of all its citizens and so skillfully encourage a balanced expression of interests that the general will is readily called forth as a guide for governing officials. But in Rousseau's view the effort is worth the result: a system that has no masters but only public servants who labor to perceive and follow the general will. The governing system developed by our Founding Fathers comes close, but, as events on our political scene demonstrate from time to time, the battle to preserve it never ends.

Was Rousseau's social contract a futile conjecture? Not if one takes seriously his conditions of a free society. The citizen must think, speak, act, and vote—striving always to rise above personal interests, never permitting fellow citizens to have their way except in the advancement of the public good. How can this be? Rousseau himself conceded that people are by nature self-serving. But he also insisted that people are by nature social beings and therefore capable of social as well as self-serving actions. That fact was the bedrock upon which he grounded the concept of democracy as expressed through the general will.

Having conceded the natural capacity of people for brutishness, for greed, avarice, plunder, and all the other evils, Rousseau showed how people's natural capacity for acting in the social good might be dominant in a system in which citizens have equal rights under a body of law that they make through legislators chosen by themselves. Rousseau's social contract could never be sufficient by itself. There must be social and political conditions that make it a reality: an abhorrence of bosses; a hunger for personal freedom and self-government; a tolerance of conflict and disorder, of lengthy debate and endless compromise, of "messy" democracy.

The general will emerges from a vectoring out of contending forces in the vigor of free political competition. It also emerges through an orderly system of justice in which quarrels are arbitrated in courts of law, through a legislative process responsive to the electorate and immune to domination by private interests, and through an executive pledged to administer the law.

Social and political conditions of the United States in 1789 were fortuitously right for Rousseau's model of democracy. There was a tradition of entrepreneurial freedom in a new land where people generally owed their livelihood and their achievements to themselves individually. The monarch was abroad, remote, impersonal, and, in the end, an enemy of their common interests. He also proved to be a tyrant and a stranger, taxing without direct consent, imposing upon citizens' rights, exploiting their commerce and responding to their protests with violence. Many of the colonists felt justified in armed rebellion, to which they pledged their lives, their fortunes, and their sacred honor. Hence, they declared their independence and launched a revolution.

Like present-day Americans, the colonists were a mixture of peoples who had come to America seeking a new life, economic opportunity, personal and religious freedom, and adventure. As a people they were vigorous, self-sufficient, independent, and ambitious, not to be oppressed by any government presumptuous of its authority beyond their consent. They were a practical people whose philosophers spoke of freedom and justice in the context of daily living.

Their Declaration of Independence was brief, specific, and incisive. Its signers were men of substance and property; some were men of considerable learning. Their Constitution, written after an eight-year war of revolution, proved enduring because it was a practical document of fundamental principles designed as a framework for the body of law to follow. It was unencumbered with protective legislation for special-interest groups.

The Founders created a system of government in which powers were shared among independent branches at the national level and between the national and state governments. In a stroke of political genius emerging from compromise, the states were reserved in the Tenth Amendment all powers not specifically delegated to the national government, although the powers delegated to the latter were sufficiently general and flexible to permit as strong a central government as the people desired.

The separation of powers among the branches of the national government and the limitations on the powers of the Congress and the president were meant to guarantee the sovereignty of the people, insofar as any charter of government can be of itself a guarantee.

The peoples of the new nation were also parochial in their interests and outlook. They wanted local self-government. They wanted diversity and flexibility to accommodate varieties of local custom existing at the time of the founding. They wanted local control then and more so in the two centuries that followed, as the nation continued to attract peoples from every part of the globe.

As new immigrants came, they settled in communities where they were welcomed or, as with the Mormons and others, they founded new ones. The agents of the national government rarely intruded in local communities even when local law and custom were contrary to the national charter and to the law of the land. Thus the general will spoke against the imposition of uniform law, custom, or principles of justice. For nearly two hundred years these latter aberrations lay dormant in the soul of a nation not yet in full maturity.

Rousseau's postulate of the general will is no mere abstraction. It is a reality of political society everywhere. While it can be manipulated, distorted, or suppressed by artful politicians, it is present and operative in every form of government. Even a dictator, if wise, will find ways to read it.

As Rousseau insisted, and as the Founding Fathers recognized, the general will emerges in purest form in a society whose people are sovereign and whose leaders are their servants. In simplest form, the general will is the sum of individual wills expressed through overt political action. It is a playing out of free political forces operating in a free political system.

The general will finds it strongest expression in a consensus, but marginal expression is no less one of the general will when it is expressed. The stability of any governmental policy, however, rests on the stability of the general will with respect to that policy. The regime of necessity takes into account the marginality of the general will and the extent to which it appears weak or unstable. The regime seeks through coercion and/or persuasion to strengthen support for it—or to put off implementation pending a broader expression of support.

Political freedom and spontaneous expression of the general will are genuine social contracts initiated by leaders whose highest personal aspiration is liberty and who understand that liberty is maximized only in a system in which the people are sovereign and that popular sovereignty is the crucial element in the full play of the general will. Representation in the formal councils of government is a primary condition. But, as Rousseau pointed out, the legislator must never be in a position politically or constitutionally to preempt or override in either the short or the long term the will of the people. Likewise, the executive is directly elected and answerable to the people, provided his or her election is frequent and the executive cannot constitutionally serve beyond a reasonable period, and provided he or she may be turned out of office by impeachment, and may have his or her actions reviewed and amended by the legislature and the courts. These checks on the executive ensure that he or she is never in a political or constitutional position to usurp the power of the sovereign people.

In the U.S. system, the president's constitutional command of the armed forces, his sole authority in foreign affairs (except in the ratification of treaties), his veto power over the legislature, his acquired authority to impound funds appropriated by Congress, his access to and potential influence over public opinion combine to place him dangerously close to assumption of sovereign powers in the short run, if not in the long run.

As powerful as the legislature and courts can be in the U.S. system, or any system in which constitutional powers are divided among the several branches, the effective check on the executive is citizen participation in the governing process at all levels, especially the local. The critical aspect of participation is that it gives vitality to the organizational vehicle through which the citizen takes political action and reminds political leaders and the bureaucracies of the citizens' interest and preeminence in the system.

It is not uncommon for bureaucracies to become so entrenched and encapsulated that they dominate the processes of government, so that citizens have little or no access to the policy structure that determines their output. Citizen participation is a preventative to self-serving government, less so a cure. The entrenched bureaucracy can be inimical to regional planning in metropolitan America, where public values can be ignored. The New Jersey State Planning Act guards against arbitrary planning actions of the State Planning Commission in its "cross-acceptance" process, where counties, municipalities, state agencies, and affected citizens negotiate their differences.[2]

While the executive and the bureaucracy are the key to the delivery of the goods and services of government, the legislature creates policies and programs that reflect the concrete priorities of the community. The corruption of the legislature, unlike that of the executive or the bureaucracy, is the sellout to special interests. The legislature at its best provides the most numerous and diverse channels for shaping public policy. The extent to which members of the legislature are "owned" by special interests is the extent to which the general public is deprived of balanced consideration of issues in the larger public interest.

As we have observed, the American system of government comes closer than most to preserving the sovereignty of the governed and maximizing the expression of the general will. We preserve the sovereignty of the people primarily in our formal governmental structures at the national level, and in the dispersion of power within the federal system at the state and local levels.

The traditions through which relationships among the branches at the national level operate are under constant scrutiny by the branches themselves, by the public media, and in endless public discussion. The publicity and discussion surrounding the relations between President Nixon and Congress are a dramatic example. The abortive effort of President Roosevelt in 1936 to "pack" the Supreme Court with judges who would support his social programs is another.

The evolving relationships within the federal system between the national and state governments and between the states and their regional and local entities are never fundamentally disturbed without prolonged and tortuous debate centering on the issue of central control as the obverse of liberty—the issue that is at the heart of the relationship between government and citizens.

While our national structures are crucial in the preservation of liberty in that we have tried to guard against dangerous concentrations of power, we have done an even greater service to liberty by preserving liberty at the local level. In a nation so large in geographical area and so diverse in social culture, the decentralization of power goes far toward guaranteeing to the citizen that, with rare exceptions (for example, desegregation), if anything of consequence is to be done in domestic affairs, it is at the will of the local citizenry.

The structure of local government is the purveyor of the general will for most domestic programs and the purveyor of local law and custom—the most accurate reflection of the general will. What people want locally, they get, although in recent times a national code of justice has been imposed gradually on local law and custom and has begun to erase the conflict between the two bodies of law.

One of the critical functions of central government is to foster local institutions that are so structured as to encourage the maximum involvement of people. The U.S. system of government follows this principle more faithfully than any other. Its local institutions are assumed to possess superior capacity to comprehend and conduct local affairs. The assumption goes even further: that local affairs may be differently defined in different places. Local institutions are assumed to be instruments of political education for citizens as well as civic and political leaders. They are expected to provide for experimentation and invention in the development of institutions for keeping pace with social change.

Local institutions are seen as a hedge against centralization that might threaten liberty. Just as the national government was the custodian of our cherished principles of justice and equity during the long period of adjustments to cultural differences within the society, in the contemporary period the tradition of local self-government imparts to local institutions a stewardship of the principle of decentralized political power.

In days gone by, local law and custom were sometimes grossly at odds with fundamental principles of democratic citizenship and participation. These principles might have been subverted had national leaders dedicated to these principles not prevailed. Indeed, a civil war had to be fought to settle the issue of slavery, which was only the worst form of antidemocratic localism. Left entirely to their own devices, local communities can as quickly produce a class structure as characterized by economic exploitation and political corruption as any national polity. Even so, opportunities for self-governance are best provided at the local level and a powerful central government can be a counterforce to corruption at its roots.

We are describing a political system in balance, in which central and local institutions mutually prevail in the preservation of the integrity of a political system whose aim is a blend of individual liberty and social good. The U.S. system of government has achieved this balance, or largely so. Yet it is inherently an unstable balance, subject to the vagaries of historical circumstances and to the uncertainties of new combinations of political leadership.

In America, the habit of self-government was established with the arrival of the first colonists, who, in the most practical sense, were on their own. Their realization of this fact took on the form and substance of government in the Mayflower Compact, which was a true social contract among the people who were about to establish a new community in a new land. Thus, participation in the affairs of the Massachusetts colony by all of the settlers was not only taken for granted but promulgated into seminal law.

By 1835, a French observer of the American political scene, Alexis de Tocqueville, found a local system of government in the United States whose citizens credited their country's power and prosperity to strong local institutions. A populace accustomed to freedom in local consensus, he observed, know then how to apply the same freedom in great affairs.[3]

As the nation matured politically, one of the trademarks was the proliferation of political clubs, civic associations, and interest-group organizations of all sorts. There being no discouragement of such groups in the American system except for certain restrictions having to do with ethical behavior in contacts with public officials, they are ubiquitous in their efforts to influence the making of public policy. Some are so resourceful that they make or mold policy in their specialized areas. The American Medical Association and labor unions are prominent examples of groups that can do this.

In addition to the voluntary, professional, and trade organizations that provide a rich variety of opportunities for citizen participation in public affairs, there are a multitude of official and quasi-official advisory boards and commissions, task-force study groups, and investigating committees that assist governmental agencies at all levels in policy and decisionmaking.

There are tens of thousands of governing units, ranging from incorporated municipalities to school districts and special authorities, all of which provide opportunities for citizens throughout the nation to have a central policy role in public affairs. The state and national legislative bodies are remarkably fluid in their membership in that, except for a relatively few immovable incumbents, the turnover rate is such as to encourage fresh candidates for most seats in all elections. For better or for worse, the terms are short and the political hazards of office are great.

The Modern Urban Condition

By the third decade of the twentieth century, it had become apparent that the American economy would be predominantly industrial and service in its orientation and that the population would be concentrated in large-scale urban areas. Later it became apparent that by the end of the century more than three-quarters of Americans would be living in those urban areas, many of which would be part of a megalopolis.

Large-scale communities breed anomie and alienation. Separation of home and work weakens family structure and leaves local government in the hands of hired professionals. Participation in local government can seem artificial except for the few who stay in one place. The loss of neighbors who move and the constant influx of newcomers take their toll on those who stay put.

Yet the longing for community persists, perhaps more consciously in the movers than in the stayers, and hungering after the permanency of local institutions—schools especially, the more local and neighborhood, the better—has become a near obsession in America. Witness the rapid incorporation of new suburban communities since 1950, and the resistance to court-enforced school-busing plans in the 1960s and 1970s that for a time threatened neighborhood schools.

People crave community as they crave the cultural opportunities of great cities. People need the intimate and they need the expansive. They need the village and they need the metropolis. They need the family hearth and they need the world. The hearth can be suffocating yet secure, the world threatening yet exhilarating. These observations are from the standpoint of the individual, but what of society and its governance?

The struggle to develop new forms of local government in which citizens can play a major role has taken many forms. In a few places since the middle of the twentieth century, efforts to make larger cities out of smaller ones have succeeded largely as a consequence of determined citizen effort. Among them were Baton Rouge-East Baton Rouge Parish, Jacksonville-Duval County, Miami-Dade County, Lexington-Fayette County, Nashville-Davidson County, Columbus-Muskogee County, and Indianapolis-Marion County. These efforts created a new scale of local government, improved planning and administration of public services, and merged city and suburban interests in a single political arena where class differences could be a direct factor in local decision-making.

But what of neighborhood and community? In Miami-Dade County (Miami Metro), the identities of municipal corporations were preserved and some governmental functions remained with them. School districts were left undisturbed. In general, the reorganizations listed above had negligible impact on community and neighborhood.

In other efforts to deal with regional problems at the metropolitan level, regional planning and development agencies were created by local leaders who anticipated the need for areawide services for water supply, sewage disposal, and other functional areas. The federal government promoted the concept vigorously in the 1950s and 1960s. Prodded by the federal government, the states began in the late 1960s to create subdistricts for planning development and decentralized administration.

These agencies are present in all metropolitan areas. They provide opportunities for local citizens and elected officials to become accustomed to area-wide cooperative efforts, thus enlarging the horizon of leaders who consider problems from a local viewpoint. Few of these agencies have decisionmaking authority that can override that of municipalities and other local units and special districts. Nor in most cases are they in a position to steer an equitable course among the myriad public and private interests their decisions affect.

Yet the regional view and regional governmental action are necessary aspects of governmental action in a nation whose economic activity is region-wide, national, and international in scope. Regional governmental action is also necessary in a nation in which the principal form of social organization is urban, now commonly metropolis and in some places megalopolis.

Management of regional forms of social organization requires regional forms of governance. Regional planning agencies and councils of government, as well as substate districts, have established citizen involvement in advisory and study committees whose task it is to investigate particular regional problems in depth, to recommend specific courses of action, and to educate citizens on problems and solutions. The most important function of such committees and task forces in regional agencies is the education of the citizen participants, thus creating a cadre of citizen leaders at the local level who hold an informed regional viewpoint. These citizens carry back to the community a viewpoint that permits them to see local problems in a larger perspective.

The regional viewpoint on local problems came into vogue in the 1960s and 1970s at the time when pressure was being brought to bear on cities for "community control." In its purest form, "community control" is the traditional demand for local self-government at the community or neighborhood level. The demand in the 1960s and 1970s called for grassroots democratic control of public services and facilities within the community. The objective was to tailor services and facilities to community needs and values: police should be transformed from a force of occupation and agent of oppression to one of service to and protection of the community.[4] Health services should be made available through clinics located in neighborhoods and by professionals sympathetic to community values as these values bear on health and medical services.[5] Libraries should be convenient and cater to the informational, educational, and recreational needs of the community.[6] All public services, aspects of which are normally administered at the community level, should be planned with community input and participation.

Community control on the model described above is an established tradition in the American system. Local political party organizations in their heyday used districts, wards, and precincts as units to manage elections. Politicians used these units as listening posts for citizen demands and complaints. They got the vote so long as their constituents got what they demanded, more or less. The trade-offs were in the mediation of conflicting demands.[7]

The suburbs of the present day are largely controlled by residents who try to make sure that services are provided in the style, quantity, and quality they desire. The close day-to-day control that politically deprived inner-city residents demand is not a characteristic of middle-class suburbs. But any substantial deviation in services from the expectations of suburban residents soon reveals the tolerance level in the community and thus the limits within which suburban governments operate.

The tradition of citizen control of public services has been taken for granted throughout the political history of the nation, except with African Americans, Hispanics, and Native Americans. These groups were the dispossessed and exploited in violation of the American creed of equality and opportunity. In recent decades, these groups have joined in the traditional demand for community control. Americans in the 1960s were shocked at the idea of turning over control of valuable local resources to political "incompetents," failing to recognize that those demands were what the dominant community was accustomed to in the traditional operation of its own communities.

Such demands were usually dismissed out of hand or rationalized out of existence. The powerless would remain so until they generated the power to win the point. Being powerless, they had no leverage—except for African Americans, who in a few places had the numbers but not the habit or custom of political organization. Among Hispanics, the race problem was less severe because their culture was intact and in it there was a psychological source of support. Individual opportunities among Hispanics were less restricted than for Blacks, for whom collective political opportunities were almost nonexistent. Most Hispanics had to make it on their own, but usually at the price of assimilation.

The color barrier and their former slave status kept African Americans physically and psychologically isolated in cities. Token representation continues to be the norm, and the tokenism is more expansive and more deliberate than ever, to the point where African Americans are vigorously sought after for choice positions.

In the 1960s the federal government, faced with a rising crescendo of ghetto riots, sought a breakthrough in President Lyndon Johnson's Model Cities Program and the War on Poverty by imposing a deliberate policy of "maximum feasible participation" in the local policy councils and in staffing these programs. These two programs and the maximum feasible participation policy resulted in a major federal impact on local government organization in the 1960s and 1970s. The two programs spawned the community-action agencies, the Concentrated Employment programs, and the neighborhood-services centers, some of which were still operating in 2005.

The Kennedy and Johnson administrations and the Democratic Party used these programs to offer inner-city residents jobs and services as a means of building party loyalty. In doing so, they deliberately bypassed the states and recalcitrant large-city administrations and set Republican Party and conservative interests against them. Also in the process, Blacks and Hispanics in some cities gained control of the new citywide coordinating agencies, much as the Irish, Poles, Italians, and Jews had earlier gained control of other municipal departments.

The War on Poverty and related programs were designed to be controlled by the poor in the neighborhoods they were to serve. The experience was as varied as the leadership these programs attracted—some of it good, and some of it disappointing. But new community leadership was spawned along with a new sense of hope and pride. The downside was that, as with the civil rights legislation of the 1950s and 1960s, the Model Cities and War on Poverty programs raised expectations beyond the nation's political or social capacity to meet. The Model Cities Program had the potential to create representative institutions with real power, and its leaders tried in vain to create territorial constituencies meant to serve as common reference constituencies for federal, state, and local officials. But the artificiality of the Model Cities areas demonstrated that HUD administrators never got beyond the bricks and mortar and physical planning and into the social planning that HUD's urban missions had intended.[8]

As experimental efforts, the Model Cities and War on Poverty programs were intended to provide access to governmental policymaking to citizens who would be affected and otherwise excluded by entrenched local interests. Maximum feasible citizen participation in the Model Cities Program required an elected policy board of neighborhood residents, and the local policy boards of the federal Partnership for Health program of regional comprehensive health planning required 51% consumer representation. These two programs marked the federal government's explicit recognition of the important role of citizen involvement in innovative local policymaking.

In requiring participation of deprived citizens, the federal government intended to ensure that benefits would not go by design or default to entrenched interests. It was also intended that politically deprived citizens should be given opportunities for practical experience in local policy decisionmaking. Once schooled in local politics, citizens would relieve their deprivation by their own efforts, and their increased sophistication would get them their share of the public largesse.

The purpose of the federal government in broadening the base of citizen participation in cities grew out of a recognition that local political structures that once served the poor and the dispossessed—immigrants from Europe—continued to serve these same groups in their acquired influence. But the new immigrants—mainly African Americans and Hispanics—were shut out and ghettoized, and by the 1960s had grown restive to the point of resorting to riots. The War on Poverty and Model Cities programs were not created in response to the restiveness of ghetto residents. Both were formulated in the Kennedy administration between 1960 and 1963. Thus they were conceived prior to the riots and were passed into law in 1964 and 1966, respectively. It is true that during the period of the riots—1964 to 1968—both programs were used to identify and develop ghetto leaders who might aid in minimizing the effects of the riots and head off organized rebellion.

Thus, when a Nixon budget in 1972 proposed cuts in welfare, education, and health, the most effective protests came from citizens who had already gained a substantial stake at the local level in these areas of public policy through the War on Poverty and Model Cities programs. In effect, the latter programs did more to politicize the poor than all the riots of the previous decade, although the riots provided the cutting edge.

The riots of the 1960s had been symptomatic of the frustration fueled by prolonged deprivation and sudden, disappointed hope. By the time the riots had spent their force in 1968, the nation had explicitly recognized (in a series of reports by presidential commissions) the social, psychological, and economic conditions inner-city and poor minorities had to tolerate. The ensuing national and local dialogue about racism and its derivative forms of deprivation generated broad public support for changes in public and private policy; thus began the long, slow process of breaking down discriminatory barriers in housing, employment, education, and political opportunity. That process is still with us as we enter a new century.

The antipoverty programs were the first to be reorganized around neighborhood and community leadership. The advisory commissions required by the Model Cities Program were elected from the neighborhoods served by the program. Some controlled planning and policymaking; others were advisory to their city administrations; a few had little effective influence on local programs. The requirement of citizen and consumer participation was an effort to widen the spectrum of interests involved in the planning and implementation of socially oriented federal programs at the local level. It was an explicit recognition of the desirability of tailoring national programs to local conditions. It was also a recognition that American policymaking had been dominated by special interests that were often self-serving at the expense of the public educators, health and medical professionals, social workers, and housing developers, to name a few. These special interests were organized; the consumer, the poor, and the public were not.

The intent was deliberate infusion of citizens representing different, theretofore previously unrepresented interests. The implementation, however faulty, helped breathe new vitality into public-sector programming. It was a new kind of education for those who participated, and it whetted the appetite of many citizens for public service. Since most of the programs that required consumer participation also included representation of professionals, consumers and professionals were exposed to the problems as seen by each other.

Most of the socially oriented federal programs of the 1960s were experimental and exploratory. The explorations paid off. Americans "discovered" poverty, not only in city slums but in smaller communities and rural areas as well. They learned about the stark differences in the quality of education between racially segregated schools and predominantly white ones. They learned to recognize that the quality of education was directly related to economic class. They learned that behind the reality of racial differentiation and discrimination a complex system of class and caste in America was in an advanced stage of development, reinforced by a system of tightly segregated city neighborhoods and suburban communities, each with its own schools and other social control mechanisms.

They learned that people most in need of social service programs did not qualify. They learned that unmanageable medical expenses sometimes impoverished hardworking citizens and that this situation was a common experience among the elderly. They learned that the U.S. healthcare system was inefficient, uneconomical, and dominated by politically powerful self-serving professionals. They learned that organized workers who served the public could hold whole cities hostage for wage increases and *reduced* output.

They also learned about the limits of money in the solution of problems. They learned that a wealthy, well-intentioned national government had to have the willing cooperation of local citizens in program planning and implementation and a responsible state government to ensure that benefits were properly allocated to all communities. They began hesitantly to demand that the welfare system be radically overhauled, the realization of which was to take another three decades.

The Nixon administration, elected in 1968, was not enthusiastic about the citizen-participation policies that Congress and the Johnson administration had introduced in the War on Poverty and Model Cities programs. Nor was Nixon himself enthusiastic about the use of the programs as instruments for consolidating the Democrats' power base in the inner cities of the nation. In addition, skeptical conservatives saw that politically deprived people did not at once take seriously an opportunity for participation or, if they tried, did not at once master the art of participatory planning. Some of them urged the new Republican administration to cancel Lyndon Johnson's Great Society programs.

Once the riots ended after 1968, and demands for community control mounted, pressures from threatened interests in city administrations to reduce or halt the programs intensified. The conservatives in the Nixon administration were quick to oblige. Subsequent attempts to dismantle the Model Cities Program along with some of the programs of Johnson's War on Poverty were guided by a policy of "benign neglect." These efforts squeezed but did not eliminate the Kennedy-Johnson urban improvement and antipoverty programs. Although underfunded by the Nixon administration and further reduced by the Reagan administration, the effective ones like Head Start and Community Action Centers survived.

These programs continued to give the poor of the inner cities a taste of involvement and a toehold in the local political power structure and in the years before Nixon got to them, the Model Cities and War on Poverty programs produced substantial numbers of new leaders who had learned the ropes at city hall and in their communities. Many of them eventually found traditional places in the political system—all the way to state houses and the U.S. Congress.

During his attempt to kill the citizen participation policies of his predecessors, Nixon embarked on a fresh agenda of centralizing political power and decentralizing social responsibility. It was a long step backward and temporarily weakened the nation's democratic base. But the affluent had been persuaded that the poor were getting too many handouts, and in the conservatives' tradition of invoking Social Darwinism, the devil could take the hindmost. The Nixon/Moynihan policy of benign neglect may have been the inevitable alternative when some of the programs of President Johnson's War on Poverty failed. In any case, the conditions in inner cities described in Chapter 2 are the legacy.

The Great Society programs had not had time to improve day-to-day life in the inner cities, and the efficacy of maximum feasible participation of the poor was hotly debated. Daniel Patrick Moynihan, a Democrat (later a U.S. senator from New York) then serving as domestic policy advisor to Nixon, insisted that the policy of maximum feasible participation only led to "maximum feasible misunderstanding," citing the sometimes contradictory goals and occasional confusion inherent in the experimental programs.[9] Moynihan's critics pointed out that clarification of the policy would have been fatal to its goals. Nixon knew full well that the goals were to politicize the poor, confirm participants as Democratic voters, and in the old style of local machine politics put money into their pockets.

Beyond the 1960s

The opportunity for citizen participation in the governing processes of the community and the nation is the essence of citizenship. Active citizenship is the substance of democracy. Democracy is the form of government most conducive to liberty, and liberty is the starting point of individual creativity. The traditions and habits of citizenship are by definition pervasive in a democratic society. Discrimination and exclusion are the marks of an aristocratic society, which by its nature assumes the high worth of the few and the low worth of the rest. In any democratic society, the process of inclusion must be continuous and deliberate and made part of the political socialization of every individual. The process of inclusion must be a principal goal of education.

The danger in taking for granted the process of inclusion is in the precarious nature of democracy itself. As Aristotle once observed, left to its natural course, societies will develop some form of oligarchy that will create a ruling class. Some people will rule and the rest will be ruled.[10] An unwatchful democracy will, from time to time, unwittingly put into positions of power leaders who try to suppress its democratic forms. Richard Nixon is a memorable example.

Such leaders begin by consolidating the power inherent in their office, diverting to themselves as much power as they can. Then they cut off, discourage, or suppress the involvement of citizens, except for those who support their goals. The remedy is an alert citizenry, jealous of its own involvement and educated to the true forms of democracy. A careless, apathetic citizenry runs the risk of losing its prerogatives and its freedom.

The experiences of the 1960s led to the initiation of a federal revenue-sharing program that became an essential ingredient in national-state-local relationships as they matured in the 1970s. To his credit, President Nixon initiated the first full-blown version of revenue sharing. Revenue sharing, of necessity limited in its early stages, made possible a functional division of responsibilities among national, state, and local levels of government in the United States. Federal sponsorship of local and regional planning; requirements of citizen participation; and presidential guidelines encouraging the states to create state-level agencies of planning and coordination; the Model Cities experiments to increase the capacity of local administrations in social services planning—all these were policies that paved the way for an effective revenue-sharing program. Some form of federal revenue sharing, as we show in Chapter 7 and revisit in Chapter 10, is the strategic mechanism upon which a process of cooperative programming within the federal system can be grounded.

Some political writers have called Rousseau a prophet of revolution. This is true. He was also a prophet of modern democracy. His concept of the general will is the culminating expression of a sovereign people. His cautions to maintain a firm distinction between the function of the sovereign (the people) and the function of the executive, as well as between the function of originating laws (the legislature) and the function of translating those laws into a code (the judicial), are crucial to the substance and operations of democracy.

He counseled that the key to a successful democracy is participation of sovereign citizens at all levels of government and in a variety of channels. Thus emerges the general will to which the executive and the legislature respond. To ensure this process, citizens must demand that every governmental policy and program have broad involvement—never less, for there is no other way for the general will to emerge within the system. The extent to which citizen participation falls short of this goal is the extent to which the system will fall prey to the natural tendency toward the rule of the few, as Aristotle warned.

The general will in full play as a governing force requires political institutions. That is to say, there must exist mechanisms of arbitration among conflicting interests, channels of expression both formal and informal, and in all this, maximum opportunities for creative political action. For the general will to emerge, there must be many and diverse kinds of institutions, political organization, and channels. As democratic nations evolve, so must their institutions. The stagnation and corruption of existing institutions is at the root of any nation's inability to solve its urgent problems.

Likewise, the importance of citizen leadership can hardly be overstated. Even citizens who are conscientious about their community obligations can devote only small portions of time to participate in politics. To make up for the marginally involved, there must be among them leaders of talent who have the ability to improve the quality of government and concentrate the energies of the political process on priority issues.

Our purpose in this book is to address the capacity of our local governmental institutions to deal with critical *regional* problems stemming from urbanization. We show (explicitly in Chapter 9) that new governmental arrangements with vigorous political and professional leadership are needed to get us beyond the problems that have resulted in the well-documented, rapidly spreading decline of our urban areas.[11]

Enhanced citizen participation in the affairs of functional agencies (those in education, public order, welfare especially) must be a priority objective. Strengthened political leadership would not obstruct this objective, but neither would it necessarily further it. Many political objectives are not fulfilled by structural reorganization, for meaningful participation is more an affair of the spirit of the polity than the legal structure of government. Strong elected leaders are more likely to favor citizen participation than are administrators, but even they are unlikely to accord it high priority unless public demand is intense. In the end, "good" structures can only enhance opportunities; the most important qualities of the system depend primarily upon the morality, alertness, farsightedness, and political energy of the citizenry rather than in formal aspects of organization.

The nation has learned from the experiments and the inner-city unrest of the 1960s. Congressional requirements of metropolitan and regional planning revealed an appreciation of the pitfalls of ad hoc, uncoordinated, piecemeal intervention. The experience gained from the War on Poverty and its attempt to foster participatory democracy suggests that other citizens might also be empowered to set local policy in decentralized federal programs. We have a long tradition of citizen participation in the nation's agricultural programs, and it has provided a precedent of direct participation of local citizens in several areas of federal administration.

We focus in later chapters on the need for reforming the structure of government at the state, regional, and local levels because a democratic system requires responsive local government to have responsive government at the higher levels. If local government fails in its responsibility to meet the needs of its citizens, the tasks at hand will be taken over by the state and federal governments. The continuing success of the American political process requires the participation of citizen voters who understand what may be expected of the several layers of their governmental system.

Notes

1. Jean-Jacques Rousseau, *Du Contrat Social* (Amsterdam: Marc-Michel Rey, 1762). Also, *The Social Contract*, trans. Maurice Cranston (Hammersmith, U.K.: Penguin, 1968).
2. N.J. Stat. § 52:18A-197 (West 1996).
3. Alexis de Tocqueville, *Democracy in America*, ed. Harvey C. Mansfield, trans. Delba Winthrop (Chicago: University of Chicago Press, 2000 [1832].
4. Alan Shank and Ralph W. Conant, *Urban Perspectives: Politics and Policies* (Boston: Holbrook, 1975), Chapter 7, "Civil Protest and Law Enforcement." See also James Q. Wilson, *Varieties of Police Behavior* (New York: Atheneum, 1968); Joseph D. Lohman, "Comments on the Relations of the Police Force to Society," West Michigan, 1980, Proceedings of the Grand Rapids Conference sponsored by television station WOOD (Grand Rapids, Michigan, March 26, 1968); Adele Harrell, The Urban Institute, "Crime Policy" (Paper presented at the annual meeting of the Urban Affairs Associa-

tion in New Orleans, March 3, 1994), cited in Ross & Levine, *Urban Politics*, 5th edn., 1996, Chapter 13, fn38.

5. Ralph W. Conant, *The Politics of Community Health* (Washington, D.C.: The Public Affairs Press, 1964).

6. Ralph W. Conant, *The Public Library and the City* (Cambridge, Mass.: MIT Press, 1965).

7. See Alan A. Altshuler: *Community Control: The Black Demand for Participation in Large American Cities* (New York: Pegasus, 1970).

8. Charles Haar, *Between the Idea and the Reality: A Study in the Origin, Fate, and Legacy of the Model Cities Program* (Boston: Little, Brown, 1975).

9. Daniel P. Moynihan, *Maximum Feasible Misunderstanding: Community Action and the War on Poverty* (New York: Free Press, 1970).

10. Aristotle, *Politics*, Book III, Chapters 6–13.

11. See Katharine L. Bradbury, Anthony Downs, Kenneth A. Small, *Urban Decline and the Future of American Cities* (Washington, D.C.: The Brookings Institution, 1982); David Rusk, *Cities Without Suburbs* (Washington, D.C.: Woodrow Wilson Center Press, 1993, 1995); and Robert J. Waste, *Independent Cities* (New York: Oxford University Press, 1998).

Chapter 7

Federal Urban Planning Policy

The preceding chapters focused on the social and political conditions in urban areas that have produced autonomous government units of a variety of types and sizes. The discussions focused on proposals for dealing with public service problems that are areawide in scope and require some form of areawide planning and administration. These proposals include consolidation of existing cities, annexation of adjacent municipalities and unincorporated territory, substate districts, special service districts, and so forth. Consolidation and annexation have in most places proved politically unfeasible. Some that *did* succeed were later overtaken by growth spilling over new boundaries.

A reasonable alternative to local governmental reorganization is comprehensive regional planning administered by substate districts on the model described in Chapter 9. In addition to regional planning responsibilities, the substate districts would be set up to deal with aspects of public services and facilities that call for administration on a metropolitan or regional level. The administrative and planning model at the regional/substate level described in Chapter 9 would be initiated by the states and would benefit from federal support in the form of federal revenue sharing featuring fiscal equity among local communities. The substate districts would be single counties in the smaller metropolitan areas or groups of counties in the larger ones.

This chapter reviews the history of national urban development and planning policy and provides the rationale for the development of substate districts. We show that a strong regional planning and administrative capability in comprehensively structured substate districts is a feasible course for federal, state, and local policymakers who have responsibilities for meeting urban public service needs.

Planning before the New Deal

Historians recognize three distinct lines of urban planning prior to the 1930s: the "City Beautiful," led by Daniel Burnham and Frederick Law Olmstead; the "City Functional," initiated by George B. Ford, which emphasized economy and efficiency; and the "Social Reformers," led by investigative reporters and writers such as Lincoln Steffens, Upton Sinclair, and Jacob Riis and by social-service leaders like Lillian Wald and Jane Addams.

Examples of the "City Beautiful" were civic centers, parkways, forest preserves, malls, public gardens, and fountains. The "City Functional" was characterized by a reliance on statistical and engineering solutions, usually at the expense of aesthetics and community attitudes. The "Social Reformers" were active between 1880 and 1930. Their major contributions were to expose the corruption of machine politics and its big-business allies and the latter's abuse of working people: slums, child labor, sweatshops, and excessive population density. The three movements competed vigorously with each other, coalescing into comprehensive planning several decades later. Nonetheless, the combined pressure on the politicians was sufficient for the leaders of the three movements to start experimenting with primitive forms of zoning, beginning about 1900.

In 1924, the U.S. Department of Commerce gave strong impetus to the infant zoning movement by issuing the Model Standard Zoning Enabling Act. Within a year, the model act was adopted almost verbatim by eleven states. By the mid-1920s, two hundred municipalities had some form of zoning, but the state courts were divided over the constitutionality of such regulations. In 1926, the case of *Village of Euclid v. Ambler Realty Co.* was decided by a 4–3 vote of the U.S. Supreme Court.[1] The majority upheld local zoning as a valid exercise of the police power. Subsequent legal history indicated that state enabling laws would be required if zoning was to be valid, and so most states adopted the Model Standard Zoning Enabling Act.

Herbert Hoover had a continuing interest in zoning and planning as a cabinet officer and subsequently as president. (He had been secretary of commerce when the department issued the Model Standard Zoning Enabling Act.) He also encouraged the issuance in 1928 of the Model Standard City Planning Enabling Act. This document was adopted almost verbatim by forty states. Although the impact on the planning movement was not as great as that of the Model Zoning Enabling Act, it spread the idea of a general plan as a guide to city growth.

New York and Chicago developed regional plans under private auspices; Los Angeles established a county planning commission with jurisdiction from the Sierra Madre Mountains to the Pacific Coast. Boulder, Colorado, developed one to control development of the adjacent foothills. The primary concerns that gave rise to those agencies included uncontrolled subdivision and land development, transportation, sanitation, water supplies, flood control, and various local issues.

Concurrently, interest was developing among local and state policymakers in regional planning. The small but influential Regional Plan Association of America (RPAA) began in the 1920s to advocate the "regional city" as an alternative to the emerging patterns of metropolitan centralization and suburban development. RPAA, led by such prominent citizens as Lewis Mumford, Clarence Stein, Henry Wright and Benton MacKaye, argued for the regional city as an approach to building cities in metropolitan areas. Several regional planning groups initiated during the period disappeared in the Great Depression.

FDR's New Deal: 1932–1945

The national planning strategy adopted by President Roosevelt's New Deal focused on the nation's monetary policy, its industrial resources, and infrastructure development. The theory of New Deal planners was that large-scale federally sponsored projects would breathe new life into the economy, increase productivity of factories and, in the process, put people back to work.

In a major shift in public attitudes, government intervention in the economy became acceptable during the Great Depression, and the New Deal was able to make important strides toward formulating national- and regional-development policy. The lasting example of New Deal comprehensive regional planning was the Tennessee Valley Authority (TVA, established by the Tennessee Valley Authority Act of 1933), with its broad, cooperative approach to regional development. The TVA experience was not extended beyond that single region because powerful economic and bureaucratic interests prevented similar developments in other major river basins.

Thus, years before most American cities and their suburbs began to cooperate in providing public services and to engage in regional planning, the federal government was experimenting with planning as a basis for launching the New Deal programs of the 1930s. The Great Depression with its threat of economic disaster was sufficient impetus.

The federal government took the first major step in national planning in 1933 when it established in the National Industrial and Recovery Act[2] and the National Planning Board in the Public Works Administration. The PWA was set up to coordinate efforts to deal with such problems as massive unemployment, floods, and dust storms. The National Planning Board, under a series of similar titles, lasted until August 31, 1943, when it was disbanded. The causes of demise commonly cited by historians include irrelevance to the war effort, loss of political support, and internal dissension.

During the eleven years of its existence, the National Planning Board, also called the National Resources Planning Board (NRPB), was the planning arm of the executive office of the president. NRPB was charged with preparing for the president and Congress plans, programs, and information that would promote "wise use and fullest development of national resources; develop six-year programs of public works; and certain responsibilities for national defense." Its publications covered energy consumption, housing, industry, land, public works, regional planning, research as a resource, state planning, technology, population, urbanism, postwar planning, and water—a comprehensive list indeed.[3]

NRPB also issued a series of reports on national and regional resources and their relationship to the physical and socioeconomic development of the country. NRPB's publications and policies helped shape thinking about the problems of the nation. For example, one publication made explicit that criteria for approval of federally funded local public works were the relation of the project to coordinated planning and its social desirability, and that the project be consistent with a state plan.

In 1933, the PWA offered consultants to aid the states in planning, provided the governor established a state planning board, developed a planning program, and cooperated on interstate planning. Within a year, forty state planning boards were created.

In 1937, NRPB issued a report entitled *Our Cities—Their Role in the National Economy.*[4] The report examined the trends of population growth, movement, and urbanization and called for a balanced growth policy aimed toward producing a nation equally divided between rural and urban populations. Its recommendations had a lasting influence among policymakers and urban planners. The following are some of the salient ones:

- The federal government should continue its policy of cooperation and assistance to social welfare programs, including public assistance, crime prevention and control, use of leisure time and cultural activities.
- A section for urban research should be set up in some federal agency to perform for urban communities functions comparable to those performed for rural communities by the Department of Agriculture.
- A clearinghouse of urban information should be created in the Bureau of the Census. Consideration should be given to the urgent necessity of coordinating at Washington and in the field the related services and activities performed by federal agencies operating in urban areas.
- A study should be made of best methods and administrative techniques for bringing about the closer coordination of federal activities in urban communities and for improving and facilitating collaboration between cities and the federal government.
- A permanent national policy should be adopted to ensure rehousing of low-income groups at acceptable minimum standards as a cooperative undertaking among federal, state, and local government and private enterprise.

- The federal and state governments should extend financial assistance to local authorities conditioned on the existence of a comprehensive city plan and housing program meeting satisfactory standards. Such a policy should be designed to stimulate local initiative, recognize differences in local circumstances, and vest the control in local authorities—to the end that urban slums may be outlawed.
- A permanent national planning board should be established to extend encouragement, cooperation, and support to state, regional, and local planning agencies; to continue, systematize, and improve long-range programming of public works in cooperation with state, regional, and local agencies; to prepare in collaboration with state planning boards and federal agencies the broad general plan of a coordinated transportation system directed toward economically more effective and socially more desirable urban patterns and distribution of economic activities.

Also, the report recommended that Congress pass legislation encouraging the adoption of interstate compacts enabling the communities within the same metropolitan region but in separate states to deal jointly with regional aspects of health, sanitation, industrial waste regulation, control of public utilities, planning, public safety and welfare, education, recreation, and other governmental functions of regional scope.

Here in this 1937 report were the planning concepts that thirty years later led to the creation of the U.S. Department of Housing and Urban Development, with such programs as "701" planning grants, "workable programs," Model Cities, and various housing subsidies. Here, too, one finds the concepts of Title IV of the Intergovernmental Personnel Act, the Law Enforcement Assistance Act, increased sophistication in census data collection and reporting, and even Social Security. Other reports of the National Resources Planning Board were credited with the idea of a U.S. Department of Transportation.

NRPB and its predecessor agency, the National Planning Board, created a network of state and metropolitan planning agencies tied to the national public works program. NRPD's proposals were largely ignored, however, and after the agency was abolished, most of the state—and regional—planning agencies lapsed into disuse.

The influence of NRPB continued after its dissolution. A series of publications under the title *Post-War Planning* focused attention on such issues as conversion of the wartime economy to peacetime production; employment for returning veterans and displaced war production workers; and planning for long-deferred capital needs. During the war, many units of state and local government had built up postwar development funds. Development boards were created, while some of the state planning agencies were eliminated. By the end of 1945, only twenty-eight states still had planning boards.

The Council of Economic Advisors, created in 1946 by the Employment Act, had a much narrower mission in national economic and fiscal planning than NRPB ever had.[5] The council operated wholly within the framework of national-income economics and never focused on such problems as settlement patterns and regional or urban economics.

One other important program of the era of the New Deal was the development of three greenbelt cities by the Federal Resettlement Administration in 1935, following the decision by the U.S. Supreme Court that the National Industrial Recovery Act of 1933 was unconstitutional.[6] The greenbelt towns were conceived to meet housing needs of government workers and others of modest incomes. The greenbelt towns were small in scale, but they had qualities of community design and life substantially absent in the tract developments of the postwar period. The planned new communities would be functionally related to each other and to a core city. They would be fully "balanced," with homes, industry, business, social life, and cultural activity, and physically organized to preserve the countryside for recreation and farming. New communities as a strategic federal initiative are discussed in Chapter 8.

The comprehensiveness of the TVA, the greenbelt towns, and the NRPB all succumbed to the politics of hostile economic interests, and the approach to planning they represented was readily sublimated to problem-oriented, single-purpose planning and development for which there were clamorous constituencies. As the nation emerged from economic collapse, the time for "practical men" arrived, and there were plenty around. Public housing was redefined as standard shelter, and community services and social development were forgotten or disparaged. In the postwar period, the practical men dominated the development scene in urban areas.

The Postwar Period

The planning framework initiated by the federal government during the New Deal prepared the nation to deal promptly with the transition from wartime conditions to a peacetime economy. The immediate postwar focus was the formidable task of getting millions of servicemen back into civilian life. Many resumed their prewar livelihoods; many others needed training or professional education; almost all needed housing.

The federal government responded by initiating and implementing the GI Bill of Rights (1944) to support education and training programs, counseling, and other practical benefits.[7] The Veterans Administration pitched in with low-interest-rate guaranteed housing loans and health benefits.

By the end of the war, there had been a prolonged interruption of the intellectual and political leadership for policy on development and urbanization; some of the nation's best brains had gone to war and were oriented to production. Optimism in private enterprise was restored; the birth rate was climbing; prosperity returned; and public improvements and housing that had been postponed during the war combined to reinforce the return to single-function planning and development.

Meanwhile, the economic reconstruction efforts of the states initiated at the war's end carried into the 1950s, during which time the nation was drawing on its vast store of previously written plans. But the Eisenhower administration (1953–1961) developed no new federal policy for cities and metropolitan areas. Up to the 1950s there had been a federal investment in metropolitan areas of more than $25 billion. Yet there had been no effort to coordinate these federal programs and interests, in spite of the earlier, specific recommendations of the National Planning Board.

Nevertheless, support for comprehensive public planning persisted. The concept was reintroduced into federal policy as an appendage of the Housing Act of 1949 and in relation to certain specific grant-in-aid programs.[8] There was no attempt before the Housing Act of 1954[9] to restore an emphasis on comprehensive state and regional planning for development. There was no effort before 1954 to develop a national urban-growth policy.

The main element of growth policy was the federal mortgage-insurance program administered by the Federal Housing Administration, established by the National Housing Act of 1934.[10] The FHA accepted the pressures of the real estate market as its own standards and, through its programs, subsidized the suburbanization and racial segregation of metropolitan areas.

The consequences of rapid suburbanization in the years immediately following the war, combined with the rapid deterioration of central cities, led to establishment of the urban renewal program in the Housing Act of 1949. The urban renewal program was an attempt by Congress to restore and reinvigorate central cities. However, urban renewal was authorized concurrently with support for suburban development. At the same time, public-housing production continued to lag far behind needs and even authorizations.

Federal urban renewal subsidies were used in the 1950s and 1960s in such a way as to deplete the scarce low-rent housing supply and to build in its place commercial space and expensive high-rise apartments. Subsidies were used to redirect investment in metropolitan areas to central business-district locations. The federal government followed the logic of the competitive struggle for property-tax revenues and, owing to political alliances between federal officials and local officials, no one protested. In many cases, both sets of officials were businessmen who were serving short terms in key government positions and carried their business norms with them into the public sphere. Thus, explicit national purposes were distorted, sidetracked, or ignored in their application at the local level. These anomalies are documented in Gans's *The Urban Villagers*[11] and in Martin Anderson's *The Federal Bulldozer.*[12]

The Housing Act of 1949 established the Housing and Home Finance Agency (HHFA), which was assigned the task of approving grants-in-aid to the local redevelopment agencies that administered urban renewal projects. The emphasis of the Housing Act of 1949 was housing. Although slum clearance and renewal were authorized, even here the purpose was to provide new housing. The act mentioned but did not emphasize comprehensive planning, and the mention of planning was construed by administrators in narrow terms. Neither federal nor local administrators made any attempt to influence the form or direction of accelerating suburbanization.

Comprehensive planning as reestablished as federal policy in Section 701 of the Comprehensive Planning Assistance Program of the Housing Act of

1954 was administered by HHFA. The 701 program was designed to encourage comprehensive planning in cities with populations of less than 25,000, in cities struck by disasters, and in metropolitan areas that had an official planning agency.

The 701 grants provided federal assistance for state, local, and metropolitan planning and were awarded on a 50% matching formula. Under 701, a few metropolitan planning commissions were organized, and some states reestablished state planning offices. Planning programs assisted under the 1954 law were to be comprehensive in physical terms, and they were to cover entire urban areas. They were, however, advisory and not authoritative initiators of growth policy.

Succeeding federal housing acts extended both the coverage and the matching proportion. Thus by March 1972, the Department of Housing and Urban Development (HUD, successor to HHFA) regulations listed the following groups as eligible: states for statewide planning and management; counties, cities, and municipalities for planning support; groups of adjacent communities with populations of less than 50,000; Indian reservations; disaster areas; federally impacted areas; and metropolitan and nonmetropolitan areawide planning organizations. Eligible entities also included metropolitan and regional agencies involved in comprehensive planning and district agencies composed of public officials representing political jurisdictions within the district; cities within metropolitan areas having populations of 50,000 or more; and interstate regional planning agencies.

The Nixon administration shifted the emphasis of the 701 program to improvement of planning, management, and decisionmaking of state, local, and areawide officials and their staffs. The purpose was to help urban and rural agencies solve development problems, realize opportunities, and formulate and implement policies related to community development and growth. The shift in emphasis was intended to add human resources and governmental-services planning to traditional physical planning. Planning was to become a part of decisionmaking in the agencies served. Feedback from these agencies was to be used in federal budgeting.

The 1954 Housing Act required a "workable program" for urban renewal. The concept of the "workable program" was straightforward: if a locality was to qualify for certain grants in housing and urban renewal, it had to have a "workable program for community improvement"—evidence that a city conducting an urban renewal project had a general plan, a zoning ordinance, and other management tools, as assurance of its ability to carry out the program. The purpose was to ensure that communities applying for federal housing and renewal funds demonstrate an understanding of the conditions that create urban blight and a willingness to take practical steps to mitigate those conditions. The objective was to eradicate blight and prevent its reoccurrence. The workable program was limited to central cities using urban renewal grants.

The effort to coordinate federal administrative action had a parallel in congressional requirements for planning, discussed in later sections. Starting with the "workable programs" of urban renewal, the scope of planning requirements was step-by-step extended to metropolitan areas. The requirement that plans exist was made operative by the requirement of referral to a regional agency with authority to plan at the metropolitan level.

Federal policy contained language that spoke of plan implementation as a condition of federal funding. Beginning with Bureau of the Budget Circular A-95, issued in 1969, the federal government published a series of guidelines requiring state-level coordination as a prerequisite of state-local participation in certain federal programs. A-95 contained the principal federal guidelines for regional planning until the Reagan administration let it die in the 1980s.[13]

The workable programs required that a local agency responsible to the chief executive supervise the program. It also required certain concrete actions: (1) adoption of housing, building, and related codes with effective enforcement; (2) establishment of comprehensive planning aimed at overcoming major physical, social, and economic problems related to the slum and blighted areas of the community; (3) development of a coordinated program for assisting in relocation of persons and business concerns displaced by community-renewal programs; and (4) establishment of citizen involvement programs to include poor and minority groups in planning and carrying out community-renewal programs.

While workable programs might have helped local officials anticipate future problems, they had marginal value in helping cities cope with changes occurring in their populations. They were of almost no value as instruments of regional development policy. As the number of urban-renewal projects grew and the program was regularized, workable programs became routine work for consultants and mere hurdles for federal grants, rather than vital processes of decisionmaking at local and regional levels.

The experience with the "workable programs" requirement of urban renewal was not encouraging. The necessity of carrying out federal programs through local agencies, the piecemeal nature of the programs, and the absence of state or local agencies responsible for coordination resulted in fragmentation and inequities. The confusion of conflicting and unreconciled federal-planning requirements compelled the federal government to develop a coherent national urban development policy. But efforts by the federal government to do so were fitful and unsuccessful.

The experiment of the workable programs came early in the federal government's long struggle with the problem of how to implement federal programs intended for the benefit of urban communities. President Dwight D. Eisenhower recognized the interest of the White House in urban problems in his appointment of a special staff assistant to deal with cities. Years later, President Lyndon Johnson delegated to the vice president, Hubert Humphrey, a former mayor, the task of maintaining White House liaison with cities. Succeeding presidents continued the practice of a staff liaison with cities but federal coordination of federal programs has never been systematically pursued by any administration nor has a president ever successfully promulgated a comprehensive urban policy. President Nixon came closest with the help of his domestic advisor, Daniel Patrick Moynihan.

President Kennedy's Committee on Juvenile Delinquency and many of the local programs of the Office of Economic Opportunity during the 1960s were federal efforts to structure some local coordination of federal and other related activities. In 1970, President Nixon took steps to devolve to city government some of the stringent controls the Department of Housing and Urban Development had imposed in the Model Cities Program.[14] This program was intended as a prime means of coordinating federal categorical grant programs for welfare services at the local level. However, none of these efforts had the political staying power to achieve lasting success.

The National Defense Highway Construction Act of 1956, popularly known as the Interstate Highway Act, was the single most influential federal program affecting urbanization patterns.[15] The act was written as a single-function program and provided no effective measures for participation by localities in highway planning. Yet the effect of an Interstate highway on the cityscape and the urban economy was to be immense.

By 1962, central-city mayors and others aggrieved by the insensitivities and maladroit effects of the Interstate Highway program lobbied for an amendment to make highway planning subordinate to areawide comprehensive planning. The aim was to harness the mammoth, well-funded highway program to serve broader ends than the movement of vehicles.

The protectors of the highway program prevailed. The Federal Aid Highway Act of 1962 required only a continuing, comprehensive transportation planning process, leaving to the cooperative action of federal, state, and local officials the specific arrangements and relationship of transportation to other aspects of planning.[16] HHFA and the Bureau of Public Roads agreed on joint funding of planning programs, and this step facilitated the creation of effective coordinating processes in some areas. While the Federal Aid Highway Act of 1962 did not fully integrate transportation into a comprehensive urban-growth policy framework, it did contribute to coherent federal metropolitan-growth strategies.

This trend is exemplified in other federal categorical grant programs enacted in the early 1960s. Each was narrowly oriented to some particular "problem" but also required the existence of a comprehensive planning process to qualify for the federal aid. The open-spaces legislation in the 1963 Housing Act, for example, established standards that required a rudimentary regional open-space plan.[17] The Urban Mass Transportation Act of 1964 required that federal assistance be granted only as part of "a comprehensively planned development of the urban area."[18]

Social aspects of comprehensive planning were launched by the federal government in a series of Community Renewal Programs, authorized by the Housing Act of 1959.[19] These programs were important in the evolution of federal planning policy. The purposes of these programs were to (1) analyze the condition of housing in the community to determine if it was standard, needed conservation, or should be demolished; (2) inventory the community's resources and relate them to the costs of solving the problem; (3) prepare a comprehensive project map, with supporting data, discussing the conditions in each project area and the type of remedial action required; and (4) establish a priority system for carrying out the projects.

The principal changes brought about by the Community Renewal Programs included development of new techniques for local urban analysis; development of innovative techniques for using urban renewal; initiation of steps to ally local physical planning with social planning; changes in the methods of local government administration and planning in those new methods.

In 1960, President John F. Kennedy had proposed the creation of a cabinet department to deal with urban problems. HHFA never had cabinet status, and it did not help with Congress that Kennedy had appointed a distinguished Black, Robert Weaver, to be administrator. When Lyndon Johnson succeeded to the presidency in 1963 and then was elected to a full second term in 1964 by a sizable majority, Congress finally created HUD, in 1965, and Weaver became secretary.[20] This step alone did not solve the problem of uncoordinated federal aid to urban areas, much less the severe housing problems of the inner-city poor.

Bernard Frieden wrote in 1967:

Federal housing policies seem to be at odds with other federal objectives. Some programs—chiefly FHA mortgage insurance, federal aid for highways that facilitate suburban growth, and aid for suburban water and sewer systems—accelerate the pace of new housing construction in the suburbs and turn-over of central-city housing. Others—principally urban renewal and aid for mass transit—aim at reviving the central cities and stemming the flight to the suburbs. Urban renewal in turn depletes the supply of low-cost housing and thus slows the turn-over effects stimulated by the national housing policy. The programs that favor urban growth promote population dispersal along racial and economic lines, setting the stage for race segregation between central cities and suburbs, which runs counter to national civil rights objectives. The same dispersal handicaps the central cities in their efforts to provide adequate services for low-income groups, countering other national goals in the war on poverty and in providing equality of educational opportunity.[21]

Creation of HUD encouraged broader thinking about federal programs. HUD began to sponsor councils of governments in preference to metropolitan planning commissions as a way to involve local officials in regional planning. Ironically, the Department of Transportation may have been a stronger influence on such thinking than HUD, as the DOT's secretary began to question the consequences of the national addiction to the automobile and to pursue an interest in comprehensive development.

President Johnson's War on Poverty and other related federal programs, launched in 1965 in the aftermath of President Kennedy's assassination, were the first to involve in planning the poor people who were to be the beneficiaries of the programs. That was when "citizen participation" was first introduced into national and local planning. As we noted in Chapter 6, citizen participation was an innovation that ensured a permanent role for social and physical planning in the development of American cities. Rarely again was planning seriously questioned as a framework of policymaking in metropolitan communities.

The experience with citizen participation in local policymaking was as varied as the leadership that the War on Poverty programs attracted. But new leadership from the neighborhoods of inner cities spawned a sense of hope and pride. Along with the civil rights legislation Lyndon Johnson pushed through Congress in the late 1950s and the 1960s, the poverty programs raised expectations far beyond the nation's political and social capacity to fully implement. The riots of the late 1960s were symptomatic (especially among inner-city Blacks) of the frustration fueled by deprivation and unfulfilled hope.

The Economic Opportunity Act of 1964 introduced a consciousness of poverty into American politics.[22] There was a widespread recognition that metropolitan planning was ineffective and that no effective national urban-growth policy existed. Yet in the wake of President Kennedy's New Frontier and the energetic activities of the Great Society there emerged a national commitment to solve such problems—problems that, however, persist to the present day. While there was not yet a conscious effort at formulating a national growth policy, by 1965 a trend could be discerned away from the narrow functionalism of the past and toward a coordinated use of federal powers in urban development.

The year 1965 was an important watershed in federal policy affecting urban development. Until then federal policy had been almost exclusively problem oriented. While the programs mentioned above had some comprehensive planning requirements, they were essentially separate from each other, and they were not well coordinated. The Housing and Urban Development Act of 1965 authorized a water and sewage grant-in-aid program that required that local projects be related to growth needs of the area.[23] A water and sewage program had to be part of a unified system serving the urban area and be necessary to orderly community development. The Advisory Commission on Intergovernmental Relations had schooled members of Congress, governors, and local officials in regionalism, intergovernmental cooperation, and the virtues of general government as opposed to special-purpose agencies. It was apparent by 1965 that a decade and a half of urban renewal had not materially arrested the deterioration of central cities, in spite of some architectural and economic successes.

By the time the riots of the 1960s had spent their force, the nation had recognized in a series of reports by presidential commissions the social, psychological, and economic conditions minorities had to tolerate. The reports stimulated public discussion about racism and its derivative forms of deprivation. The discussion generated broad public support for changes in public and private policy that began the long, slow process of breaking down discriminatory barriers in housing, employment, education, and political opportunities—a process that continued in American society into the twenty-first century.

A congressional response to critics of federal urban policy (or lack of one) was the Demonstration Cities and Metropolitan Development Act of 1966, especially Title I, which authorized the Model Cities Program.[24] The program in the grant-receiving cities was meant to improve the quality of urban life in a coordinated attack on all types of social, economic, and physical problems. The political heads of the city government were to mobilize federal, state, local, public, and private resources to accomplish the task. The new program was to marshal resources from a wide variety of federal programs, piggyback on urban renewal for the necessary land assembly and funds, and deal with a sufficiently large segment of the city to bring about physical and social improvement.

A plan was required, and the first year of a grant was designated for its preparation. The Model Cities grant could be used to match federal "categorical" grants. Federal agencies were directed to work with the program, and for this purpose HUD had "convenor" powers. A Washington Inter-Agency Coordinating Committee was established along with regional interagency coordinating committees. Typically, the core federal agencies involved were HUD; Health, Education, and Welfare (HEW); Labor; and the new Office of Economic Opportunity (OEO), established to run President Johnson's War on Poverty.

As initially conceived, the Model Cities Program was to be used in a limited number of cities to demonstrate financial, administrative, construction, and other techniques that could be extended to other cities. The initial "demonstration" idea was stillborn as congressional and mayoral pressure combined with bureaucratic caution to greatly enlarge the number of cities given Model Cities grants. The larger number of cities among which the funds were distributed reduced the funds available to each and thus fatally reduced the chances of careful experimentation in each of the recipient cities. The Model Cities Program became, in effect, just another grant program, bogged down in procedures, requirements, deadlines, and reports.

In spite of the problems and drawbacks, the largest federal impact on local government organization in the 1960s and 1970s came from the Model Cities Program and the antipoverty program. The programs encouraged new organizations outside the framework of the existing administrative and political establishment—the community action agencies, the concentrated employment programs, and the neighborhood services centers.

In political terms, Democratic administrations used the programs to offer jobs and services to build party loyalty and deliberately bypassed the states and hostile or recalcitrant large-city administrations. In the process, Blacks and Hispanics in some cities gained control of citywide coordinating agencies, much as Irish, Italians, and Jews earlier had gained control of other municipal departments.

These programs did little to improve life in the inner cities. The efficacy of "maximum feasible participation" by the poor was hotly debated. Daniel Patrick Moynihan insisted that the programs led only to "maximum feasible misunderstanding" because of their contradictory goals and confusion.[25] As we observed in Chapter 6, clarification of the citizen-participation policy would have compromised the goal of politicizing the poor, of confirming participants as voters for Democratic candidates, and of putting money into their pockets.

Title II of the Demonstration Cities and Metropolitan Development Act dealt with the problems of metropolitan coordination. As we explain later in this chapter, Section 204 of Title II required that a broad range of federal grant applications from local governments be reviewed by an areawide agency. Since the same Congress accepted a rider preventing the use of any HUD appropriations to administer this section, the Bureau of the Budget (BOB) assumed responsibility for establishing the standards for designating the regional agencies and the programs to be reviewed.

In 1967, BOB issued Circular A-80 encouraging state and local planning agencies to work together in using common planning bases.[26] These included statistical and economic estimates, sharing planning facilities and resources, using common boundaries for planning and development districts, and making such districts consistent with state planning and development regions and districts.

BOB never officially suggested that the Standard Metropolitan Statistical Areas (SMSAs) be the planning districts, although they would have been an acceptable alternative. The importance to the federal government of defined territories in urban areas—such as the SMSAs—was their value as a geographical area where serious planning could be accomplished. BOB was concerned that federal, state, and local programs be put into a manageable framework of priorities in the context of regional planning. The statistical base was present in the SMSAs, and the clusters of contiguous municipalities within the SMSAs suggested the potential for cooperation among the local officials for some areawide problems. Substate districts were not yet prominently on the scene in most areas of the country.

Treating metropolitan regions as territorial areas for federal decentralization and coordination would have contributed to the evolution of national urban development policy. The SMSAs would have been suitable for comprehensive planning purposes because they comprised labor markets, housing markets, transportation, and other integrated systems that required at least the scope of a metropolitan region for coordinated development action.

BOB added policies (1) to facilitate state and local initiative and responsibility for developing organizational and procedural arrangements to coordinate comprehensive and functional planning activities; (2) to discourage overlap, duplication, and competition in state and local planning activities required under federal programs and to maximize state and local resources available for development planning (leadership, manpower, and money); (3) to minimize inconsistency among federal administrative and approval requirements placed on state, regional, and metropolitan development planning activities; and (4) to encourage the states to take the lead in establishing a system of planning and development regions to coordinate federal, state, and local development programs.

Subsequently, BOB issued Circular A-82, which stimulated the formation of forty new metropolitan review agencies, most of them modeled on councils of governments.[27] By the end of 1969, there were 171 areawide planning agencies to handle the Circular A-82 planning review mandate. Most had jurisdiction over all or part of 208 SMSAs. Fourteen had planning jurisdiction over two or more SMSAs.

The Intergovernmental Cooperation Act of 1968 broadened the scope of federal policy aimed at requiring that national, state, regional, and local viewpoints be taken into account and that plans be consistent with the objectives of state, regional, and local comprehensive planning "to the maximum extent feasible."[28] The act also required federal agencies to consult with each other and required system planning by individual federal programs to be made part of comprehensive local and areawide development planning.

The act required that the state governors approve functional plans for federal assistance and extended coverage of federal programs to human concerns such as health planning, juvenile delinquency prevention and control planning, community action planning, and community renewal planning.

The scope of the review mandate was extended to environmental standards in the National Environmental Policy Act of 1970.[29] The review mandate was again extended in 1971 by the Office of Management and Budget (OMB) (successor to BOB). In federal public works, disposition, acquisition, and use of public land were to be checked against local and state plans and any deviation justified.

In sum, the councils of governments, state planning offices, and governors' reviews of state plans were intended to give a voice to the states, metropolitan areas, and cities in federal decisionmaking. The effectiveness of the system depended on the willingness of federal funding agencies to accept clearinghouse recommendations.

The mandatory referral system may have given de facto veto power over other local governments when that power had no other basis than control over federal purse strings. The Office of Management and Budget always emphasized the service aspect of the relationship, but autonomy of decisionmaking was circumscribed by the mandatory referral system.

In 1969, OMB issued Circular A-95, expanding the number of federal programs covered and incorporating requirements for state and regional clearinghouses required by the 1968 Intergovernmental Cooperation Act and issued pursuant to Title II of the Demonstration Cities and Metropolitan Development Act of 1966. A-95 proved to be the single most important statement of federal policy on urban development prior to Title VII of the 1970 Housing and Urban Development Act.[30] That is because it reinforced the mandate of the Intergovernmental Cooperation Act, which required metropolitan agencies to make reasoned choices and priorities in the federal grant programs they approved.

A-95 should be read in combination with HUD Circulars MD 6415.1 through 3. These documents established the requirements that areawide agencies had to meet, and they provided process guidelines. They did not establish substantive standards for metropolitan planning or development policy, and some federal agencies continued to recognize agencies independent of the A-95 review agency as program agencies for specific activities.

Section 204 of Title IV, OMB Circular A-95, and HUD Circulars MD 6415.1–3 provided an opportunity for a new kind of political process in metropolitan areas. Section 204 allowed jurisdictions previously denied participation in bilateral agreements between local and federal agencies to examine these proposed agreements and to comment upon them. While an A-95 agency could not deny a grant application, unfavorable comments could impair the chances of funding. The real power, however, was in the development of regional plans against which individual applications would be judged.

Section 205 offered substantial leverage for interjurisdictional bargaining, but it did not produce a regional development policy in more than a few areas because it was never funded. If it had been funded, it could have provided the needed element to induce regional development policies. This section offered a 20% supplement to basic federal grants to areawide projects. These "override" grants were dependent on meeting criteria for metropolitan planning, programming, and local implementation in accordance with those plans. In short, Section 205 would have established the basis of regional capital improvements programs and budgets and provided the sine qua non for an effective public policy for regional development. That Section 205 was not funded reflected the ambivalence of federal policy toward urban development: growing concern that there was no federal urban development policy, and a reluctance to take the federal actions necessary to ensure that such a policy could become a reality.

As a consequence of this ambivalence, federal policy toward urban development tended to concentrate on processes of developing policy rather than its substantive content. At the time there was a trend toward regionalizing these processes in spite of some backtracking during the inner-city riots of the 1960s. There was also an uninterrupted drift in federal policy toward requiring more comprehensive and fewer functional political and technical processes to develop regional and even federal urban development policy. Two planning programs in functional areas illustrate this trend in federal urban policy. These were the planning programs in health and manpower, both initiated in the mid-1960s.

In the years following development of the "701" planning assistance program, the Community Renewal Programs, and the "workable programs," the federal government went on to apply the requirements of comprehensive planning to such functional areas as health and manpower. The development of comprehensive planning in the health field, starting with the Partnership for Health Act in 1966,[31] proved an especially difficult area for publicly sponsored planning because the field had always been dominated by powerful private interests—physicians, hospitals, insurance companies, and, in more recent years, hospital corporations, health maintenance organizations, and managed-care groups, all of which have traditionally resisted government-imposed planning.[32]

Planning got started in the health field in a variety of private and public efforts. Community-sponsored health and welfare councils and hospital councils were among the earliest. The federal government edged into health planning with the Hill-Burton Act of 1946, which provided hospital construction funds sometimes conditioned on community health planning and hospital cooperation or mergers.

The Partnership for Health Act was designed to establish comprehensive regional health planning for coordination of existing and planned health services, facilities, personnel, and capital equipment. The program required a regional health-planning agency and a state health-planning agency. Planning activities at the state level included establishing health goals, identifying problems, inventorying resources, setting priorities and a timetable for action, providing information to policymakers, preparing and periodically revising a comprehensive state health plan.

Functions of the regional comprehensive health-planning agencies (CHPAs) included encouraging institutions to develop planning programs consistent with regional objectives, creating a system of data collection and analysis, studying area problems and resources, contributing to the state CHP effort, and reviewing and commenting on local grant applications.

By 1970, 90% of the areawide CHP councils were nonpublic. Most were former hospital planning councils or former health and welfare planning councils. The general urban planning agencies had difficulty establishing meaningful relationships with them, in spite of the federal review requirements then in effect. Little interest was evidenced by the manpower services planners in coordinating with the urban-planning function beyond the required review process, despite areas of common concern, such as economic development and intra-urban transportation (the home-to-work journey).

The development of comprehensive planning in the manpower field is another example of the federal government's efforts in the 1960s and 1970s to introduce comprehensive planning in an important functional area. Comprehensive planning in manpower services at first existed without a legislative mandate and was funded from appropriations under the Manpower Development and Training Act of 1962, as amended in 1966.[33]

Manpower planning councils, which operated in substate areas and at the state level, had the mission of reporting annually on the nature of unemployment and underemployment problems, trends in the job market, and plans for job matching. For years, the Cooperative Area Manpower Planning Service (CAMPS) system routinely issued reports but findings were not related to federal grant patterns. The "plan" part of the report was a wish list of several participating agencies that delivered manpower services.

In 1970, the Domestic Council was established in the White House to coordinate formulation of policy in domestic affairs, which focused on urban policy. This was about the time the Bureau of the Budget became the Office of Management and Budget, with the mission of strengthening oversight of all federal policies and programs.

There remained a substantial gap between legislative and administrative declarations about urban development policy and the funding of appropriate programs. The penchant for "processing" problems could be seen in the Nixon administration's reorganization plans for a proposed Department of Community Affairs and the president's revenue-sharing program.

President Nixon was elected (in 1968) before any of the cities selected for the Model Cities Program were funded. His analysis of the program led to these actions: the Washington coordinative function was upgraded to an Urban Affairs Council, comprising Cabinet-level secretaries. Uniform regions were established, initially for the four "core" agencies and subsequently extended to the Economic Development Administration and the Small Business Administration. Limited decisionmaking was vested in the new regional offices.

In addition, President Nixon reinforced the role of mayors in the leadership of the central cities and metropolitan areas. In the latter, mayors got check-off powers over awards of federal grants and staffing grants. A clear strategy to reinvest in the states and local government responsibility for areawide urban planning and plan implementation were coupled with efforts to centralize and coordinate decisionmaking and policy formulation at the federal level.

President Nixon introduced the concept of general revenue sharing in 1969 as a way of providing state and local governments with the fiscal resources for meeting and solving urgent service needs, and as a way of overcoming inconsistencies, duplications, and gaps in the categorical funding system. Nixon also saw his revenue-sharing plan as a return to Jeffersonian democracy and a repudiation of the Johnson administration's "creative federalism" by returning control of federal programs to local government.

The idea of revenue sharing was by no means new with Nixon and his advisors. As Robert Freilich reminds us, the federal government tried to implement a revenue-sharing program in 1837, an initiative that was canceled by a major recession the following year.[34]

The revenue-sharing grants were intended as a means of dispersing federal surpluses during the few years in the 1960s when there was a surplus and at the same time of relieving state and local government tax shortages. The initiators of the Nixon revenue-sharing plan also thought that by making state and local government responsible for increased spending, a greater fiscal administrative capability would be developed. "A more progressive federal-state-local tax system, less dependent on regressive property and sales taxes was another hoped-for benefit."[35] Federal budget experts expected surpluses at the conclusion of the Vietnam War. As it turned out, the last year of federal surpluses was fiscal year 1969, three years before the Paris Peace Accords were signed ending the Vietnam War.

The theory of federal revenue sharing was developed in 1964 by economists Walter W. Heller, then chairman of President Johnson's Council of Economic Advisors, and Joseph A. Pechman, director of economic studies at the Brookings Institution and chairman of a task force appointed by President Johnson to study revenue sharing. The theory held that, because of the income elasticity of the federal revenue structure, federal government revenues tend to outrun federal government expenditures (in years of surplus revenues), thereby dragging down the national economy's total expenditures to suboptimal levels. The menace of "fiscal drag," so the argument went, could be averted by dispersing unanticipated surpluses to state and local governments. In a program of revenue sharing the federal government would distribute a "specified portion of the Federal individual income tax to the States each year on a per capita basis, with next to no strings attached."[36]

Nixon made revenue sharing the centerpiece of his New Federalism program. The Nixon plan, known as the general revenue-sharing program, was passed into law as the State and Local Fiscal Assistance Act of 1972.[37] The program continued to benefit cities until President Ronald Reagan terminated it in 1986.[38]

The Nixon administration's New Federalism program was explicitly designed to encourage decentralization of responsibility for planning and policy to the states and localities. This program was the Nixon administration's key urban policy. An important feature was decentralization of decisionmaking for local use of the new general revenue-sharing funds. In preparation, the Nixon administration in 1969 created ten federal regional councils. The regional councils survived with modest support in the Carter administration but were disbanded in 1983 by the Reagan administration. The New Federalism program was a deliberate strategy to make planning palatable to conservatives. The strategy worked and the Nixon policy to foster local and regional planning was never reversed, although the funding and regional structure disappeared.

Nixon's general revenue-sharing program had one major drawback from the standpoint of prospects for future consolidation of some services at a regional/substate district level. By the 1970s, some small and sparsely populated local jurisdictions—notably townships and incorporated villages—were increasingly hard put to make ends meet and many were ripe for areawide arrangements for some local services. The Nixon revenue-sharing program deliberately gave the states and all 38,700 local jurisdictions in America a piece of the action. This was a windfall of new and unexpected largesse—negating any incentive for areawide consolidation of services.

No federal revenue-sharing program could legally have "no strings attached" as the Heller-Pechman theory stipulated, and so the State and Local Fiscal Assistance Act of 1972 included the restriction that recipients "adhere to all applicable Federal laws in connection with any activity, program, or service provided solely or in part" by the allotments. This provision was intended to include the various federal planning requirements such as those associated with the "701" planning grants, "workable programs," Model Cities, and various housing subsidies discussed earlier in this chapter.[39] The act also restricted the use of the shared funds to nine areas: public safety, environmental protection, public transportation, health, recreation, libraries, social services for the poor and aged, financial administration, and capital expenditures.

Though Nixon's general revenue-sharing program was terminated by the Reagan administration, Congress developed a modified form of revenue sharing in the Housing and Community Development Act of 1974 (HCDA)—the Community Development Block Grant (CDBG).[40] HCDA was a hybrid between a no-strings-attached special revenue-sharing measure proposed by the Nixon administration and the extensive application of federal oversight requirements of replaced programs. This program consolidated several existing grants-in-aid programs: urban renewal, neighborhood development, Model Cities, water and sewer grants, open space, land rehabilitation loans, and construction of public facilities.

The primary purposes of HCDA and the CDBGs were decent housing, a suitable living environment, and expanding economic opportunities primarily for people of low and moderate income. The act required a three-year community plan, a housing-assistance plan, A-95 review, and citizen participation in the planning process. The grants were awarded according to a formula based on population, housing overcrowding, and poverty levels.

A year earlier, Congress had consolidated several Great Society programs in the Comprehensive Employment and Training Act.[41] The two block-grant programs were popularly known as special revenue sharing. "Compared to the earlier General Revenue Sharing program, CDBG (Special Revenue Sharing) proved more popular and durable . . . and has emerged over time as the number one urban-aid program," writes Waste.[42] The funding levels of CDBG increased from 1974 to 1996, although President Jimmy Carter, by executive order, reversed Nixon's decentralization of CDBG decisionmaking to require monitoring by HUD.

President Carter's major urban initiative was the Urban Development Action Grant, popularly known as UDAG, created by the Urban Development Act of 1977.[43] UDAG was intended as a complement to the Community Development Block Grant program. The UDAG program was designed to help eliminate physical and economic deterioration in severely distressed cities and urban counties by offering federal resources to leverage private capital investment, create new employment opportunities, and increase the local tax base.[44] UDAG applications had to demonstrate compliance with CDBG requirements for citizen participation and consistency with Community Development and Housing Assistance Plans.

The UDAG program came on line just after federal grants to states and local governments peaked in 1978. In that year the federal-aid system, which had expanded 100% from 1969 to 1978, began to relax highly intrusive standards and controls and to shift the burden for program growth to state and local government. Federally imposed planning standards also began almost imperceptibly to fade. In the years that followed, A-80 and A-95 guidelines fell into disuse and were eventually dropped.

The gradual shift in responsibility for urban development programs became federal policy in the Reagan administration, which used the shift of programs to the states as a way to keep in check burgeoning federal deficits. In fiscal year 1982 federal aid to state and local government showed the first absolute decline in a quarter-century.[45] After 1982, Democratic congresses resisted some of the most damaging cuts initiated by the Reagan administration. The Urban-Rural Recovery Act of 1983 responded to housing needs with new CDBG funds over three years and new funds for the UDAG program over the same period. Under the new law HUD was authorized to make grants for rental projects in targeted low-income neighborhoods where the existing supply of rental housing was insufficient for the need.[46]

As we have seen, federal responsibility for planning and development in cities and metropolitan areas was essentially piecemeal during the three-decade period from the late 1940s through the 1970s, as cities burgeoned from unprecedented migrations from rural areas and from immigration. There were exceptions: planning for public housing, begun in the prewar New Deal and revived in the postwar years, was expanded to address the growing problem of housing the poor in cities. Hospital planning initiated by the Truman administration in the Hill-Burton Act[47] paved the way for the initiatives in regional-health planning, Medicare, and Medicaid (1966), initiated by the Johnson administration.

Throughout the 1950s and 1960s, the major problem for the federal government in regional and local planning was the widespread negative attitude of local political and civic leaders to publicly sponsored development planning. It was an attitude akin to that of opponents of the New Deal in the 1930s and 1940s, which killed the National Resources Planning Board. In the 1950s and during most of the 1960s, many local leaders ignored federal planning initiatives or, when the initiatives could not be ignored, were hostile to them. But as more and more federal requirements for local and regional planning were promulgated in the 1960s and 1970s and the benefits became apparent, the climate of acceptance among local leaders improved.

Most citizens and local officials who served on the new regional planning commissions and on the councils of governments represented local or private interests. Very few of them adopted an areawide planning point of view. An areawide perspective was for a long time not only unpopular but in conservative communities risky to one's public reputation. Planning was seen to be socialist or downright communist. The communist governments in the Soviet Union and the People's Republic of China had their centrally controlled five-year plans and systems of governance that carried out these plans. These programs gave planning a bad name in America and so to many Americans, comprehensive planning seemed the antithesis of private property rights and personal freedom.

Nevertheless, federal initiatives to improve cities persisted, and federal grants-in-aid became convenient for implementing federal initiatives at the local level. From the standpoint of federal officials from Congress and the president on down, the grant-in-aid as a tool of revenue sharing had the great advantage of establishing uniform guidelines (as is required by the equal protection clause of the 14th Amendment to the U.S. Constitution), improving state and local management and planning capacity, and whetting local appetites for enhanced social programs.

The Nixon initiative on national urban policy, formulated in 1970 by Moynihan, contained the following points:

- The relative ineffectiveness of urban government to respond to urban problems derives from the fragmented and obsolescent structure of urban government itself. The federal government should encourage and provide incentives for the reorganization of local government in response to the reality of metropolitan conditions. The objective of the federal government should be that local government be stronger and more effective, more visible, accessible and meaningful to local inhabitants. To this end, the federal government should discourage the creation of para-governments designed to deal with special problems by evading or avoiding the established jurisdiction of local authorities, and should encourage effective decentralization.

- Federal policy should seek to equalize the provision of public services among different jurisdictions in metropolitan areas. The federal government must assert a specific interest in the movement of people, displaced by technology or driven by poverty, from rural to urban areas, and also from densely settled populated central cities to suburban areas. State government has an indispensable role in the management of urban affairs, and must be supported and encouraged by the federal government in the performance of this role. The federal government should support extensive research into urban problems. The federal government, by its own example, and by incentives, should seek the development of a sense of the finite resources of the natural environment and the importance of aesthetics in urban growth.[48]

The Moynihan statement was the Nixon administration's policy framework for formulation of new urban programs and adjustments to existing ones.

Congress was also concerned with a national growth and development policy and so it enacted two landmark statutes, the Agricultural Act of 1970[49] and the Housing and Urban Development Act of 1970.[50] Title IX of the Agricultural Act proclaimed in Section 901(a) that Congress commits itself to a sound balance between rural and urban America, that Congress considers this balance so essential to the peace, prosperity, and welfare of all citizens that high priority must be given to the revitalization and development of urban areas. The act called for annual reports to Congress by the federal agencies responsible for aiding rural areas through location of public facilities, planning assistance, information and technology, government services, and financial assistance.

The companion act was the Housing and Urban Development Act of 1970. Part A of Title VII dealt with development of a national urban growth policy.

Section 702 outlined population trends and the influence of federal programs on those trends and declared that the federal government must assume responsibility for the development of a national urban growth policy incorporating social, economic, and other appropriate factors consistent with the responsibilities of state and local government and the private sector. The policy was to serve as a guide in making specific decisions at the national level which would affect the pattern of urban growth and was to provide a framework for development of an interstate, state, and local growth and stabilization policy.

Title VII directed the president to develop a national growth policy and to make a biennial report to Congress. This report was envisioned as the urban counterpart of the president's Economic Report and would be a major state paper to be used as a basis for urban growth policy. The act required the report to be prepared by the Domestic Council and provided for establishment of an advisory board to assist in preparation of the report.

A national urban growth policy was to favor patterns of urbanization and economic development and stabilization that encouraged balanced use of physical and human resources in large urban regions and in smaller urban places with a potential for accelerated growth; foster economic strength in all parts of the United States, including central cities, suburbs, smaller communities, local neighborhoods, and rural areas; help reverse trends of migration and physical growth that reinforced disparities among states, regions, and cities; encourage planned, large-scale development of new communities; treat comprehensively the problems of poverty and unemployment associated with disorderly urbanization and rural decline; and develop good housing for all Americans "without regard to race or creed."

Title VII called for an urban growth policy that would lead to strengthening state and local governments to manage urbanization and improve federal program coordination of urban and community development. Title VII also called for a policy of "wise and balanced use of physical and human resources," and one that would "foster the economic strength of all parts of the United States" and "encourage good housing for all Americans."

In addition, the act specified seven elements of data and analysis a presidential report should contain:

1. Information describing urban-growth characteristics and trends.
2. A summary of significant problems resulting from those trends and developments.
3. An evaluation of federal efforts at meeting the problems.
4. An assessment of interstate planning, policies, and programs.
5. A review of relevant state and local policies.
6. Current and foreseeable needs and policies to meet them.
7. Recommendations for carrying out such policy.

A national urban growth policy should refine the role of the federal government in revitalizing communities and encourage planned, large-scale urban and new community development to strengthen the capacity of general governmental institutions to contribute to balanced urban growth and stabilization. It was also meant to improve coordination among federal programs and to encourage desirable patterns of urban growth and stabilization, prudent use of natural resources, and protection of the physical environment.

The first presidential report was submitted in 1972. It fell far short of its statutory mandate and as a contribution to federal policy on urban growth. Nonetheless, the report was the Nixon administration's most comprehensive statement of urban growth policy.

The most influential tool the federal government had in shaping the policies of local, regional, and state entities was the federal grant-in-aid. The shortage of fiscal resources at these levels combined with a multiplication of responsibilities during the 1960s and 1970s intensified the impact of federal grants-in-aid programs. In fact, the availability of earmarked federal funds tended to dictate local priorities. In the planning area, the principal thrusts were the Comprehensive Planning Assistance Program, the Community Renewal Program, the "workable program," and comprehensive planning in such programs as health and manpower.

By the early 1970s, local leaders had become accustomed to federal planning requirements and to the review powers of regional planning agencies. Elected officials whose concerns were primarily local were in fact in control of regional planning. In some metropolitan areas, local officials were brought to a regional orientation through participation in regional planning required by the national government, suggesting the value of the federal involvement in promoting local and regional planning. Local leaders found that areawide projects from which they benefited were easier to coordinate through the regional mechanisms, that federal funds flowed with fewer delays, and that the planning the special interests had feared carried no extraordinary authority except that which local authorities lent to it. Thus, regional planning became an accepted tool in the federal system.

President Carter, faced with economic and diplomatic crises (inflation on the domestic front and hostages in Iran), managed little more than the UDAG program for inner cities and tightened federal control over the Community Development Block Grants and Nixon's CETA program. The Nixon administration's efforts to decentralize federal programs were reevaluated during the Reagan administration. Reagan's objective was to induce states and municipalities to shoulder the burden for domestic problems and to reduce and decentralize federal support for them. This policy resulted in large federal cuts or minimal increases in housing, education programs, planning, and other programs and services.

President Clinton came into office in 1993 at the start of an unprecedented period of economic expansion and national prosperity, and so his prodigious efforts to restore a federal domestic agenda produced some successes. However, the Clinton administration also favored shifting control of urban aid to state and local governments. Decentralization of the federal government and enhanced flexibility to state and local governments were recurring themes in Clinton administration proposals. The momentum toward decentralization that Clinton supported was reflected in the Welfare Reform Act of 1996. The year before Clinton's election in 1992, federal planning policy made some limited gains in the Intermodal Surface Transportation Efficiency Act of 1991 and the Transportation Equity Act of 1998. President George W. Bush in his first term showed equally strong support of devolving responsibilities to state and local government, notably in his signature education bill, the No Child Left Behind Act of 2001, in which state departments of education and local school districts were required to carry out (and in many cases fund) federal mandates to administer performance tests intended to measure the effectiveness of public schools in teaching the children enrolled in them.

Conclusions

During the 1960s, the Kennedy and Johnson administrations initiated a number of programs requiring local jurisdictions to change accustomed procedures. Some of these programs did not live up to expectations. Duplication and waste accompanied the energetic pace of activity of the Johnson administration. The inefficiencies prompted a federal call for improved planning by federal agencies, the states, metropolitan areas, cities, and suburbs. In consequence, planning agencies proliferated.

Thus, a key feature of the federal government's urban planning policy as it evolved in the 1950s and 1960s was a coordinated approach among federal, state, regional, and metropolitan agencies in local development objectives. The mandatory referral programs associated with the early councils of governments, later written into the Demonstration Cities and Metropolitan Development Act of 1966, were a manifestation of this policy.

As we have seen, that act provided that most applications for federal grants or loans be reviewed by a designated areawide agency. If a special-purpose unit of local government made an application, it also had to be reviewed by the unit of local government with authority to operate in the area within which the project was to be located. Comments and recommendations were to be forwarded to the appropriate federal agency.

Comments were to include information on the extent to which the project was consistent with a comprehensive plan developed for the metropolitan area or to the unit of general local government, and the extent to which the project contributed to the fulfillment of such a plan.

The federal agency was to use the comments and recommendations to determine whether the application was in accordance with the federal law governing the grant. Federal programs covered by the policy included open-space protection; planning and construction of hospitals, airports, libraries, water supply and distribution facilities, and law enforcement facilities; and water development and land conservation projects.

The councils of governments and metropolitan planning commissions are the principal vehicles for coordinating metropolitan planning. Multistate planning agencies and development commissions are the principal vehicles for water-resource development and for economic development. Substate planning agencies are the principal vehicles for land use and economic development planning. In the future, substate planning and administrative districts on the model described in Chapter 9 could be the vehicles for drawing together and implementing federal and state urban growth and development policies.

Urban planning at the regional level has expanded from its traditional concerns with the physical environment to include social, economic, managerial, and financial aspects. Citizen participation in the planning process, especially participation of the poor and the minorities, has become standard in public planning. Evaluation of interactions among programs has led to the demand for a coherent national growth policy.

The 1970s and 1980s were years of consolidation, evaluation, and reorganization in public planning. The theme of the period was economy and efficiency, and the emphasis was on managerial competence and the cost/benefit ratio of programs. The focus was on devolution of authority and responsibility to general and local governments rather than to special districts; strengthening the role of the states in planning, coordinating, and supervision; shifting from citizen participation to increased power for elected policymaking officials; and substituting local initiative and responsibility for national policy leadership.

The policy thrust of this period was the opposite of that of the preceding two decades. The net effect was to institutionalize the reforms of the 1960s, to eliminate some of the excesses and failures of that period, and to give the country time to become accustomed to a changed national climate. The upshot was that the urban policy trends of the 1970s and 1980s persisted into the twenty-first century and provided the foundation for structural improvements at the substate level.

Notes
1. 272 U.S. 365 (1926).
2. National Industrial and Recovery Act of 1933, 73rd Congress, Session 1, Chapter 90.
3. In 1941, the NRPB also assumed the functions of the Economic Stabilization Board pursuant to the Federal Economic Stabilization Act of 1931.

4. National Resources Committee, *Our Cities: Their Role in the National Economy*, 1937.
5. P.L. 79-304, Employment Act of 1946.
6. *Schechter Poultry Corporation v. United States*, 295 U.S. 495 (1935).
7. P.L. 78-346, Servicemen's Readjustment Act (GI Bill of Rights).
8. P.L. 81-171, Housing Act of 1949.
9. P.L. 83-590, Housing Act of 1954.
10. P.L. 73-479, Housing Act of 1934.
11. Herbert Gans, *The Urban Villagers: Group and Class in the Life of Italian-Americans* (New York: Free Press, 1982).
12. Martin Anderson, *The Federal Bulldozer: A Critical Analysis of Urban Renewal, 1949–1962* (Cambridge, Mass.: MIT Press, 1964).
13. Bureau of the Budget, Circular A-95; P.L. 89-754, Demonstration Cities and Metropolitan Development Act of 1966; P.L. 90-557, Intergovernmental Cooperation Act of 1968.
14. P.L. 89-754, Demonstration Cities and Metropolitan Development Act of 1966.
15. P.L. 84-627, National Defense Highway Construction Act of 1956 (embedded in the Federal Aid Highway Act of 1956).
16. P.L. 87-866, Federal Aid Highway Act of 1962.
17. P.L. 88-158, Housing Act of 1963 (Housing for the Elderly).
18. P.L. 88-365, Urban Mass Transportation Act of 1964.
19. P.L. 86-372, Housing Act of 1959.
20. P.L. 89-174, Department of Housing and Urban Development Act of 1965.
21. Bernard J. Frieden, "Housing and National Urban Goals: Old Policies and New Realities," in *The Metropolitan Enigma: Inquiries into the Nature and Dimensions of America's "Urban Crisis,"* ed. James Q. Wilson (Cambridge, Mass.: Harvard University Press, 1968), pp. 170–171.
22. P.L. 88-452, Economic Opportunity Act of 1964.
23. P.L. 89-117, Housing and Urban Development Act of 1965.
24. P.L. 89-754, Demonstration Cities and Metropolitan Development Act of 1966.
25. Daniel Patrick Moynihan, *Maximum Feasible Misunderstanding* (New York: The Free Press, 1970).
26. Bureau of the Budget (BOB) Circular A-80.
27. Bureau of the Budget (BOB) Circular A-82.
28. P.L. 90-557, Intergovernmental Cooperation Act of 1968.
29. P.L. 90-190, Environmental Protection Act of 1970.
30. P.L. 91-609, Housing and Urban Development Act of 1970.
31. P.L. 89-749, Comprehensive Health Planning and Public Health Services Amendments of 1966.
32. Ralph W. Conant, *The Politics of Community Health* (Washington, DC: Public Affairs Press, 1968).
33. P.L. 87-415, Manpower Development and Training Act of 1962; P.L. 89-792, Manpower Development and Training Act of 1966; P.L. 90-636, Manpower Development and Training Act of 1968.
34. Robert Freilich, "Current Developments in Local Government Law," *Urban Lawyer* 6, no. 2 (1974): 289.
35. Ibid.

36. Walter W. Heller, *New Dimensions of Political Economy* (Cambridge, Mass.: Harvard University Press, 1967), p. 145. See also Heller, "A Sympathetic Reappraisal of Revenue Sharing," in *Revenue Sharing and the City*, ed. H. Perloff and R. Nathan (Baltimore: Johns Hopkins University Press, 1968), p. 6.

37. P.L. 92-512, State and Local Fiscal Assistance Act of 1972.

38. Cannon, "Federal Revenue Sharing: Born in 1972. Died 1986: R.I.P.," *New York Times*, Oct. 10, 1986, 9A at p. 31, col. 1.

39. See also four works by J. Pechman: *Federal Tax Policy* (Washington, D.C.: Brookings Institution, 1966); "Financing State and Local Government," Reprint #103 (Washington, D.C.: Brookings Institution, 1965); "Money for the States," reprinted in Joint Economic Committee of Congress, Subcommittee on Fiscal Policy, *Revenue Sharing and Its Alternatives: What Future for Fiscal Federalism?* 90th Cong., 1st Sess., at 786, 790.

40. P.L 93-383, Housing and Community Development Act of 1974.

41. P.L. 92-203, Comprehensive Employment and Training Act of 1973.

42. Robert J. Waste, *Independent Cities* (New York: Oxford University Press, 1998), p. 60. For a description of the Nixon administration's special revenue-sharing proposals and an analysis of the potential impact of community development revenue sharing, see Jeffery Pressman, "Political Implications of the New Federalism," unpublished paper, 1974, cited in *Urban Lawyer* 9, no. 1 (1977): 62n4.

43. P.L. 95-128, Urban Development Act of 1977.

44. Kenneth W. Ellison, "The Urban Development Action Grant Program: Using Federal Funds to Leverage Private Investment in Distressed Communities," *Urban Lawyer* 11, no. 3 (1979).

45. Robert H. Freilich, Paula C. Acconia, James E. Martin, "Judicial Federalism and State Sovereignty: Trends and Developments in Urban, State and Local Government Law," *Urban Lawyer* 16, no. 4 (1984): 572.

46. P.L. 104-193, Urban-Rural Recovery Act of 1983.

47. Hospital Survey and Construction Act of 1946 (Hill-Burton Act).

48. President Nixon's National Urban Policy Report (prepared by Daniel Patrick Moynihan), (Washington, D.C.: U.S. Government Printing Office, 1970).

49. P.L. 91-524, Agricultural Act of 1970.

50. P.L. 91-609, Housing and Urban Development Act of 1970.

Chapter 8

New Communities in the Future of Urban Growth Policy

The History of New Communities

One important initiative of federal urban policy in the 1960s and 1970s touched upon in Chapter 7 was the New Communities Program. This initiative was introduced in Title IV of the 1968 Housing Act and given substance by Congress in Title VII of the Housing and Urban Development Act of 1970.[1] For reasons that will become clear in this chapter, the New Communities Program never got beyond a handful of new towns sponsored by private interests and has not been an integral part of federal, state, or local urban development planning in the years since the 1970s. But the concept is a practical one and should be revisited as the nation considers strategic ways to deal with the future growth of urban areas and the redevelopment of central cities.

The idea of planned new communities is not new: St. Petersburg, Russia, founded by Peter the Great in the early eighteenth century, was one. The concept was introduced in the United States by nineteenth-century utopians and by pioneers who wanted comfortable, functioning communities that were aesthetically pleasing. Their utopian settlements—Brook Farm in Massachusetts and New Harmony in Indiana, to name two—did not endure, but their social experimentation was a powerful idea in American culture: to start from scratch and build a better community. Both utopian and pragmatic, the exploration and settlement of frontiers stirred the American imagination and energized its entrepreneurial inclinations.

Some early American cities that drew upon European experiences were soundly planned from a physical standpoint. Historians often mention Philadelphia, Savannah, Charleston, and Annapolis as examples. Washington, D.C., was a planned city designed to serve as the capital of the new nation. The strengths of the plans for Savannah, Charleston, Annapolis, and Washington have withstood revolutionary changes in urban technology and life styles to remain dominant in their cityscapes.

Frederick Law Olmstead (Olmstead, Vaux, and Company) laid out Riverside, Illinois, in 1869. Riverside was built on a two-square-mile section twelve miles west of Chicago on a commuter rail line and was the first planned "commuter" community in the United States. It was incorporated in 1875 and reached a population of 8,000.

Regional planning and new-town concepts grew more slowly in the United States than in other countries. The U.S. has always been more concerned with growth than with planning. In spite of antiplanning attitudes, however, several milestones were reached during the second quarter of the twentieth century.

In the early years of the twentieth century, the Regional Plan Association of America's "regional city" concept, briefly described in Chapter 7, was strongly influenced by the British New Towns movement initiated by Ebenezer Howard and exemplified in Welwyn Garden City.[2] The Americans Henry Wright and Clarence Stein set out to demonstrate their own "new-town" ideas in the development of Radburn, New Jersey. But the Great Depression brought the project financial trouble and it was terminated after only 600 homes were constructed. Radburn has nevertheless remained an influential example of advanced community planning, with its superblocks, pedestrian circulation, green space, and community control of common areas. The two experiments were influential in the new-towns movement after World War II in America and Europe.

Coordination of physical and social planning were central to RPAA's concept of using the site selection and planning process as a means of achieving an economic and humane distribution of population, good quality services, and local self-government. RPAA's concepts also embodied the principle of government intervention in the economy, an unpopular idea in the 1920s.

The regional planning and new-towns movement, when first introduced, attracted a substantial intellectual following in the United States but very scant political support. As a consequence, when migration to cities gathered momentum during and after World War II, and urban areas were inundated by population growth, few states or localities had any effective regional planning machinery or new-town plans to cope with that growth. Nor, in the political climate of the day, could they have used them.

In the post–World War II years, small-scale homebuilders, supported by Veterans Administration and Federal Housing Administration low-interest mortgage insurance programs, erected new subdivisions with dispatch. Little attention was paid to such factors as journey to work, public facilities and amenities, land planning, macroeconomic factors, and environmental impacts, much less social relationships.

The FHA and VA, following the practices of the marketplace, reinforced racial and class segregation during a period when Black migration, white population mobility, and rising birth rates were generating massive changes in the demography and morphology of metropolitan areas. Policies of state and local governments in the decade or two after the war reinforced the private market in suburban development. Small-scale operators flourished. Land ownership was fragmented and town-sized developments were rare because the costs of assembling sites required quick turnover to finance marginally capitalized ventures. HHFA did not encourage new towns in those years, although they could have been authorized under the Housing Act of 1949.[3]

By the mid-1950s, the structure of the housing industry began to change with the emergence of a few large-scale community builders: William Levitt, the developer of the Levittowns; Philip Klutznick, the developer of Park Forest, Illinois; and several West Coast developers (such as Park LaBrea in Los Angeles).[4] Some of the large-scale developers started with ownership of extensive lands, like Don Bren of Irvine Ranch in Orange County, California.

While the suburban boom was under way in the United States, the picture was entirely different in Europe. The United Kingdom and the countries of northern Europe developed highly rationalized methods to deal with growth problems, partly in response to the need to rebuild a war-ravaged housing stock, and partly in response to a new consciousness of the inadequacies of prior patterns of urbanization. Building on the "pragmatic idealism" of Ebenezer Howard's garden cities movement and the imaginative work of such men as Patrick Geddes, Britain adopted the New Towns Act in 1946 and set about establishing satellite communities near major metropolitan centers. New towns were buttressed by strict developmental controls, industrial expansion, location policies, and housing priorities.

In the Netherlands and Sweden, similar efforts were under way, and by the late 1950s there were impressive new towns for American planners, architects, and businessmen to visit and ponder. New towns were working in Europe, but there were doubts that they could be viable in the less regulated U.S. economy. Nonetheless, the new-towns idea in America resurfaced. The new respectability of regional planning and the emergence of a planning profession helped inject the new-towns idea into the general search for solutions to metropolitan problems.

New Communities in the 1960s

By 1960, Washington and Baltimore's regional planning agencies had proposed a series of satellite cities supported by radial transportation corridors. The satellite form of the "new community" became, in the minds of some visionaries, a cure-all for urban sprawl. The new concern with sprawl was exacerbated by the recognition that urban renewal had not been an effective counter to suburbanization. Moreover, the decline of American central cities seemed irreversible in the face of market-based land-use decisions and conflicting public policies.

New towns were still held back as a generalized approach to urban growth policy by the opposition of central-city mayors and the home-building industry. Several influential big-city mayors saw suburban new towns as a danger to their eroding revenue base. The smaller operators among the homebuilders (who constituted 90% of the industry) viewed new towns as an opportunity only for large-scale developers who could assemble the land required for a new town. Some policymakers and social scientists doubted the ability of new towns to handle America's more difficult urban issues, such as poverty and race relations, or to provide the freedom of choice for the homebuyer in a planned environment.

Reston and Columbia are outstanding examples of the new towns of that era. In 1960, Robert E. Simon, the owner of Carnegie Hall, sold the property. He was compelled under the Internal Revenue Code to reinvest in real estate in the same tax year to avoid heavy capital-gains taxes. He acquired 7,600 acres in Fairfax County, Virginia—the Sunset Hills property—where he decided to build the new town of Reston, derived from the initials of his name.[5] The idea was consistent with the Washington region's Year 2000 Plan satellite city proposals. But there was no basis for a new town in local or state land-use and public facilities policy. Moreover, Simon's project was not viewed favorably by HHFA and other federal agencies. Its design was unconventional and therefore suspect from the point of view of investors. Fairfax County officials were uncertain of the merits of Simon's project, although in the end they approved it.

Simon proceeded to develop Reston, but he was inadequately capitalized. The community's first homes came onto the market just as interest rates began to climb. Sales lagged and control of the project passed to its principal backer, the Gulf Oil Corporation. After a careful financial analysis, Gulf Oil continued the development more or less as conceived.

Reston was important to the contemporary new-towns movement because it reintroduced the ideas of mixed land uses and housing types as an alternative to prevailing patterns of homogeneous suburban residential subdivisions. In spite of financial reverses, Reston's creative design made it a national landmark and it inspired new adherents to the new-towns movement. Reston's proximity to Washington, D.C., was also important, as national media and opinion leaders focused national attention on the development.

Shortly after Simon founded Reston, James W. Rouse launched Columbia in Howard County, Maryland, halfway between Washington and Baltimore. Rouse was a mortgage banker, shopping-center developer and urban improvement activist who combined a flair for financial packaging and marketing with a missionary's zeal for new towns and socially oriented private enterprise. The land for Columbia was secretly assembled through many separate purchases, and the assembly and development program were well financed by the Connecticut General Life Insurance Company.

Unlike Simon, whose concern was with the architecture and physical design in Reston, Rouse placed his emphasis on community planning and management of the development process. The rapid acceptance of Columbia by home seekers and industry were persuasive arguments for the new-town approach. The Columbia experience demonstrated that new towns could be profitable and could offer a humane suburban environment.

Neither Reston nor Columbia addressed any of the difficult problems of central cities. Both demonstrated that racial integration in housing was practical, but within middle- and upper-income groups. Jointly they lent impetus to making new towns practical as business ventures. Both developments were major influences on the thinking of local governments regarding land-use policies.

During the period of the early 1960s, the housing industry underwent another transformation. Several of the country's major industries and new conglomerates were entering community building: ITT absorbed homebuilder Levitt. Boise-Cascade, Westinghouse, General Electric, Chrysler, and Humble Oil also embarked on the development of several full-scale new towns. Big-city mayors' opposition to new towns began to soften in light of arguments that new towns had the potential of solving some of their problems by relating jobs to housing, whereas conventional suburbs were limited to providing one-class housing and rarely could do anything to address employment.

Although attempts were made in the early 1960s to provide mortgage insurance for large-scale land acquisition and development of new communities, opposition of real estate organizations, builders, and mayors was successful in preventing legislation on the subject until 1966. Finally, Title X of the 1966 Housing Act allowed FHA to insure loans for land development that met certain criteria, but it would not insure loans for land acquisition.[6] No new communities were approved under the program, although a few small projects were attempted. It seemed apparent that this limited program offered little incentive for new-town development.

Interest in a national urban-growth policy continued to intensify in the 1960s and 1970s as the federal government tried to deal simultaneously with the problems of urban poverty and migration of people from rural areas. During his presidency in the 1960s, Lyndon Johnson focused on the problem, and his secretary of agriculture, Orville Freeman, proposed a "balanced" growth policy aimed at distributing the population between urban and rural areas. Members of Congress from both parties sponsored various proposals to stem rural migration and to promote a more "rational" distribution of people and industry.

In response to the growing concern, the U.S. Advisory Commission on Intergovernmental Relations (ACIR) conducted a study of urban growth policy. Its 1968 report, *Urban and Rural America: Policies for Future Growth*, offered three major recommendations for federal and state policies:

1. Development of a national policy to guide specific decisions at the national level which affect patterns of urban growth and the assignment of growth policy responsibility to an executive agency and a congressional committee.
2. Redirection of multistate economic planning and development agencies to charge them with carrying out national urban growth policies through their regional programs.
3. Development of state policy on urban growth including (a) coordination of planning activities and relating them to national and regional policy; (b) conformity of programs of state agencies to state urbanization plans; (c) formal review by the state of metropolitan, multicounty and local comprehensive plans and implementing ordinances and projects which have impact beyond the jurisdiction's borders to assure their conformity with the state plan.[7]

ACIR's report suggested the components of a national urban growth policy, including federal tax and contract incentives to influence industrial locations; federal building and facility location criteria to serve growth objectives; resettlement allowances; training programs and job banks for migrants from and residents of labor-surplus areas; elimination of state or regional variations in public assistance programs; and family planning.

Such policies directed at people and industries were to be put with a new program of federal assistance through low-interest loans and capital grants for land acquisition; direct federal involvement in large-scale urban development;

federal assistance and tax incentives for new communities; and development of experimental new towns on federal lands.

ACIR recognized the importance of complementary state policies to deal with urban growth. Its report emphasized establishing state and local development agencies to undertake new communities as public ventures; coordinating state capital improvements to further state urbanization policy; and developing new types of ordinances and regulations to facilitate planned development. States were also urged to provide credit facilities for desirable development; reform property taxes that might adversely affect new communities; strengthen county and municipal governments; and exercise control of development at highway interchanges and over rights-of-way.

The ACIR report lent credence to ideas of urban growth policy and new towns. It also analyzed the political and policy constraints that held back development of new towns and helped lay a political foundation for efforts to produce urban growth and develop new-towns policies.

The ACIR report and mounting interest in new towns helped allay opposition, so Congress enacted Title IV of the 1968 Housing Act, which contained provisions for federal debt guarantees for land acquisition and development of new communities. The program was confined to private developers, however, and the term "new communities" was emphasized to avoid the connotation of independent new towns.

HUD established guidelines for Title IV assistance and by 1973 had issued debt guarantees to Jonathan and Cedar Riverside, Minnesota (the latter a high-density in-town development in Minneapolis); St. Charles City, Maryland; Flower Mound, Woodlands, and San Antonio Ranch, Texas; Maumell, Arkansas; Riverton, New York; and Park Forest South, Illinois.

In the fall of 1968, Albert Rains, recently retired from Congress, where he had chaired the House Banking and Currency Committee, and Laurence Henderson organized the National Committee on Urban Growth Policy. The committee was sponsored jointly by the National Association of Counties, the National League of Cities, the National Conference of Mayors, and Urban America, Inc. The committee comprised congressmen, mayors, governors, and county commissioners.

The committee toured European new towns under the auspices of Urban

America and conducted a series of conferences and a major symposium on urban growth policy. The resulting publication, *The New City*, contained symposium papers and the report of the committee.[8] The report concluded that population pressures would worsen urban conditions and that the needs of city, suburban, and rural residents could be addressed by a comprehensive national growth policy.

The report also concluded that a new-communities policy was an essential element and that existing provisions for them were inadequate. The report called for new forms of public financing to intensify interest in new communities. It proposed federal assistance for the creation of 100 new communities of 100,000-plus population and ten new cities with populations of a million each. The committee also proposed new machinery in the executive branch to deal with urban-growth policy, state-urban development agencies, and a federal program of loans or loan guarantees for new-town development. The report called for model state legislation and research on building techniques that could be applied to new-community development.

In that same year (1968), President Johnson initiated development of 300 acres of surplus federal property in Maryland as a "new town in town," specifically to establish a socially and economically integrated community. The town was to be called Fort Lincoln. In this move, the president gave legitimacy to a new-town strategy of physical revitalization of inner cities. Johnson demanded full cooperation in the project, although the community would not be eligible for assistance under Title IV of the 1968 Housing Act if it were *publicly* developed. Negative reaction in the neighborhood prevented the project from going forward.[9]

By 1969, the opposition of mayors around the country had turned to limited support, and the U.S. Conference of Mayors, the National League of Cities, and the National Association of Counties all urged establishment of a national urbanization policy. Changes in the housing and development industries, the successes of Reston and Columbia, and the deficiencies in Title IV as a vehicle for new-communities programs all had begun to turn opinion in Congress. The Nixon administration, in pursuance of the Nixon urban growth policy, decided to support a new congressional initiative for new-communities development. The initiative became Title VII of the Housing and Urban Development Act of 1970 (discussed in Chapter 7). Thus, there were efforts by both the executive and legislative branches of the national government to formulate policies to guide the growth and development of urban areas, including social, economic, physical, aesthetic, and management considerations.

The operative part of Title VII was the New Communities program. Part B increased the authorization for federal debt guarantees provided initially in Title IV of the 1968 Housing Act and extended this program to public as well as to private developers. To be eligible, however, a public development agency could not use tax-exempt bonds for the portion of debt guaranteed by the federal government. As a practical matter, this restriction virtually precluded use of this section by public developers, but public agencies appeared to be eligible for the other benefits of Title VII.

New-community developers were also eligible for grants and long-term federal loans to meet interest payments on the financing needed to undertake land assembly and development. Grants-in-aid were authorized to state or local agencies to enable them to cover the cost of providing essential public services during the initial years of development before a sufficient assessable base had been established. Supplementary grants to public agencies of up to 20% of project costs were also authorized to assist in providing public facilities in new communities.

Technical assistance was authorized to aid public and private developers in carrying out new-community programs. Planning assistance was made available, especially for programs responsive to social and environmental problems or which encouraged the use of new or advanced technology. The act also permitted the federal government to use federal lands to undertake demonstration projects in new-community development.

Title VII proved to be the high point of federal policy on urban growth and new communities. It stimulated great interest in new towns and by mid-1972, HUD extended debt guarantees to all private developments.

1972: Nixon Turns Back the Clock

What Congress left murky in Part A of the 1968 Housing Act, the administration obfuscated in the first presidential report on urban growth, which seemed to return the discussion of urbanization policy to pre-1960 levels. The basic issues a national growth policy should address include the following: (1) interregional distribution of population; (2) spatial distribution of urban activities in national, regional and metropolitan terms; (3) an appropriate measure of urban-rural balance and a plan of growth centers as a means of achieving such a balance; (4) optimum size for cities, especially free-standing and satellite new communities.

While the 1968 ACIR report—and Congress in its declaration of policy in Title VII—recognized the problems of rural-urban migration and suggested that industrial location incentives were needed to alter trends, the Nixon administration insisted in its first *Report on National Growth, 1972*, that "there is no place in our country for any policy which arbitrarily dictates where and how citizens will live and work and spend their leisure time."

At that time there was no other policy or incipient policy that tried to direct the destinations of rural migrants, or which tried to reduce the rate of growth of major metropolitan areas. The irony of the Nixon administration statement was that no urban policy *was* the policy. Location of both public and private employment centers and economic base activities was optimized at the micro level of the individual agency or corporation. Only in special cases, such as Appalachia, a designated federal poverty region, was any attempt made in the 1970s to provide federal funds for facilities and contracts as investments in area development. Even in Appalachia, incentives for industrial location were not complemented by disincentives for locating elsewhere. The level of public investment remained too low to produce major changes in migration patterns and employment center locations.

President Nixon's *Report on National Growth, 1972*, emphasized the difficulty of fashioning national policy on urbanization and concluded that "it is not feasible for the highest level of government to design policies for development that can operate successfully in all parts of the nation." In making this point, the report observed that people disagree about whether or not urban sprawl is a poor form of development. The report's conclusion: "Low-density living appears to be the style of living preferred by our population."

Where Are We Now?

In the early years of the twenty-first century, there was still no official national policy on urban growth nor has a new-communities program been made a viable tool for organizing development. Neither did the Nixon administration or any subsequent one actively encourage public agencies to utilize the program. The public service grants were not funded and no encouragement of state or metropolitan urban growth policy developed.

Thus "new communities" has been a neglected federal program since the 1970s. No guidelines or policies govern where new communities should be constructed. The development of new communities has been left entirely to private initiative, with local, regional, and state agencies maintaining the right of veto through the now-defunct A-95 review process.

From the standpoint of the federal and state governments, new communities are not a preferred form of development. Areas organizing growth in such nodes receive no better federal treatment than those that allow the market to determine the course of development. The "new communities" of Title VII have demonstration and experimental qualities, but they have not been a serious federal stratagem or means of addressing national or regional growth problems.

Much lip service and misplaced money was spent on the concept of "balance" in the 1960s and 1970s. As used in Title VII, in President Nixon's *Report on National Growth, 1972,* and in rural development legislation, "balance" was more of a political than an economic concept. In practice, "balance" meant distributing federal dollars evenly among congressional districts, regardless of the effect on population distribution or economic and urban development.[10]

Rural-urban migration trends have been what they have been. As farms mechanized and consolidated, farm jobs became scarce and farm workers had to find work elsewhere. Nearby cities, in spite of their problems, seemed to offer a broader range of employment, educational, cultural, and housing opportunities than rural areas and small towns. The metropolis, with its large component of service industries, offers steady jobs at wages that are not usually found in rural and small-town areas.

The other side of the "balance" issue is that industries seeking to relocate are likely to be highly capitalized enterprises in need of highly trained workers. Unskilled workers in a labor-surplus area are no longer an attractive resource to such industries. Labor-surplus areas are also likely to have weak assessable bases, and as a consequence low levels of public services. Thus these areas are not attractive to the managerial and professional people who are required for operating modern industries.

Policy Implications

This analysis leads to some politically difficult conclusions: some rural and urban areas probably cannot grow; some will continue to lose population. If the stream of migrants to major metropolises were to be diverted, growth centers of substantial size would be required so that sufficient diversity and opportunity for employment of unskilled and semiskilled labor would be possible. Such centers should be within the orbit of larger urban growth centers. Also, an important public role is improvement of community facilities and services, whether to provide magnets for people and industry or to serve populations that continue to live in both metropolitan and nonmetropolitan areas.

The first of these conclusions evokes the issue of optimum city size. In a rational growth policy, this issue relates not only to new towns but to existing cities as well. Some cities may already be so large as to be dysfunctional, and reducing their size is an almost insurmountable problem. The architect Peter Calthorpe and the urban economist Anthony Downs propose specific plans to contain urban sprawl in two separate works published respectively in 1993 and 1994. Downs's critique of Calthorpe's work in a lengthy appendix lends a sense of realism to the concepts of both authors.[11]

As indicated above, larger cities provide higher personal incomes, even when the cost of living is held constant. Ironically, attitude surveys consistently report that people prefer small towns, but their behavior suggests that only a few can afford them. Thus, since the present system of city sizes is relevant to economic life, trying to change it may require substantial changes in the national economy.

The growing concern with diseconomies of scale, however, has produced counter-pressures to urban aggregation. Environmental and energy costs have discouraged expansion of cities at the rates of the recent past. The social costs of bigness are great but difficult to calculate, and there are benefits from size that offset some of the social costs. Cultural, leisure, and recreational opportunities tend to be more varied in larger metropolises, as do educational opportunities. Health systems are more sophisticated and extensive.

One stratagem for dealing with the problems of optimum size proposes that migrants be deliberately attracted to *middle-sized* metropolitan areas that are in rapid economic growth. In such areas, new communities can help organize growth in ways that avoid the environmental and fiscal problems of the larger metropolises, and the economic growth rate is sufficient to absorb rural or inner-city migrants into the work force with minimal dislocation. New-community development would become a means of creating an upwardly mobile population.

The logic of this stratagem is straightforward: such metropolises already have rapid growth rates and so require less subsidy or incentive to develop. Natural trends can be captured. Some are closer to labor-surplus areas, such as Appalachia. They consistently have lower rates of unemployment than major metropolises. Many of them are reaching the capacity to compete with larger urban areas in cultural and educational facilities.

Such areas should be a primary focus of a national growth policy that aims at maintaining an interregional population balance, limiting expansion of large metropolitan areas, and addressing the critical socioeconomic problems of urbanization. Such a strategy could also be used to reorganize urban systems.[12]

A secondary element in dealing with migration patterns and interregional distribution of population could be establishment of moderate-sized new communities centered on large public investments or specialized economic activities where good transportation and land are available.

Two such projects were built in the Appalachia region: Midlands, Kentucky, and Timber Lake, Tennessee. Both were responses to federal investments in flood control, power generation, and recreational development. Projects by the Corps of Engineers, U.S. Forestry Service, and the Tennessee Valley Authority generated sufficient economic activity to produce urban settlements capable of supporting sizable populations. Such enterprises might be marginal, however, and depend on linkages to larger metropolitan areas.[13] In most rural areas, a principal function of new communities would be to provide basic community services.

Such was the case of Soul City, North Carolina, approved by HUD for Title VII support in 1972. The size of the development (25,000) was insufficient to support substantial economic-base activities, but it might have become one element among the urban settlements in the North Carolina Piedmont economic region (which includes the cities of Raleigh, Durham, and Winston-Salem), thus aiding economic mobility for the rural Black population.

A third element in the strategy of urban growth would deal with super-metropolises. These huge aggregations of urban communities require special attention in two respects. First, their limited space must be better organized, and, second, the generative forces of growth must be captured to provide major assistance in dealing with social issues. This means that for both environmental and social reasons, new urban development should be restricted to planned new communities consistent with regional and state policies. It also means that new communities in metropolitan regions should be linked or paired with redevelopment and relocation programs of cities and inner suburbs. Whenever people are to be displaced by redevelopment schemes, public or private, new communities to accommodate them should be built before actual displacement takes place. The principal thrust of the planning and construction of new communities in central cities should be to replace old, run-down areas where structures have outlived their usefulness. The sequence of the redevelopment should be deliberately planned to avoid harmful consequences to neighborhood communities such as those Herbert Gans describes in *The Urban Villagers*.[14]

In the preceding pages, we have reviewed some of the problems of developing a national urbanization program and we have touched briefly on the shortcomings of comprehensive regional planning. Most multistate planning has concentrated, as in Appalachia, the Ozarks, and New England, on general economic development and provision of public infrastructure. Where growth centers have been an element of planning, the resources available to achieve such objectives have been largely absent.

On the substantive level, state planning is little better. New York's Urban

Development Corporation (UDC) proposed a state growth policy centered on new communities, arguing that at least half of the increase in the population of the state over a projected thirty-year period should be housed and employed in new communities. UDC projected costs, made a preliminary reconnaissance of sites, and outlined the legislation that would be required to bring such a program into being.

The UDC report recommended state and federal funding to support such development. UDC also recommended establishment of a new-communities site-selection process, review of and coordination with related state programs, a research-and-development program for new development and urban systems, measures to assure availability of an adequate labor force for each new town, incentives for industrial development, and management training for public and private new-town developers.

From the state/regional comprehensive planning viewpoint, site selection is central. Under existing policy, site selection is almost entirely a private activity. In most new-town projects approved for Title VII support, state and local planning officials were unaware that a developer was about to propose a new town, let alone the location of sites! Few if any states have adopted criteria against which to judge new-town sites. Such criteria would include ecological or environmental impacts; public costs and benefits, such as regional airports; or capacity of a site to serve labor or consumer markets and be able to work in a regional or statewide system of urban settlements.

Beyond criteria for assessing proposals, a minimal urbanization policy would involve selection of optimum sites or areas for new communities as an element of comprehensive regional planning. The institutional weakness of this one element of comprehensive planning is scarcely improved upon at the local or town level. Most planning and zoning patterns do not envision new-town development.

Relatively few jurisdictions have zoning ordinances under which new towns could be developed, as most continue to rely almost exclusively on "Euclidean" zoning.[15] Little attempt is made to provide industrial or commercial land in locations suitable for new towns or to pursue public policies that will protect coherent development such as new towns from parasitic peripheral development that provides few of the facilities or services needed by the development itself and consequently overuses those of the new town. In almost every instance the land-use regulation process is geared to deal with the small-tract builder rather than the long-term process of new-town construction.

In another respect, local planning does not comprehend going beyond land use. Great care is taken to review master plans of development and site plans of particular sectors of the new town as they reach the development stage. However, too little attention is given to the economic, fiscal, social, or institutional aspects of the development, largely because many local jurisdictions lack the staff or financial resources to hire the expert consultants. As a consequence, many jurisdictions are dependent on the input of private developers. Local jurisdictions can legally command compliance with land-use designation but generally have to negotiate (and even barter for) acceptance of conditions relating to social, economic, and institutional aspects of development.

Land-use and development law is mostly a product of an earlier and simpler era and generally provides little basis for assurance that a new community is well balanced from an economic or social point of view, or that an adequate internal bus system will be in place, or that there will be a functioning health system, or that recreational facilities will be properly financed and operated. Local governments are rarely prepared to deal with such questions.

While most developers have little interest in the comprehensive planning a successful new-town venture requires, the sophistication of private new-town planning has made impressive progress. Especially with the advent of the pre-application and application processes of Title VII, some social planning is undertaken by the developers, whose enterprise has to show economic viability to qualify for assistance. Ironically, more can be done through federal regulations to produce a functional new community if its developer seeks federal assistance than can be done through local planning and regulatory processes if he does not.

Planning and designing a new town are intricate processes. They start with site availability. Development objectives must constantly be tested for their economic feasibility. The new community must achieve a reasonable balance between the local labor force and available jobs for a substantial and varied population. A population of 100,000, for instance, requires employment for 30,000 to 40,000 workers and about an equal number of dwellings.

These very basic objectives must be tested against market absorption rates over a reasonable period and against cash-flow requirements to sustain the pace of development. They also determine, based on the sectors of the economy likely to be served by the new town, the probable income mix needed to balance the system. The mix of income groups in a development is usually determined by the price structure for housing. In a new town, however, a conscious effort to supply a proper share of moderate- or low-cost housing requires an analysis of the probable labor force as well as the conventional housing market.

Whereas most subdivision developments tend to attract a homogeneous population, the new town strives to attract a range of ages and incomes—especially as it matures. This objective is achieved in part by producing homes for both rent and sale, and homes of different types and sizes to serve the more diverse markets it seeks to attract.

The demographic and economic profile projected for the new town provides the basic numbers that directly influence plans for public services such as schools, recreation, health, and transportation. Such projections must also operate as constraints or opportunities in the design of neighborhoods or other social elements of the new town, such as the extent to which neighborhoods will contain similar or dissimilar types of housing, and distribution throughout the community of low-income housing or special types of housing for the elderly or singles.

Such planning leads to consideration of the social-physical hierarchy of the community and its basic design concepts. Most American new towns have followed the Columbia model, using the neighborhood as the basic social and physical unit and then combining several neighborhoods into a "village" at the level below that of the entire town. The typical social organization of cities is neighborhoods within villages and villages within the city.

The units in the hierarchy are normally given identity and cohesion in a similar hierarchical system. A school, a convenience shopping center, and a neighborhood recreation center are linked to their neighborhoods by vehicular and pedestrian ways. The village center provides more diversity than the neighborhood center, is probably surrounded by denser housing, and offers specialized commercial or community services. The town center itself aspires to be a regional commercial and office center. This basic physical system is also linked to specialized districts for industrial employment or facilities such as lakes, golf courses, or institutions of higher learning.

A new town can deal differently with landform than a conventional tract development. The ability to cluster and vary densities within some overall average and to adjust the location of industrial and commercial districts permits the new-town developer to respect the constraints of the environment and ecology. Before moving past the design-concept stage, careful analyses must be made of the landform, microclimate, soils, geology, vegetation, and wild-life. These analyses permit a more intelligent use of environmental features such as vistas, stream valleys and flood plains, stands of trees, marshes, and so forth than when maximum yield per acre shapes the land.

Care in environmental planning also is necessary to produce a marketable environment and prevent high-cost consequences of improper development that can damage subsequent stages. A new town can expect to use less than 50% of its total acreage for construction if it is carefully planned and to reduce such external costs of development as storm-water management, air and noise pollution, and traffic congestion.

New-town planning provides the missing links in most local planning: urban design and scheduling. Most local plans contain very generalized classifications of land, road networks, and location of public facilities. The new town must be designed in greater detail to include such elements as pedestrian systems and centers. The gap between general planning and detailed design of structures permits testing of general objectives and more precise programming of facilities and services. It also allows advance acquisition of private and public open spaces. Since the detailed design of a new town anticipates a schedule of development, this also can facilitate public budgeting.

Planning a new town is subject to the discipline of the cash-flow curve whether its developer is a public or private corporation. Production must meet a schedule sufficient to pay debt service, at the very least. If a new town takes twenty years to build, it is likely that more money will be spent in the first ten years for land development and construction than will be returned to the developer in sales and leases.

Thus, the problem of "front-end" money remains the most difficult aspect of new-town development—the biggest deterrent to the private sector. Because the amount of money required to assemble and develop enough land for a new town is so great, anything that prolongs any stage of the development, or adds risk through uncertainty of public action, increases the amount of interest paid to financing institutions funding the project.

Land assembly is an important aspect of this overall economic and financial picture. If a developer must undertake prolonged negotiations to purchase land, its value increases, producing both higher costs and higher property taxes. If the land cannot be assembled in a reasonable period of time, the developer may be forced into premature and partial development through conventional methods—with adverse environmental and fiscal consequences.

For new towns to become a principal thrust of federal or state urbanization policy, public assistance may be necessary in identifying sites and in land assembly. Sites suitable for development and in single ownership are rare, especially in major metropolitan areas. One approach to the problem is a state authority that has powers of condemnation to assemble land for development. The substate administrative planning districts we propose in Chapter 9 could be the alternative to a statewide authority, especially in states where urban development varies from region to region.

Either a statewide authority or a substate administrative and planning district could be positioned by law to use public powers to assemble land and to obtain favorable interest rates through tax-exempt bonds. Such an authority would reduce the time and costs associated with new-town development. If public developers may also sell or lease to private enterprise for all aspects of development and lend assets for special elements, such as low- and moderate-income housing, the discipline of private profit can be retained in the production of new towns which also serve important public purposes. Such efforts could be combined with Title VII debt guarantees to private participants in the venture.

The government's role could be limited to creating incentives and conditions for private investment. For example, say to the private sector, "If you want cheap land for development, it must be according to local or regional planning guidelines and you have to pick up a portion of the costs of the infrastructure." Local authorities could use tax-increment financing (explained in Chapter 3) to keep infrastructure ahead of needs with real estate tax guarantees.

One of the front-end costs of new-town development is the production of public infrastructure. The highest-cost elements—trunk sewers, water production and transmission systems, and major access roadways—should be in place before construction commences—well before the population or assessed values are created to support them. Under normal development practices, the developer makes a "contribution" to the sewer agency or the roads department for extension of service, that is, pays the initial costs for construction, which are then added to the price of each lot as it is sold. This arrangement works well when a few hundred lots are the total development and are marketed within a four- to six-year period. In a new town the cost of the infrastructure cannot be borne by the first lots sold, which might be a tenth of the total development served by the basic system. These elements would cause an early negative cash flow and therefore the developer might find them to be intolerable.

Title VII sought to alleviate the problem of cash flow in the debt guarantee provisions, in the long-term debt-service loans, and in the supplemental grants-in-aid for public facilities. The 1972 Housing Act also provided for community-development block grants that were designed to make possible public-sector investment in the public infrastructure of new communities. Very little use was made of these latter grants during the Nixon administration or in subsequent administrations.

Each of the financial elements discussed above has always raised questions about the capacity of local and state governments to work with the development of new towns. Coordination of capital improvements with a development plan and construction schedule is of great importance—so much so that some developers have preferred to incur the cost of turnkey construction rather than to rely on the public sector to have the facilities in place on time.

State and local agencies are notorious for operating without due regard for anything other than their special function and its clientele. Thus, a state college may seek to locate in a new town at a different location and at a different time than is specified in a regional or state development plan. Such a move can increase infrastructure costs and radically compromise the financial viability of a new-town project. For example, a state roads agency may give a low priority to an interchange needed in the first five years of a new town to enhance industrial development. The school system may bus new-town children to vacant classrooms elsewhere rather than build schools that would not be filled immediately, thus compromising for new families a sense of community and identity within the new town.

To meet such problems, it would seem desirable during the development stage of new-town planning and building to establish a new-town development district with the power to coordinate, and if necessary construct, all public facilities and works in the new town. This agency could operate the facilities.

There are three economic tests of feasibility for a new community: (1) It must serve the economic objectives of the region in which it is located, in terms of what it adds to the housing supply, employment opportunities, and the general economic health of the region. (2) It must be a financially sound investment, with its housing, commercial, and industrial sectors so well balanced that it will earn a profit or surplus sufficient to pay debt service and debt retirement. (3) It must be fiscally desirable to state and local governments.

The experience with new communities during the last four decades of the twentieth century leads to the conclusion that a new-town strategy should be given serious consideration as a national—indeed local, regional, and state—policy for management of urbanization. However, the critical dimensions of new-town planning, development, and financing run contrary to most existing governmental practices. New-town planning is comprehensive; local and state planning has always been functionally fragmented—catering to the "vertical autocracies" of federal, state, and municipal governments.[16] The substate districts proposed in Chapter 9 would solve this problem.

New-town financing and development requires a long-term commitment; public regulation and budgeting is short term, and often *post factum*. In many cases, local governments lack the professional capacity to understand, much less evaluate or participate in, a proposed new town. A physical plan and a good design provide the spaces for social and civic activity to occur. They provide some constraints and opportunities for social contact. They do not provide the processes and the institutions that give a place its sense of community, or lack of it, or which impart its character.

Some basic aspects of the social system can be planned, or at least planned for. Racial integration is an example. Title VII assistance requires an affirmative equal-opportunity program in management, home sales and rentals, business leasing, and so forth. Generally, new towns have demonstrated that open housing policies work and that below-market housing in a neighborhood need not affect its desirability or property values.

Such planning is rudimentary and has long been assumed by new-town developers. What seems more important is provision of community services and fostering of associations of residents capable of knitting them together as a community. Providing for adequate healthcare, for instance, may involve intricate arrangements with hospitals, insurance companies, employers, and a local medical association. Providing for the religious life of the community goes beyond reserving lots for churches. Columbia, Maryland, residents chose to foster an ecumenical movement. Other new towns may seek to accommodate other forms of worship and religious practices.

Such considerations feed back into physical plans and capital improvements. If neighborhood is to be emphasized, can churches and schools be made multipurpose institutions? Can arrangements be made for the care of the children of working parents? Can mechanisms be created to meet problems that cannot be anticipated before people arrive? In some cases, rudimentary structures may be necessary. Community associations and/or municipalities may be needed to perform basic services. As Kraemer and others have cautioned, the social/community issues can be very difficult to manage in a new community.[17]

In Columbia, a panel of experts helped formulate the new town's objectives and outlined some of its basic social arrangements. A vice president of the development firm was charged with responsibility for institutional development. This person worked with regional and national institutions to facilitate their location and activity in the new community. He also served as a point of access for citizens who needed advice on establishing community groups.

This is the function of a catalyst to help new groups get started or to provide backing, seed money, or technical assistance for institutional development.

Alternative approaches would be a community foundation independent of both the developer and local government, or the involvement of a university in a continuing community action program in cooperation with the new community's citizens and developer(s).

Planning for civic institutions and for community governance is often less well articulated than for social institutions. The governmental aspects of a new town involve both production functions and civic ones. The production functions usually are accounted for in the development plan itself—capital improvements and basic services such as education, public safety, and sanitation. Special arrangements may be needed for private governance, such as a homeowners association to manage common lands and recreational facilities or a health-insurance program.

The civic functions relate to how the new town operates as a polity and the extent to which citizens share responsibility for the future of the community. The civic functions include providing for meaningful experience in democratic governance. The Twentieth Century Fund in a 1971 report, *New Towns: Laboratories for Democracy*,[18] recommended that new towns become laboratories for testing new forms and processes of local self-government and that they experiment with novel means of broadening and strengthening participation by people in planning, developing, and governing their urban environment.

These proposals suggest the need for a plan of governance as a part of the comprehensive plan of new-town development. The proposals also suggest that the plan be flexible so that the governing institutions can be adjusted with each new stage of development. New-town governance offers an opportunity to demonstrate improved techniques of local governance, which could be copied by older cities and suburbs.

Finally, the need for state policy regarding new-town planning and development is of crucial importance, for in the end it is the states that control local government and so only the states can give new towns legal status as self-governing communities—or the license to experiment with new approaches to local self-government.

All these elements of the new-town planning and development process—its design, economics, social institutions, and governance—have ramifications for public policy. Substantial institutional changes are needed to aid a new town in the transition from an experimental stage of development to the main thrust of urbanization policy. At the national level, an entire range of urban-development programs must be refocused toward new towns, and federal favoritism should be accorded the ones sponsored or endorsed by state- and regional planning authorities. This would, in turn, involve amendments to federal law to support creation of state-development agencies and the development of statewide, multistate, and substate regional new-town development programs. It would also mean federal emphasis on the pairing concept, whether the new town or growth center is paired with a central city or a rural labor-surplus area. Finally, federal fiscal reform would be needed to make it affordable for some areas to lose population without suffering reduction in intergovernmental aid. Tax reform could also provide incentives for locating and investing in new towns.

State policies on new-town location and size should be developed in concert with environmental and transportation policies. States must also organize their capital programs to use effectively the enormous investment required to develop new communities and to realize the sought-after social benefits and revenue.

Roads, mass transit, universities, hospitals, and airports are useful to new towns only when such facilities are well managed. This means strengthening state planning, budgeting, and administrative processes along the lines suggested in Chapter 10. It also means creation of development authorities or substate districts with the necessary powers to assemble land, coordinate public services, and, if necessary, produce new towns themselves.

Revenue reform is needed at the state level to reduce gross disparities in service levels and revenue yields, which lead to inefficient competition among local jurisdictions for high-yield development. The adverse effect of property taxation and assessment practices on front-end financing should be studied to devise ways to assist new towns and prevent escape from legitimate taxation. Some new towns should be permitted to experiment with land-value taxation or to create special taxing areas to support additional services.

Land-use law and regulations need reform to reconcile them to the vast changes in the development industry and the new time horizons and necessary flexibility of new-town planning and building. Local authorities also need new powers respecting urban design and new towns, ability to consider the fiscal consequences of a development, and the powers to oversee fulfillment of the social objectives of a new town.

In combination with revenue reform, states and localities should experiment with pricing systems for new-town services to attempt improved measurement of the externalities of development and to influence such behavior as commuting modes and water consumption.

The substate planning and administrative districts we propose in Chapter 9 are the type of regional structure needed to aid in the assembly of land, to help coordinate development at the local level, and to provide a financing mechanism for new-town land development and construction. Substate districts may also offer a means of maintaining public equity in new towns. Comprehensive planning will have to be strengthened vis à vis functional planning and extended to include social, economic, and governmental aspects of new-town development.

More important, the public sector, if it is to obtain a fair public benefit from new towns, must abandon its traditional adversary relationship with the private sector and participate directly in planning and development partnerships. The public should assume the role of entrepreneur and increase its planning competence and its credibility based on superior performance.

Creating a single new town is a process that blends public and private interests. Creating a system of new towns linked to regional cities is a formidable but necessary undertaking. But it should not be too difficult for so diverse a nation as the United States to attempt, for the inertia of existing patterns of urbanization is destructive of the environment and destructive of the social fabric of the country. As we have shown in earlier chapters, metropolitan and regional planning is well enough established in most urban and some rural places to provide the basis for considering how new-communities programs might be put to work in and adjacent to our cities.

There are good reasons why the new-communities idea could be made to work as an approach to the redevelopment and repopulation of central cities: (1) Land is available in the form of abandoned or unneeded/unwanted industrial, railroad, and commercial areas—many located near the heart of the city.

(2) Near-in areas of many cities have been gradually depopulating in recent decades. (3) The previous two factors mean that large-scale displacement of population and valuable urban properties may no longer be necessary. (4) The young and upwardly mobile ("yuppies") who have pioneered the "gentrification" of old, run-down inner-city neighborhoods have demonstrated that living in the city can be fun, safe, and profitable. Investments in city condos and loft apartments can be financially rewarding with value appreciation on resale. (5) A strong market for housing has developed in some large cities that takes most of the risk out of new-community projects. For example, condos in and near downtown Chicago were selling out (in 2000) before they were constructed or completed. Recovery of front-end costs has been quick. (6) Cities are competing for tourism and conventions, which has prompted continued investment in public amenities and city beautification projects. (7) The performing arts, museums, and educational institutions are of growing importance in American cities. In 2000, Chicago outranked Los Angeles and New York in "off-Broadway" productions and in the generation of new talent. This situation is changing the popular perception of "mainline" American cities. Chicago also outranked East and West Coast cities in percentage increases in recent years in attracting vacationers and tourists from Europe.

The new-community concept as a direction for urban development in the future will require focused policymaking and planning in a closely coordinated effort by federal, state, and local officials. The federal government will be crucial to the up-front financial underwriting essential to getting any of these projects off the ground. The state governments hold the key to the coordination and planning of the state resources critical to the phasing of public infrastructure and services in the practical matter of building new communities. Those new communities that are developed within the boundaries of a central city will need the planning support of a regional agency positioned to coordinate regional infrastructure and services that are outside the legal purview of the city. The prospects for moving in the direction of new communities and new towns to accommodate expanding urban populations will be greatly facilitated by the creation of the competent multipurpose substate planning and administrative districts described in Chapters 9 and 10.

Notes

1. New Communities Acts of 1968 and 1970, P.L. 90-448 (1968) and Urban Growth and New Community Development Act, P.L. 91-609 (1970).
2. See Ebenezer Howard, *Garden Cities of Tomorrow* (London: Sonnenschein, 1902): The book was first issued in 1898 under the title *Tomorrow: A Peaceful Path to Real Reform*, and has been reprinted under its present title by MIT Press, Cambridge, Massachusetts, 1965. The New Towns Movement is discussed in Sir Frederick J. Osborne, *The New Towns: Answer to Megalopolis* (London: McGraw-Hill, 1963). For American thinking on the subject, see Clarence Stein, *Toward New Towns for America* (Liverpool: Liverpool University Press, 1951), reprinted by MIT Press, Cambridge, Mass., 1966.
3. P.L. 81-171, Housing Act of 1949.
4. Edward P. Eichler and Marshall Kaplan, *The Community Builders* (Berkeley: University of California Press, 1967).
5. A careful analysis of the history of Reston's planning and development may be found in Kathryn Stone, *Reston: A Study in Beginnings* (Washington, D.C.: Washington Center for Metropolitan Studies, unpublished MS., 1966).
6. P.L. 89-754, Demonstration Cities and Metropolitan Development Act of 1966.
7. U.S. Advisory Commission on Intergovernmental Relations, *Urban and Rural America: Policies for Future Growth* (Washington, D.C.: U.S. Government Printing Office, 1968).
8. Donald Canty, ed., *The New City* (New York: Praeger, 1969).
9. Martha Derthick, "Defeat at Fort Lincoln," *Public Interest* (Summer 1970): 3–39.
10. *Report on National Growth, 1972* (Washington, D.C.: U.S. Government Printing Office, 1972).
11. Anthony Downs, *New Visions for Metropolitan America* (Washington, D.C.: Brookings Institution, 1994); and Peter Calthorpe, *The Next American Metropolis: Ecology, Community, and the American Dream* (Princeton, N.J.: Princeton Architectural Press, 1993).
12. See Marcou, O'Leary and Associates, Inc., *New Community Development: Location Analysis of Potential Sites/Economic and Legal Settings* (Washington, D.C.: Marcou, O'Leary and Associates, 1972).
13. Canty, *New City*.
14. Herbert Gans, *The Urban Villagers: Group and Class in the Life of Italian-Americans* (New York: Free Press of Glencoe, 1962).
15. The term "Euclidean zoning" derives from the U.S. Supreme Court case *Village of Euclid v. Ambler Realty Co.*, 272 U.S. 365, decided in 1926 by a 4–3 vote in which the Court first upheld the validity of zoning.
16. The term "vertical functional autocracies" was coined by David B. Walker, formerly executive director of the Advisory Commission of Intergovernmental Relations.
17. For a well-informed discussion of this point, see Kenneth L. Kraemer, "Developing Governmental Institutions in New Communities," *Urban Lawyer* 1, no. 3 (1969). Kraemer's footnote citations also yield valuable insights into the problems of governance in new communities.
18. Twentieth Century Fund, *New Towns: Laboratories for Democracy*, 1971. (The Twentieth Century Fund was renamed The Century Foundation in 2000.)

Chapter 9

States' Responsibility for Urban Development

Our cities and their environs must be made comfortable, energizing, culturally stimulating, and convenient places for everyday living—for residents and visitors alike. Americans have worked toward these goals for all of their history, but they have never before had the wealth of resources that are present in our day. To achieve the goals of a better life in our cities, the services that make our cities work must be made optimally efficient by improved planning and administration at the governmental levels best equipped to manage them. We have the knowledge and skills to make such improvements, and they can be achieved incrementally. What we lack is the focused leadership of policymakers to make the necessary adjustments in our planning and administrative systems at the state and local levels.

This chapter proposes a model substate planning and administrative mechanism that could fill the partial void that exists in metropolitan areas between the state governments and local governments. The model stands on its own conceptual base and could be applied in any urban region in America. The problem is political acceptance—how to get local leaders to accept any new multipurpose metropolitan or regional governance structure. Hence, we propose that the model be built upon the traditional structure of county governments and their equivalent in Connecticut, where counties have been eliminated, and in Hawaii, where the state government administers regional services. The authority of the substate districts must, of course, derive from their states. Their operational authority would be enhanced by a federal policy requiring the states to coordinate all federal grants and funds for regional and local programs through these substate planning and administrative districts. Anthony Downs makes a similar suggestion in his 1994 book *New Visions for Metropolitan America*, where he observes that "coordination of federal agency funding has the ... advantage of requiring only a single political action by Congress."[1]

Areas of State Responsibility

As we saw in Chapter 7, the federal government in the past has vigorously promoted a restructuring of local governance in response to chronic urban needs. Yet the major role for originating and implementing actual changes in local governance falls to the states, because they are in the first instance responsible for the structure and functioning of local government. Within the limitations of the U.S. Constitution and their own constitutions, the states are at liberty to determine the kind of local government suitable to meet the needs of their citizens. The Tenth Amendment to the U.S. Constitution is explicit: "The powers not delegated to the United States by the Constitution, nor prohibited by it to the States, are reserved to the States respectively, or to the people." Professor Charles L. Black once wrote that an enormous advantage of our federal system is that the "state governments *are* omni-competent; no plea of *ultra vires* can prevail against them."[2]

The Eleventh Amendment addresses the sovereign immunity of the states: "The Judicial Power of the United States shall not be construed to extend to any suit in law or equity, commenced or prosecuted against any one of the United States by Citizens of another State, or by Citizens or subjects of a Foreign State." Recent Supreme Court decisions have moved toward a literal interpretation of the Tenth and an interpretation of the Eleventh that favors the states, thereby strengthening the position of the states in the federal system.[3] Since the Nixon years, most of the states have accepted responsibilities for local and regional problems, but much remains to be done. The time has come when the states need to create new multipurpose planning and administrative districts in the no-man's-land at the substate/regional level.

The objective is to provide for the planning and administration of selected local and state functions, especially where there are gaps and overlaps in regional planning and services. For this purpose, we propose that the substate planning and administrative districts be based on existing counties or groups of counties. If they are based on counties, the new substate districts will enhance the power and functioning of existing jurisdictions and therefore could be supported rather than opposed by local political leaders.

The new substate districts will provide states, towns, and the federal government with effective planning and administrative capacity for addressing problems that are of mutual concern. This chapter explores alternative models of the proposed substate districts and recommends one. We lay the groundwork by reviewing the principal areas of state responsibility for local and regional services.

Education

Vocational education, technical institutes, and manpower training and retraining are strategic means by which local communities can improve their economic base. Cooperation among educational institutions in regions can make a significant contribution to manpower requirements for regional economic development. Regional economic plans that take into account the regional labor market are essential to educators in projecting the job mix that guides vocational education. Community colleges and technical institutes can influence the location of industry, for these educational facilities train manpower and provide pools of professional and skilled talent.

The substate districts could be given the responsibility for planning and administering those economic-development-related educational services. They could benefit from a regional approach, utilizing regional resources and taking advantage of economies of scale. These are critically needed educational services in the ongoing task of maintaining and expanding economic opportunities, both locally and nationally. It is up to the states to take the strategic initiative; neither the federal government nor local governments have the constitutional authority.

Health Services

Health services are subject to economies of scale and so comprehensive area-wide planning of health facilities should be reasserted in federal and state policy. Many communities have neither the resources nor the markets to justify provision of even minimal health services. Regional planning should include measures to provide health services sufficient to meet regional needs. A state's health plans should envision a regional system of delivery that sets a floor under available services. State initiative in creating multipurpose substate planning and administrative districts can facilitate regional cooperation and can be the mechanism through which minimum state standards are established.

Substate districts would be the means by which regional health planning and operations are coordinated with related state responsibilities for education, welfare, code standards, enforcement, and sanitation, and with mental health and preventive medicine. A major value of state planning through substate districts can be to provide guidance and incentive for regional planning and operation in bringing about effective interrelations among otherwise compartmentalized functions. For example, a major contribution of the federal poverty program in the 1960s was the discovery of the close correlation between sickness and dropouts, ill health, and chronic unemployment and dependency among minorities.

Public Safety

Public safety is a basic responsibility of the states. In many cases public safety has been delegated to local governments, which in some jurisdictions provide primitive service at best. Even where specialized full-time personnel are available, competence may be substandard. As a practical matter, the states have a responsibility to see that adequate levels of public safety are provided to all their citizens. Many urban counties have not developed crime task forces and rely on municipal police, who are in many cases ill-prepared to investigate homicides and organized crime. Incentives for regional cooperation in the provision of communications, technical services, and training can be a beginning. For communities unable to meet their police protection needs, one option is to contract with other jurisdictions or a regional facility of state police. Some communities have taken this course. The sensible answer is to place such responsibilities with the proposed substate districts, where they can be addressed comprehensively by professional administrators.

Water Supply

Water supply has traditionally been the responsibility of households in rural areas and local governments in cities and incorporated suburbs. Faced with a chronic scarcity of water resources in urban areas and some rural ones, this function cannot be left to chance or to the limited capacity of local governments. Many states plan water needs on a state or interstate basis; others are moving in that direction. At the state level, such planning means state acquisition of major water resources and the state functioning as the wholesaler of water.

At the regional level, the state could deliver water to regional special districts incorporated by contiguous towns and cities. Special water districts can also function as wholesalers to town, municipal, and private water agencies. Since provision of water is a major factor in determining economic development, land use, and land values, a state capability in water supply provides a significant instrument in state development planning. The proposed multipurpose substate districts could serve statewide water planning needs and eventually replace water districts.

Water Pollution

Concern with water pollution as well as basic sanitary needs requires state concern with sewage and trash-disposal facilities. Inadequate local arrangements can be costly and hazardous; economies of scale can be significant. State control and development of drainage basins is in many states the only satisfactory way to secure their efficient, sanitary, and recreational use. These drainage basins are unlikely to coincide with regional boundaries for other purposes, and, where this is the case, the state should provide for the interregional development of these basins. The siting of mainline sewers and the management of water resources are major tools of land use and development. These tools should be used to further state and regional development and land-use planning and could be administered by the proposed substate planning and administrative districts.

Solid-Waste Disposal and Recycling

Solid-waste disposal and recycling are a major local expenditure. Local governments have for years been running short of locations for disposal such as landfills. Incinerators, unless of very costly design, contribute to air pollution. New devices that municipalities cannot afford may be within reach of regional or state agencies. The search for promising new technologies is a responsibility of state planning. Regional planning should include in its objectives the proper siting of solid-waste-disposal facilities. This task is a responsibility of state planning as well. The proposed multipurpose substate districts could plan the siting and administration of regional facilities for solid-waste disposal.

Regional Transportation

A state role in regional transportation has rarely been considered in states that do not have commuter railroads. State highway departments have seldom planned their grids with a serious concern for regional transportation systems. Even where state and city highway engineers work together, they do not always give attention to modes other than trucks and automobiles.

The potential of mass transit has traditionally been neglected in planning both highways and traffic control. Yet, along with sewers and water supplies, highways are major factors influencing land use and economic development. The state highway grid should be an instrument for realizing the state's development plans, and it should be a means of giving authority to regional planning. The Intermodal Surface Transportation Efficiency Act of 1991 gave state and local governments their first committed source of funds that could be used for a variety of transit and traffic improvements, not just for highways.[4] The Transportation Equity Act of 1998 (TEA-21) was designed to expand funding of ISTEA.[5] The planning objectives of these important federal initiatives could be fully realized in states that create substate planning and administrative districts and assign them responsibilities for planning and coordinating all highway and mass transportation projects except purely local ones.

Planning for Regional Economic Development

Much of state planning can be effectively applied only at the regional and local levels. Regional economic development planning must be coordinated and supervised by a state planning agency, as is already the case in some of the states. Indeed, regional planning agencies must be the connecting link between local and state planning. Regionalized state administration in highways, water, sewers, conservation, education, and other areas can back regional plans and provide a parallel linkage between state administration and local governments. The substate districts could be given the responsibility for planning and administering these strategic regional economic development functions.

State policy can do much to make regional development planning more than a competitive scramble for tax base. State fiscal policy needs to be developed in such a way as to reduce pressure on the property tax. In addition, ways need to be found to provide local governments with incentives to pool resources in creating joint industrial parks, organizing the regional labor market, and designating one or more member communities as regional growth centers. Again, the proposed substate districts would be appropriate planning and administrative mechanisms to achieve statewide objectives of regional economic development planning.

Environmental Policy

With federal encouragement (and mandates), the states have taken on responsibilities as custodians of environmental quality. These responsibilities include regulation of air and water pollution, preservation of natural and manmade things of beauty, recreational needs for open space, even some aspects of urban design. The federal government has imposed mandates in most of these areas and provided funds to the states for carrying out these responsibilities. The mandates are spelled out in the National Environmental Policy Act of 1969, the Water Resources Planning Act of 1965, the Clean Air and Water Acts of 1973, and the Clean Air Act Amendments of 1990.[6]

Most of the states carry out their environmental responsibilities and federal mandates through state environmental agencies and are aided by councils of governments and regional planning agencies, as well as special districts with a variety of functions that touch on environmental concerns. The multipurpose substate planning and administrative districts proposed here would bring order to the administration and enforcement of complex federal state environmental laws and regulations and ease the coordination of research and the application of new environmental technology.

Housing

Where local governments lack land and resources to meet low-income housing needs, the states have a responsibility to ensure that adequate stocks are available. A half-century of experience with federal urban renewal programs has taught local policymakers that, if low-income housing needs are left to local governments, they may play musical chairs with the poor to avoid service costs, attract development, and increase tax yields. A sad reality is that local officials are always under pressure to prevent the incursion of "undesirables" into local communities.

An effective approach to the problem of providing low-income housing requires identification and organization of the regional housing market. Of course, a cooperative regional agency made up of local communities could meet regional needs for low-income housing. In any event, the state should take responsibility for determining low-income housing needs in the state and the feasible alternatives to meet them. This responsibility requires that regional planning develop regional housing needs and alternatives. State support of regional planning should provide the funds for housing studies.

The states should accept responsibility for creating a legal climate conducive to economic and social progress in housing. That is their unique mission. The resolution of the basic economic issues of housing technology and productivity are largely in the hands of industry, finance, and the federal government. What is required of the states is a periodic reexamination of the legal and administrative practices that affect individuals and families in relation to their housing and housing options. There is a need for an urban dwellers' "bill of rights"—a radical change in the rules of the game to ensure fairness in housing, especially for people who are affected by urban development and redevelopment programs.

All of the issues discussed in the previous paragraphs could be addressed comprehensively by the proposed multipurpose substate planning and administrative districts, because the problems are primarily administrative and most of them call for research and planning. All of them would benefit from regional rather than local administration, which is the purpose of the proposed substate districts.

Fiscal Reform

The temptation to put land to immediate and intensive use in order to shore up the municipal tax base is a deterrent to the concept of the land reserve and to sound urban/environmental planning. There can be no sound environmental planning and no urban modernization without land resources. Thus, scarcity and cost of land are key to urban redevelopment. For lack of an adequate fiscal base, municipalities are often forced to subvert their planning programs to strategies for enhancing revenue yields and broadening the property tax base (the main source of "collateral" for municipal bonds to finance major infrastructure improvements). As a remedy, the states should devise systems of taxation and borrowing that would give municipal officials options to choose among competing urban development and redevelopment goals based on civic needs and benefits.

Illinois, for example, permits a variety of special municipal taxes, and so Chicago levies a local sales tax, hotel tax, parking tax, utilities tax, even a head tax on employees. These special taxes give municipal officials incentive to welcome a variety of development. Thus, a local sales tax encourages retail development because the municipality will receive revenues from retail sales. A local hotel tax encourages hotel development, and so forth. The point is that the more diversified the sources from which the municipality benefits, the freer local officials are to choose among different kinds and intensities of development. As long as revenues are related to the development, the municipality will be a winner financially, so it might as well choose the projects that officials consider to be in the public interest.

In pursuit of this goal, the states should aid municipalities in achieving sound planning by relieving them of fiscal pressures that deny the premises of land planning. Serious consideration should be given to forms of revenue, including revenue-sharing programs, which would make possible a reduced reliance on the direct tax on real estate as the predominant component of the municipal tax system. Once relieved of immediate fiscal pressures, local planning programs can become strategies for remedying environmental defects and for anticipating new environmental and functional requirements.

The proposed substate districts could play an important role in local development planning by establishing a revolving loan fund to be used by municipalities for the infrastructure required for new development. Such a revolving loan fund could be initially funded by the state legislature or as a piece of a regional shared tax base such as in the Minneapolis-St. Paul and Portland, Oregon, plans described in Chapter 4.

Fiscal reform is also needed to support the housing goals discussed earlier. Contradictory taxation policies and practices tend to cancel each other out and make difficult the achievement of housing goals. For example, there is an inconsistency between the declared national policy to provide low- and middle-cost housing and those local practices that increase shelter costs. The property tax on real estate is a fixed charge on housing that has a direct impact on the housing market. The tax on property in major cities accounts for 15 to 20% of the average monthly mortgage or rental payment. Reduction or withdrawal of the property tax would thus result in a reduction in the cost of housing. The major beneficiaries would be low-income families, since they pay a disproportionate share of their income for shelter compared to middle- and high-income families.

The so-called housing or tax-incentive legislation enacted at various times in such states as California, New York, New Jersey, Connecticut, Missouri, and Wisconsin is evidence of sensitivity to this problem in urban states. Such legislation has taken the form of tax abatement, a freeze, or subsidy and is generally available only to new construction. We described in Chapter 3 tax-increment financing that has been authorized in thirty-four states for redevelopment of blighted areas in central cities. Our point is that tax policies should be reviewed to determine whether alteration would achieve lower costs of existing housing. The proposed substate planning and administrative districts, once established, could be assigned the task of reviewing local tax policies throughout their jurisdictions.

Land Policy

The capacity of local communities to cope with growth and change will be increasingly strained in the early decades of the new century. That is because the construction boom in the late years of the twentieth century preempted many available large parcels of vacant land in cities. Thus it is imperative that the states create strategic land reserves both within central cities and in adjacent and nearby urban areas.

The land reserves can be maintained tax-free as publicly owned property for future development for either public or private uses. The intent would be to balance constant absorption of land and to offset intensity of use by a permanent program of creating and stockpiling new vacant land. The creation of land reserves can be achieved through demolition of existing improvements, as in slum clearance; forest preserves and green-belt zoning; reclaimed land, as in landfill and other reclamation projects; and purchase of improved properties as well as continued maintenance of those improvements (through lease arrangements) until the land is needed for new uses.

The problems of development timing that inner-city land reserves could meet are often brought about in peripheral zones of metropolitan areas through questionable zoning practices. No doubt the methods used by some states to acquire scenic easements are practical, justifiable, and legal, to the end that land reserves are achieved at low cost outside central cities. In the process of acquiring land reserves, states should avoid abuses of the power of eminent domain.

A next step would be enactment of state programs providing revolving funds for acquisition of private lands to hold for future urbanization—the replacement dollars to be provided upon the subsequent sale at a write-down or at market value to private developers. Not only would such acquisition programs tend to assure development in accordance with state or regional land-use plans; they would allow the states to exert an influence upon the character and nature of regional development programs. The regional land bank has operated successfully in some areas where the environment is highly valued by local citizens. In Martha's Vineyard and Nantucket, a regional land bank is financed by a 2% tax on real-estate sales. Local residents say that increased demand for land has offset the costs of the tax.

In 1971, the federal Council on Environmental Quality prepared a background report for President Nixon's proposed National Land Use Policy Act (never adopted) titled *The Quiet Revolution in Land Use*, which reported a shift in governmental regulation of land use from local government back to the states.[7] The report traces pioneering land-use legislation in thirteen states, from Hawaii's prototype in 1961 to Maryland's in 1992.

A unique feature of Hawaii's land-use law was the implementation in 1979 of the Hawaii State Plan. The only such state plan enacted in its entirety, it requires state agencies to conform their land-related actions to the provisions of the statute. However, state plans are merely guidelines for county and municipal planners.

In 1971 Vermont had an Environmental Board and Environmental Commission that required regional reviews of certain land development decisions. In 1988 the legislature established statewide planning goals and required review of the plans of state agencies and local governments by regional planning commissions. A year later mandatory conformance to the statewide goals was eliminated, but review by the regional planning commissions and confirmation of conformance to statewide goals was retained.

Florida ventured into statewide land-use controls with its Environmental Land and Water Management Act of 1972. Implementation of the act targeted four areas of critical state concern: Big Cypress, Green Swamp, the Florida Keys, and Apalachicola Bay. The State and Regional Planning Act of 1984 mandated a state comprehensive plan as well as regional plans in Florida's eleven planning regions, the latter to be consistent with the state comprehensive plan. Amendments in 1985 required local governments to adopt local plans consistent with state and regional ones. Local plans had to include future land use, capital improvements—sewage; solid waste and potable water facilities; drainage systems—aquifer protection; conservation; recreation and open space; housing; traffic circulation; intergovernmental-cooperation; coastal zone management; and mass transit. The 1985 amendments also required infrastructure programming and specified that a proposed development must meet the service standards established by the local government to be approved.

In the Planning Act of 1989, Georgia established a comprehensive state-regional-local "consistency" program similar to Florida's but without the mandatory features. The Department of Community Affairs and the Governor's Development Council were charged with creating a state plan and working with state, regional, and local governmental entities on land-use planning and siting of public facilities. The Department of Community Affairs could deny state grants and other funds to local and regional governments that failed to produce a comprehensive plan in accordance with state and regional standards. Eleven Regional Development Centers prepare regional plans and review local plans for conformity with state and regional standards. The Regional Development Centers also review local land-development regulations for conformance to state and regional standards and to local comprehensive plans.

In 1973 the Oregon legislature established the Land Conservation and Development Commission and Department, responsible for promulgating statewide land-use planning goals which all the cities and counties in the state must observe. In response, local comprehensive plans, zoning, and subdivision ordinances had to be revised to comply with the statewide goals. State agencies are bound by the statewide planning goals and by local plans and implementing regulations. In 1979 Oregon established a Land-Use Board of Appeals, an administrative court with powers to review all land-use decisions of local governments, state agencies, and special districts.

New Jersey's State Planning Act of 1985 was a legislative effort to bring order to land-use planning in the state and to deal with the urban growth pressures of the Northeast Corridor. The resulting 1989 New Jersey State Plan established statewide planning goals for land use, housing, economic development, transportation, natural resource conservation, agriculture, farmland retention, recreation, urban and suburban development, historic preservation, public facilities and services, and intergovernmental coordination. Until 1992 implementation had to be by a process of "cross acceptance," which meant achieving a consensus of interested parties. The consensus process proved to be impractical and was abandoned in 1992 in favor of certification by the State Planning Commission that local plans conformed to the state plan.

In 1990 the legislature of Washington followed Oregon's lead in adopting the Growth Management Act, which required that counties with populations of 50,000 or with 10% to 20% growth rates prepare comprehensive plans with the following mandatory elements: land use, housing, capital facilities, utilities, rural lands, and transportation. A second Growth Management Act followed in 1991, which added protection to sensitive and natural resource lands. The high-growth counties were required to work with their municipalities in a mutual planning effort. Land-use regulations had to conform to the comprehensive plans.

The Rhode Island statewide land-use control system also uses strict conformance between compulsory local plans and state-planning goals. These goals are in the Comprehensive Planning and Land-Use Regulation Act and the State Comprehensive Plan Appeals Board Act, both enacted in 1991. The former lists the state goals with which local government comprehensive plans must be consistent: development of affordable housing; open space; recreational, cultural, and historic resources; protection of natural resources; economic development; and compatibility of growth with the natural characteristics of the land. Local plans must also be consistent with regional goals such as providing public facilities and financing transportation. All state agency plans and projects must conform to the state comprehensive plan. Rhode Island has a Comprehensive Plan Appeals Board appointed by the governor.

The Maryland Economic Growth, Resource Protection, and Planning Act of 1992 requires all local governments to conform to goals set forth in the act and lists mandatory elements of local plans: land use, public facilities, transportation, mineral resources, critical areas, and a "streamlined development application" in designated growth areas. If a local government does not adopt these elements in its plan, state standards apply instead.

The governor of Illinois announced in April 2000 a voluntary program to combat suburban sprawl, reduce traffic, and preserve open space. The program, Illinois Tomorrow, would coordinate efforts to achieve "balanced growth" focused on environment and natural resources. The governor announced two new state programs to develop distressed urban areas and encourage affordable housing near mass transit. The governor said the effort was designed to deal with the loss of agricultural land, decaying urban centers, and increased traffic. The Illinois programs aimed to avoid dictating land-use policies to local governments or penalizing towns for annexing and developing farmland.

The programs summarized above are all based on state plans. Most require that local comprehensive land and facilities planning be in accord with state standards. Moreover, most of the states offer incentives for local governments to engage in comprehensive planning. About half impose sanctions for non-compliance. Approval of a local plan by a state agency usually results in a measure of local control over state decisions in the local jurisdiction.

Leadership in land-use planning positions the states to move statewide development policy toward planned new towns, both "in town" and outside the built-up areas. As we will show in the concluding chapter, an emphasis on new towns—new communities—is likely to be the future of urban development in the twenty-first century.

New towns could be housing programs in their own right to meet the needs of an expanding population and relocation destinations for families displaced by redevelopment projects. Most urban communities, especially in the more populous states, lack the elbowroom of large tracts of vacant land, especially in suitable locations, that make possible the rehousing of displaced populations. The federal government provided support and encouragement in the little-used New Communities Acts of 1968 and 1970.[8] We explored the "new communities" concept in Chapter 8 and we discuss its potential for the longer range in Chapter 10.

A half-century ago redevelopment programs benefited from high public receptivity to any program promising an improved urban environment. Thus, the public accepted the pains of population displacement and relocation. Later, the federal courts changed the perspective of people dislocated by urban development projects. Partly as a consequence of the 1960s inner-city riots, public receptivity diminished and legal challenges increased. Also, federal regulations were promulgated that cast doubt on development schemes that lacked an adequate rehousing plan. As a consequence, cities have not been able to displace large numbers of people since about 1970 and urban renewal programs have been slowed.

If urban renewal and slum clearance are to move ahead with the vigor they had in the 1950s and 1960s, new ideas and new programs are needed to make relocation of families in blighted areas an opportunity for rehousing of poor families in new and more desirable environments. Planned new towns could serve this purpose, provided they are conceived as open communities available to the displaced and others as well. The upgrading of housing for displaced families would thus be part of a larger program to provide better housing and more housing for the expanding general population.

If land-use planning is to be taken out of the impasse of intergovernmental competition for real estate taxes, states should remove the cause of the competition by preempting the tax on commercial and industrial real estate. In lieu of these taxes, the states should be able to provide local governments with equivalent revenues on the basis of some equitable formula. Since the capacity for self-taxation is related to the capacity for self-government, some local revenue source is needed for a sense of serious participation in local government. The residential property tax, the earnings tax, and the sales tax suggest themselves as major sources of local revenue.

The important objective is to find a way to divorce local concern with land use from preoccupation with maximizing tax revenue. The other side of the coin is that local concern with land use may produce a sizable population whose service costs are high and whose tax returns are low.

In view of the critical importance of low-income housing, states may wish not only to assist in its construction but also to provide incentives to local communities to zone land for such use. Recognizing the costs to the community of this kind of property, the states could provide grants to encourage communities to accept the costs for some part of their total land use. For this purpose, the states must have some form of regional planning agency to provide data on the regional requirements of low-income housing and how they are to be met. Substate planning and administrative districts, described later in the chapter, could serve this purpose.

Code Standards

The states should encourage preservation of sound housing through effective building-code enforcement. Only the states have the legislative power to promulgate a strong building-code policy. This is done by enactment of unusual remedies to secure code compliance, and state grants to municipalities to fund compliance programs are a corollary need. The conservation of existing housing is dependent upon the ability of local government to prevent blight through police powers. An alternative arrangement is to delegate to the proposed substate districts responsibility for monitoring code enforcement on behalf of the state and for allocating state code-enforcement grants to municipalities.

Traditional municipal procedures and penalties for dealing with infractions of local standards relative to dwelling maintenance and use are too cumbersome to cope with the willful neglect of property. The result is a lowering of housing quality, sometimes on a large scale. The crux of a code enforcement problem is the lack of means to assure swift restoration of neglected housing to an acceptable condition. In most localities there is an absence of penalties of sufficient severity to deter violation of code requirements. Several states have legislation that enables municipalities to petition for the appointment of "rent receiverships" for properties in the hands of recalcitrant owners.

The value of such legislation is limited. Local governments are usually reluctant to be receivers for purposes of code enforcement and rehabilitation. After all, the deterioration and abandonment of urban property is more likely to have stemmed from externalities than from owner greed: a poor business climate, inferior city services, a weak transportation infrastructure, poor schools, transient populations in the labor pool, and in some cities lack of political organization and leadership.

The states should back up municipalities by extending grants to municipalities to fund receivership programs, much as states have provided grants for conventional renewal programs in some urban states. The availability of state funds for this purpose would encourage the use of a more selective approach to slum prevention and rehabilitation.

Some states have provided unusual remedies to control blight through direct intervention in management and disposition of properties. Aggressive statewide policies of legislative experimentation with unusual remedies for backstopping the enforcement of local building, housing, health, and zoning codes should be basic to the state/local partnership in redevelopment. Among the major requirements for extraordinary remedies are prompt action by courts of higher jurisdiction, putting the recalcitrant owner in contempt of court, and eliminating violations by municipal repair-and-demolition projects with liens attached to the property.

The roots of the problem of slum prevention and code enforcement run deep in our national habits and can be traced back to an earlier preoccupation with economic development. Our cities have been despoiled by mobile populations that exploited but failed to replenish resources as they moved from place to place in search of better locations, better neighborhoods, and better housing—much as earlier generations searched for more productive soils and better grazing lands.

The maintenance of community planning, design, and preservation standards and housing quality can be difficult in periods of rapid population growth, when pressures mount for relaxation of community standards to ease temporary shortages of shelter. This also happened when states (Illinois, for example) deinstitutionalized people from mental hospitals and other mental facilities. These people overwhelmed some neighborhoods, turning apartment buildings into rooming houses and the like. These are crisis periods for cities because, in the wake of such pressures, whole sections of cities are devalued for the sake of short-term relief, or worse, the lack of any return. This process occurred in many cities during and after World War II, and it was not until the mid-1950s that improved code-enforcement programs tried to roll back the damage, often too little, too late. The damage is still occurring in the newer metropolises of the nation.

Social and population mobility has historically been pronounced, and practically all urban areas are still in transition. Only the velocity of turnover and the economic capability of local populations differ from area to area. At some point, local enforcement of building, housing, and zoning codes breaks down under the alternating impact of population vacuums and pressures, and the development/redevelopment of urban areas becomes a rescue operation to relocate people from conditions that imperil health, safety, and morals.

In operational terms, redevelopment is a costly effort to repair the damage of the past and to conserve land, location, and valuable urban artifacts. A century ago, the nation began to face up to the need to conserve its natural resources—its farms, forests, waterways, and mines. At the dawn of the twenty-first century, the nation and the states should recognize a similar need to conserve the country's urban resources in consideration for public costs and public morale.

It is critical that permanent ends not be confused with immediate operational results, whether they be the abatement of specific nuisances or the elimination of uninhabitable dwellings. The objective is to arrive at a condition in which public authorities and the institutions of the marketplace come to accept as customary property standards that require the threat of legalized action to secure compliance.

The conversion of law into custom is likely to occur when the public has reason to demand a consistent performance in code enforcement. A high level of public expectation is a function of community education. Support of code standards by the courts, by administrative action, and by statements of legislative intent is a rudimentary form of communication of community standards and is essential to the education of the public. Participation of the states in code-enforcement activities is vital because only the states possess the authority to act. The states could assign responsibility for code enforcement to the proposed substate planning and administrative districts.

Substate Planning and Administrative Districts

For decades policymakers and urban scholars have seen metropolitan areas as unique communities awaiting visionary political leadership to inspire their citizenry to form supermunicipalities capable of addressing areawide problems efficiently and economically. A more promising approach looks at metropolitan regions as territorial units for decentralizing state administrative and planning functions that impact urban areas. As states identify functions, including planning, that require implementation at the regional level (ones that cannot be managed by local government), one solution is to establish multipurpose substate planning and administrative districts in all the states.[9]

In efforts to deal with pressing regional problems in the early 1950s, a handful of states established a limited form of substate planning districts. The federal government recognized the value of these pioneering districts and supported them with matching funds authorized by Section 701 of the Housing Act of 1954.[10] The first state to experiment with substate planning was Connecticut, following the disastrous 1955 floods. The Connecticut Development Commission became involved in planning assistance with the help of 701 funds for preparation of flood-prevention plans for three river valleys. This experience proved valuable in revealing the weaknesses of planning in a portion of the state and in revealing the need to involve local communities in regional developmental planning. So in 1958, the Connecticut General Assembly authorized the establishment of statewide regional planning areas. The Housing Act of 1959, which included the 701 planning assistance program, stimulated a renewed interest in regional planning. The 701 program made federal funds available to state planning agencies for the purpose of implementing statewide or interstate comprehensive planning.

Connecticut's early actions were followed by similar actions in Georgia, which passed legislation in 1961 authorizing financial assistance to area planning commissions. Other states authorizing similar regional planning programs included California, Massachusetts, Pennsylvania, New York, Tennessee, and Wisconsin. These states all shed passive roles in regional planning and charted courses leading to substate regionalism.

The state planning agencies fostered by federal 701 planning assistance soon recognized the opportunities offered them by the substate district concept. Accordingly, they established state-sponsored planning districts to discharge state agencies' planning responsibilities. The later federal grant and aid programs (mostly after 1964) to multijurisdictional areas led to a broadening of the functions of the new substate districts.

The Public Works and Economic Development Act of 1965 authorized another form of substate district.[11] In January 1966, shortly after establishment of the federal Economic Development Administration, the governors of thirty-seven states were offered federal assistance to establish economic development districts. Twenty states were initially funded for this purpose. The need for substate districts received further emphasis in Section 204 of the Demonstration Cities and Metropolitan Development Act of 1966, which, as we have noted, required review of federally sponsored local projects by a regional planning agency.[12]

In April 1966, the ACIR issued a report in which it recommended that states create multipurpose regional planning agencies to undertake physical, economic, and human resource planning and development programs over multicounty areas; and that where states had taken action, federal agencies responsible for such programs be required to use the same geographic base and to the maximum extent possible the same regional agencies.[13]

These recommendations led directly to President Johnson's issuing a memorandum (September 1966) calling for coordination of development programs in planning at the federal level and for federal cooperation with state and local agencies in establishing common planning bases and sharing facilities and resources. The memorandum stated in part that "Comprehensive planning covering wide areas is a promising and extremely important beginning to the solution of critical state, metropolitan and regional problems. . . . At the federal level, we must coordinate our efforts to prevent conflict and duplication among federally assisted planning efforts." The memorandum emphasized that boundaries for planning and development districts assisted by the federal government should be consistent with existing state planning districts and regions.

A few months later, in January 1967, the Bureau of the Budget issued Circular A-80 to provide guidelines to implement the president's directive. BOB's policy regarding substate districts was to encourage the states to take the lead in establishing planning and development districts for regions in each state which could provide a consistent geographic base for coordinating federal, state, and local development programs. The objective of A-80 was to discourage duplication and competition in state and local planning activities required by federal programs.

In A-80, the federal government established a policy that was intended to overcome problems stemming from the multiplicity of uncoordinated programs. In 1967 such programs included the Office of Economic Opportunity's community action agencies, created for Johnson's War on Poverty by the Economic Opportunity Act of 1964;[14] the Department of Agriculture's resource, conservation and development districts, authorized by the Food and Agricultural Act of 1962;[15] the Department of Commerce's economic development districts, established by the Public Works and Economic Development Act of 1965;[16] the Appalachian Regional Development Commission's local development districts, provided by the Appalachian Regional Development Act of 1965;[17] the Department of Health, Education and Welfare's areawide comprehensive health planning agencies, established by Section 314b of the Public Health Services Act of 1966;[18] and the Environmental Protection Agency's quality-control regions, authorized by the Clean Air Act of 1963.[19] These programs were followed by the Department of Labor's Cooperative Area Manpower Planning Service (CAMPS), established by a presidential executive order in 1968; and the Department of Justice's law enforcement assistance administration districts, provided for in the Omnibus Crime Control and Safe Streets Act of 1968.[20]

In February 1968, the Department of Housing and Urban Development offered funds to support substate planning districts. HUD's policy was that state comprehensive planning agencies should delineate "multi-jurisdictional planning and development districts covering the entire state." HUD's 701 comprehensive planning funds were made available to states for delineation studies that would determine the boundaries of a statewide system of planning and development areas. By the end of 1967, thirty states had state planning districts.

These federal efforts peaked in July 1969, when the Office of Management and Budget (successor to the Bureau of the Budget), issued Circular A-95. That policy statement implemented certain provisions of three federal acts: Part I of the Intergovernmental Cooperation Act of 1968;[21] Section 204 of the Demonstration Cities and Metropolitan Development Act of 1966;[22] and Section 102(2)(c) of the National Environmental Policy Act of 1969.[23]

A-95 encouraged establishment of state and substate clearinghouses whose purposes were to assist in coordination of federally funded projects and programs with state, regional, and local planning efforts. State governments were to designate a state agency as a clearinghouse and regional agencies as regional clearinghouses for review of and comment on applications for federal assistance in over one hundred federal programs. Part IV of A-95 instructed federal agencies to conform to the substate districts established by the states.

By 1973, there were five types of planning districts in addition to the new substate districts: (1) the regional-planning commissions with strong economic development orientations, established in the 1950s and 1960s by local governments and private groups; (2) metropolitan and nonmetropolitan councils of governments, some of which had been organized after World War II, composed primarily of local elected officials and financed by local and HUD 701 funds; (3) state districts established by the welfare and highway departments; (4) special single-purpose districts such as transportation authorities and solid-waste authorities; (5) areawide planning districts for particular functions created in response to federal programs.

The primary objectives of the multipurpose substate districts were to develop regional plans, to provide operational programs and services, to perform A-95 reviews, and to coordinate federal programs at the regional level. The purpose in creating substate planning and development districts was to bring these various district organizations together on a coordinated and geographically sound basis and to coordinate state and local plans with federal and state programs.

Substate planning and administrative agencies could have implementing powers and provide a regional alternative to metropolitan government. It would have been a big assist to regional planning if the states had not only pressed to standardize regional planning requirements through substate planning agencies but also worked to make federal regionalization coincide with their own.

At the time of their inception in the 1950s and 1960s, substate districts appealed to planners as a means of creating a new statewide planning system to supplement the few HUD-funded planning organizations then operating in some SMSAs. The idea behind the substate districts was to divide states into regions (districts), with each district providing planning and technical assistance throughout its area. The state planning organizations would further strengthen statewide planning by fostering special relationships with their substate planning agencies for statewide planning and ultimately budgeting.

The substate district concept was intended to make sense out of the geographical and organizational overlapping stemming from ad hoc federal program requirements. The substate district was to provide a consistent regional-planning base in the states and across the nation for coordinating federally supported projects. Some of the governors looked to the substate district arrangement to make administrative sense out of state planning and budgeting and delivery of some state services. Local governments hoped to increase their federal-aid receipts and gain a larger voice in state and federal decisions affecting them.

In the years following initial federal efforts to promote the substate district concept the fragmentation of planning and service organizations grew more pronounced. Substate districts were established in most of the states on three different models. The first model assumed that federal program agencies at the local level and the substate district organization were separate, with minimal interagency communication and coordination. In the second, local federal program agencies (as well as regional single-purpose, nonfederal agencies) were separate from the substate district organization, but the district organization assumed a dominant position and reviewed the budget and planning actions of the federal program agencies. In this model, there could be additional, unofficial, ties between the two bodies through overlapping board membership and shared staff. In a third model, the substate district organization assumed total responsibility for the organization, financing, staffing, and operation of the federal program agencies.

All three models have persisted in the regional planning commissions and councils of governments based in substate districts. They have concentrated on physical and economic planning and rarely have been involved in service delivery operations. Most of them have done little or no *social* planning; few have developed an integrated regional plan, even physical or economic ones. Regional social planning has been carried out by separate special-purpose planning agencies—for example, in health, manpower, and community action—and not integrated into a comprehensive plan.

In short, comprehensive regional planning has made few gains since its early years. Yet the need for a coordinated public strategy in physical and social planning has become increasingly apparent to public policymakers and even to large-scale private developers. A serious new exploration of the substate district concept is appropriate as we move into a new era of expansive economic development.

In a reformulation of the substate district concept, we consider how to restructure regional planning and administration so that it comprehends physical and social planning and links the planning function to the delivery of public services and programs. A revised substate district system should (1) be wall-to-wall in all the states and based on counties or groups of counties; (2) replace and assume the functions of the councils of governments, regional-planning commissions, economic development districts, comprehensive health planning agencies, and other special-purpose regional planning agencies; (3) combine regional planning and administrative functions of state agencies whose services and operations impact urban and economic development and populations; (4) assume responsibility for the planning review of all federal and state projects and programs that impact urban and economic development and populations; (5) reaffirm federal support for a substate planning and administrative system in a new OMB directive to resurrect, reaffirm and extend the policies described in BOB A-80 and OMB A-95.

The long-term objective in establishing multipurpose substate agencies is to create effective governance at the regional level. The new substate districts could play a key role in the federal system if they are capable of (1) taking over many of the functions (areawide in nature) ordinarily performed by local municipalities; (2) responding effectively to future demands that would otherwise unduly burden state and local governments; (3) reviewing substantial grants of delegated state and federal power; (4) attracting a high level of public interest; and (5) giving expression to regional interests in state and federal processes.

The new substate districts should be staffed and funded to undertake regional planning for the state, for municipalities, and for federal programs in the state. Integration of local, regional, and state planning is specifically encouraged in federal law and policy and should be welcomed by federal policymakers and planners. Experience with the COGs and regional planning agencies during the last half of the twentieth century showed that delegation of responsibility for metropolitan and regional planning could bring comprehensive planning to a territorial level comparable to urban populations.

The substate district concept would include the substate planning and operating responsibilities of state functional agencies such as welfare and highway departments. The governors or the legislatures would establish the substate districts as reconstituted counties or groups of counties. Thus the question of boundary lines so vexing in the establishment of the old substate districts and all of the other regional planning entities need not be at issue. Where more than one county was to be involved, as in very large metropolitan areas, the question of boundaries would be the question of which counties to include in which substate districts. In our proposal, each state would have wall-to-wall substate districts; therefore every county would be a substate district or a part of one involving two or more counties. Our proposal would guarantee that all state and federal agencies would have the same regional boundaries for substate planning and operations. The proposal would also guarantee that all state agencies would be headquartered in the same facility for substate operations. The proposal would go a long way toward a guarantee of cooperation and coordination among departments that have been traditionally autonomous. It would also go a long way toward doing away with the administrative anomaly of "vertical autocracies."

With wall-to-wall substate districts in every state in the country, the states could channel diverse federal programs through a single state-level and substate regional planning process. In short, the proposed arrangement would eliminate the confusion and duplication made endemic in state and local planning by federal planning requirements. For its part, Congress should require states and municipalities to use the substate districts to coordinate the federal funds they receive. Federal planning functions delegated to the states and coordinated by the new substate districts would benefit from the involvement of state and local elected officials in shaping and carrying out local and regional policy.

The division of authority between the proposed substate districts and existing municipalities is of central importance. The American federal system is one in which authority is shared among all levels of government, and dominance tends to accrue to those that possess resources, unity, and administrative competence. County-based substate districts should prove their worthiness in the political arena and for this reason should be accorded the leeway to develop their capacity without unduly restrictive provisions as to future responsibilities and functions.

The new substate districts should be under the supervision of a state administrative and planning department in the governor's office. This arrangement would position the department to work closely with both the governor and legislature, especially in the budget-planning process. Gubernatorial and legislative action could then transform planning into a serious tool for responsible problem solving.

The functional departments of state and local government would be required to do their planning with and through the new state/substate structure. A state planning and administrative department would therefore be in a position to plan and administer state and federal programs that have for decades operated with a minimum of planning and coordination. Forty years ago, few of the states were prepared to take on such a responsibility, but by the close of the twentieth century most of the states had developed the fiscal and administrative capacity for the task and some of them had come far enough to serve as models.

To make substate planning and administrative districts effectively representative of the state in negotiations with federal bureaucracies, states should give special attention to professional staffing and support. The substate districts would ensure that the state's viewpoint is represented in the regional-planning process. State development plans would be reflected in regional plans and vice versa. It is doubtful that many existing state planning agencies have the staff and resources to carry out development planning that would encompass a wide range of regional objectives at the state level. A state planning and administrative department would provide the intellectual basis for coordinating major state program activities.

The state planning and administrative department should correspond in function to the substate administrative and planning districts. As part of an operating agency responsible to the governor and legislature, the planning operation of such a department could provide the data and interpretive material needed for a significant gubernatorial report on the state of the state. Its trend data could provide citizens with indices as to progress in areas including employment, investment, education, health, and the like. Making such trend data salient could focus public attention on targets that are to be met if increases in population are to be effectively managed. The department should have a clearinghouse to provide information and technical assistance to the substate districts.

The proposed substate districts should be structured to serve as regional units of the operating state agencies: highways and transportation, police, health and welfare, environmental regulation, and so forth. A significant value in regionalizing state administration is that local governments would have the option of contracting with substate districts for certain local services that were not provided at the regional level. Much of what a regionalized state administration might do would probably arise from the desire of local governments to shift to the regional-level functions that were not being adequately met at the local level. The point is that different local services have different economies of scale. The size of a fire district, operating at optimum efficiency, would not be in the same area or population as a school district, a sewer district, or a library district. Thus, the substate districts could operate more efficiently than individual municipalities because they could take advantage of economies of scale available in many functions, obviating once and for all the need for regional supergovernment.

Nearly every action of state and local government influences development. The location and type of development, in turn, directly affects the social and economic quality of life for the people of any given area. For example, a regional engineer of the state highway department concerned with regional-transportation systems would be in an excellent position to interpret local needs to the department and to the region.

A regional approach through substate planning and administrative districts would make possible the application of a variety of solutions to local problems that would not be possible without such a structure. "Open occupancy," for example, is possible only where effective control over zoning, taxing, public service, and the like permits a challenge to local "exclusiveness." Similarly, control of crime is facilitated with uniform areawide protection. Industrial development and unemployment can be dealt with when tax shelters or barriers and zoning and similar influences on industrial development are undertaken for entire urban areas at once. Highway construction has an important bearing on commuting, industrial development, and residential patterns. The location of a new road or an improvement of an existing road can significantly change residential patterns by altering traffic-friction costs as measured by both time and money. Moreover, highways are probably the most important factor in decisions to locate small manufacturing plants. If highway planning is done before more general state, regional, and metropolitan planning, the effect of all the planning that follows will be either shaped or undermined by highway engineers. A regional view that is functionally defined has a far better chance of influencing and coordinating highway and street development and has a better reason for doing so than separate towns or municipalities.

A state department of education might have responsibility for providing community colleges, technical institutes, and specialized educational services. Educators in local government and the state regional office would work closely together in planning regional needs and relating education programs to the economic aspects of regional development.

Promoting a regional labor market could be an important state program that could be shared with the federal employment service. An effectively organized labor market is a key resource in regional economic development. Substate districts would enable the states to develop improved planning and administrative capabilities in water and sewers, highway construction, and other strategic functions. State police working through county-based substate districts would be in a position to provide law enforcement to smaller municipalities, which would benefit from an improved level of professionalism. Health services and a wide variety of others might be arranged by contract with local municipalities. A professional planning staff in the substate districts could provide assistance to local government in their planning and aid in relating local planning to state and regional objectives.

Administrative Leadership

If regional planning became the responsibility of the substate districts, the emerging plans of the major operational departments of the state would be coordinated in the district offices. The planning activities of the major state departments would be the work programs upon which a regionalized state performance budget would be built. Welfare, health, education, highways, police, and public works could form a core of substate district administration.

A substate district administration should have a district executive officer and a governing council. The district executive might be either directly elected (as with some mayors and county executives) or appointed by the governor. The role of the governor and legislature in the administration of the substate districts would be through the administrators of the regional offices of the state departments assigned to the substate districts. These regional administrators would continue to report to their respective state commissioners, who in turn report to the governor. The legislature's authority, of course, is in the allocation of state funds.

The role of the district executive is to assure coordination of planning and implementation of the programs and projects of the major state departments whose regional functions are assigned in his district. The district executive is primarily a mediator among the regionalized state departments and between state interests and local concerns. In a word, the district executive is a political administrator.

The district executive would have a planning and administrative staff and a district budget but not direct control over project budgets of the state departments residing in the district office. The district executive would work with the state's regional directors in the preparation of a district budget related to a regional plan. The district council would have the authority to approve or reject such plans. The emphasis of the district planning function would be on developing priorities within and among state and federal programs.

The federal government should have a "metropolitan expediter" in each substate district office. The district executive, the heads of the regional state departments, and the federal representative would serve as the regional planning committee. This committee would be a useful medium for the resolution of differences and for bargaining among the participating local governments.

Political Leadership

An important task for giving political vitality to planning regions is that of mobilizing a regional leadership that could transform regionalized state administration into regional self-government. For this purpose, the proposed district council would have authority over regional-local affairs comparable to the authority cities and counties have over local affairs.

Two principles of representation are likely to be urged by various interests: representation by officials of the constituent municipalities (as with the COGs) and representation of the district population through direct election. In our proposal, the elected district council would be a reconstituted county board of supervisors representing the incorporated municipalities of the district as well as the unincorporated areas in the traditional county mode. County-based substate districts might suggest to legislatures that both the administrator and the council be elected, following a tradition of county government.

On the other hand, regional politics in some states might require a mixed representation on the district councils such as seats for the chief elective officer of each city and town and for state legislators representing the region. A substate district council so constituted would in most regions be a large body, but large councils are the rule and not the exception in many democratic regimes. The small council of the typical American city would probably not suit the representative needs of a regional district. Such a council would function as a legislative forum were it to delegate sufficient authority to a district executive. Inclusion of state legislators on the district council would provide an opportunity for direct oversight of state functions administered at the district level.

The substate district councils would, through the district executive, have responsibility for the budget of the state district administration and oversee formulation and implementation of land-use planning, regional infrastructure planning, sewage treatment and disposal, solid-waste disposal, water treatment and supply, and public transportation. The council's chief role would be to oversee and approve regional plans and projects submitted to it by the district executive. Submission of plans and projects to the council would be the end point of the planning and negotiation function of the district executive and the regional planning committee.

While possessing no final authority, the body could be given the power to make recommendations to the state, its departments, and the local governments. If the district councils included some of the region's political and civic leaders, its recommendations would carry weight with all levels of government—state, local, and federal. The chair of the district councils would be a focus of leadership in the region. An able leader in such a post could do much to develop regional identity and a sense of shared purpose.

Substate districts could be modeled after municipal corporations with powers limited by compatibility with existing local governments. In matters of revenue, the state should assure the adequacy of essential services, but some substate districts could be empowered to raise funds for levels of services that other districts did not desire.

Legislatures should make sure that state and substate administration and planning be directed to gather data on the items the legislature considers important and that they develop plans that deal effectively with the economic and social problems of their areas. The state planning and administrative agencies should serve as staff to governor and legislature to ensure that their plans become action programs. Properly used, the substate planning and administrative agencies working between the state and the municipalities could bring order into federal programs that require regional planning. In doing so the states would be at the center of the action and not bypassed.

A joint committee of the legislature should be established to provide oversight for the planning work of the department and interpretation of its findings to the legislature. Effective cooperation between the planning operation and the state's budget office could improve the possibilities of program budgeting and give the budget process added meaning by relating it to the planning process.

The legislature, by specifying data to be gathered by the planning operations of the substate districts, would provide needed information for state planning and a means of determining how regional and state plans and their implementation are progressing. By specifying that certain data be secured and reported, the state could ensure that important facts of regional life are called to public attention. Data would be given added salience by relating their magnitude and directional change to grants or other state actions. The development of an array of regional data presented to emphasize regional identity and consciousness could encourage cooperative problem solving.

Should states decide to regionalize administration in substate districts, they could bring effective government closer to the people. Such a structure at the regional level would serve both to increase governmental scale and at the same time to reverse a trend toward big and remote government. By equipping both state and local government to deal with regional problems, the substate district could increase the vitality of local government and prevent its erosion. By providing an effective set of institutions to coordinate federal programs, the state would restore its authority in areas in which it has been bypassed by the federal government. A regionalized state administration with a local representative policy body could take on the task of working out an interrelated state, federal, and local coordination of action in which the values of self-government can be preserved and strengthened.

Conclusions

The approach to planning suggested by the substate district arrangement is aimed at increasing the capacity of states to provide the means for making more effective the management of public business at the regional and metropolitan level. The need to increase management capacity by drawing a sharper distinction between staff planning and programming functions and operations should be self-evident. The primary consideration is the need to redefine and strengthen the role of planning and programming so that they provide a framework for decisionmaking. This simple step would clearly distinguish between policymaking and implementation.

Once substate planning and administrative districts are in place in any state and an appropriate governing council of state and local officials has been established, a further step would give the council strong and independent governing powers. Such powers would have the advantage of ensuring that the district would be able to implement regionwide services and guide regionwide development for the benefit of everyone.

The first step would be for the legislature to vest the substate administrative and planning districts with the legal authority to perform any function and exercise any power *not* forbidden by state law, thus permitting local units to act on new matters without awaiting specific authorization. This action would substitute the concept of *shared powers* for the express powers of Dillon's Rule. (As noted in Chapter 4, Dillon's Rule says that the powers of municipalities are limited to those expressly delegated to them by the state.)

Care should be taken to avoid development of a doctrine of preemption, which could prevent a substate district council from acting when there is a state law on the subject. That is, a weak state law could preclude a strong substate district council action. Under the shared-powers approach, a substate district council would be able to *supplement* a state law as long as its action did not *contravene* it. The general rule, therefore, would be that the primary local unit could take any action not *inconsistent* with state law. Implementation of the shared-powers approach probably should be accompanied by strong constitutional limitations on the enactment of substate district-council laws by the state legislature.

A substantial reeducation of a state judiciary accustomed to strict construction of municipal powers would of course be necessary. Since a significant lag in the judicial construction of shared powers could be expected, the broadest feasible power should be given to substate district councils. There will always be ample grounds for denying local authorities the power to act where there is a direct conflict between local and state laws, when a power is expressly denied by the state, when there is an implied denial of power by a state law that indicates a clear policy that could be blocked by local action, or when a citizen cannot comply with conflicting or parallel laws.

The state would have the exclusive power to occupy a field by enacting a law expressly prohibiting specified substate district actions. The state could enact general laws that might require review of certain local laws by the legislature or by state agencies to ensure that they are not inconsistent with state policy. A blanket prohibition or review procedure might be established for such sensitive matters as fiscal affairs to prevent nuisance taxes or avoid imbalances in the equity of the overall revenue system. Nevertheless, if the state wished to circumscribe district authority, it would have to take positive action. It could not frustrate district action solely by inaction. It would have ample authority to provide constant assistance and to intervene in response to need.

Similarly, shared responsibility and action by state and substate district governing councils in the implementation of urban development programs seems not only practical, but likely. It would be possible to create substate planning and administrative districts that had the flexibility to proceed differently in different places to encourage coherent and varied urban design and development.

The shared-powers approach advances two basic propositions: first, state and regional administrations need unfettered initiative in dealing with the conditions of urbanization; and second, both levels of government should be able to meet the political wishes of their constituents, although, in the American political system, the interests of the locality must yield to those of the state where there is a clear conflict.

Shared powers are addressed directly to the capacity to govern. Representative machinery, sensitive administrations, and a clear understanding of the political, economic, and social function of district governing councils would be of limited value if the district did not have the legal authority to take the action its officials deemed necessary.

Perhaps the most difficult political problem associated with the shared-powers formula is the establishment of the boundaries within which the substate districts would exercise general powers. As a practical matter, the introduction of shared power for substate districts would be combined with some arrangement for state review and realignment of the initial district boundaries. In our proposal, the boundaries of the substate districts would be existing county boundaries, except in Connecticut and Hawaii, which lack counties. Boundary adjustments would come into play in our proposal in cases where a substate district would require inclusion of more than one or several counties, or the addition of one or more counties in cases where the initial substate district started out as a single county.

A permanent commission on intergovernmental relations, with power to recommend alterations in district boundaries and their powers, would be necessary in most states. Such a state commission could function as a legislative, executive, or administrative agency. Its powers might range from recommending legislation or other state action to serving as a tribunal for resolving boundary and jurisdictional conflicts. It might also have hearing and regulatory functions. Regardless of form and procedures, a process of review is crucial in shared powers to establish the adequacy of substate districts for the increased responsibilities.

In addition to deciding upon the boundaries of the substate districts and establishing a commission or review agency, each state should permit alternative methods for the mechanics of changing boundaries. For example, the state legislatures should be able to modify boundaries with the adoption of the shared-powers doctrine. Finally, joint service agreements, contracts, and other cooperative arrangements among neighboring districts should be facilitated.

As local government is presently structured, local power to produce and deliver services is distributed among a broad array of special-purpose authorities (more than 37,000 nationwide) in addition to the local governments themselves. The shared-powers doctrine would obviate the need for special authorities within a substate district. These districts could be authorized to

exercise whatever powers would be required to perform all governmental services, thus creating an improved climate for deciding priorities and allocating
resources among the public services demanded of government. The political
system would be simplified and the political processes associated with special
functions would be required to operate in the public view. Substate planning
and administrative districts wall-to-wall in all fifty states would surely bring
urban America toward the more perfect union the Founding Fathers envisioned.

Notes

1. Anthony Downs, *New Visions for Metropolitan America* (Washington, D.C.: The
   Brookings Institution, 1994).
2. "Symposium: Federalism in the Bicentennial Year of Our Constitution: A Comprehensive Analysis of Historical Perspectives, Current Issues and Creative Solutions," *Urban
   Lawyer* 19, no. 3: 431.
3. U.S. Constitution, Amendment X and Amendment XI. See *Alden v. Maine*, 715 A.2d
   172 (Me. 1998), cert. granted, 119 S. Ct. 443, aff'd, 119 S. Ct. 2240 (1999) and *Seminole
   Tribe of Florida v. Florida*: 517 U.S. 44 (1996). Also see "Returning to a General Theory
   of Federalism: Framing a New Tenth Amendment United States Supreme Court Case,"
   Urban Lawyer 26, no. 2 (Spring 1994).
4. P.L. 102-240, Intermodal Surface Transportation Efficiency Act of 1991 (ISTEA).
5. P.L. 105-178, Transportation Equity Act of 1998 (TEA-21). The predecessor legislation incorporated in TEA-21 was P.L. 102-240, the Transportation Restoration Act of
   1914.
6. P.L. 91-190, National Environmental Policy Act of 1969; Water Resources Planning Act
   of 1965; P.L. 93-15, Clean Air Acts of 1973; P.L. 93-14, P.L. 93-207, 93-243, Clean Water
   Acts of 1973; P.L. 101-549, Clean Air Act Amendments of 1990.
7. Fred Bosselman and David Callies, *The Quiet Revolution in Land Use*, Council on
   Environmental Quality, 1971. The report is summarized David L. Callies, "The Quiet
   Revolution Revisited: A Quarter-Century of Progress," *Urban Lawyer* 26, no. 2 (Spring
   1994): 197–213.
8. P.L. 90-448, P.L. 91-609, New Communities Acts of 1968 and 1970.
9. *Substate Districting Systems in Twelve States*, a study prepared for the Advisory Commission on Intergovernmental Relations, by the Southwest Center for Urban Research,
   Houston, in association with the Institute for Urban Studies, University of Houston,
   and the Lyndon Baines Johnson School of Public Affairs, University of Texas, Austin,
   Texas (Washington, D.C.: Advisory Commission on Intergovernmental Relations, November 31, 1972).
10. Portions of this section on substate districts are drawn from the following paper:
    George W. Strong, "Substate Planning Districts—A Planner's Dream," unpublished
    paper presented to the 1973 Workshop on Government for Metropolitan Areas spon-
    sored by the Southern Newspaper Publisher's Association and the Institute for Urban
    Studies at the University of Houston, May 20–23, 1973.

11. P.L. 89-136, Public Works and Economic Development Act of 1965.
12. P.L. 89-754, Demonstration Cities and Metropolitan Development Act of 1966.
13. Report of the U.S. Advisory Commission on Intergovernmental Relations, 1966.
14. P.L. 88-452, Equal Opportunity Act of 1964.
15. P.L. 87-703, Food and Agriculture Act of 1962.
16. P.L. 89-136, Public Works and Economic Development Act of 1965.
17. P.L. 89-4, Appalachian Regional Development Act of 1965.
18. P.L. 89-749, Comprehensive Health Planning and Public Health Services Amendments of 1966.
19. P.L. 88-206, Clean Air Act of 1963.
20. P.L. 90-351, Omnibus Crime Control and Safe Streets Act of 1968.
21. P.L. 90-557, Intergovernmental Cooperation Act of 1968.
22. P.L. 89-757, Demonstration Cities and Metropolitan Development Act of 1966.
23. P.L. 91-190, National Environmental Policy Act of 1969.

Chapter 10

Toward a More Perfect Union

In this closing chapter we focus on the quarter-century ahead, during which the American economy, with some temporary setbacks, is likely to continue to experience unprecedented prosperity and unprecedented opportunity for citizens and newcomers alike. The challenge is to fashion public policies and programs that assure inclusive participation in that prosperity and to develop the political and administrative capability to carry them out. From the founding of the nation it has seemed America's destiny to establish its unique system of governance across the continent to the Pacific Coast. In the third millennium, it seems to be the nation's destiny to assimilate and connect people from all the cultures of the world and to provide a global example of the value of tolerance and the rule of law. The aim of this chapter is to suggest what specific public policies and programs are most likely to realize that destiny. The importance of the proposed substate districts is to make available the planning and administrative mechanisms at the metropolitan/regional level that will be required to implement the policies and programs we envision.

In the early years of the twenty-first century, America's economic structure was reaching a critical mass and its entrepreneurs were extending their markets globally and establishing alliances with entrepreneurs in most parts of the world. America's political structure lent support to entrepreneurs when it encouraged the formation of the European Union, the South East Asia Treaty Organization (SEATO), and the Asia-Pacific Economic Cooperation forum (APEC), and took the first step toward a Western Hemisphere economic union with the North American Free Trade Association—NAFTA. In consequence, the global economy in the twenty-first century seems likely to continue development of a series of regional economic unions that in the long run will make national boundaries irrelevant: the Western Hemisphere based on NAFTA; the European Union, eventually including Russia, the Near East, and Israel; Southeast Asia, including Japan, China, Korea, Australia, New Zealand, and India. As relations among the nations of the continent of Africa stabilize, that region too will develop an economic union. The world economy will in the course of the twenty-first century come to be guided by the rule of law and the laws of trade rather than that of politics and war. The global prosperity that follows will benefit almost everyone.

The task at hand is to show that America can lead the way with the practical steps that assure success. The groundwork in the United States was laid with the Sixteenth Amendment to the U.S. Constitution, which authorized the federal income tax. That powerful engine of national revenue made possible the welfare programs of Franklin Roosevelt's New Deal: Social Security, public housing, federal welfare and unemployment insurance; as well as the temporary programs that refired the economy and got people back to work: the Works Progress Administration (WPA), the Public Works Administration (PWA), the National Industrial Recovery Act (NIRA) (popularly referred to as the NRA, later declared unconstitutional),[1] and others. The federal income tax also made possible every subsequent program that the national government has implemented from its inception into twenty-first century.

The groundwork for the period ahead includes all the federal government's experimental programs that have helped sort out what government can do to increase economic growth and to lift people out of distress and into prosperity. The experiments that have worked are established programs of federal, state, and local government: Head Start (the foundation education for small children), legal aid for the indigent, and so forth. Some of the experiments have become entitlement programs: Social Security, Medicare, Medicaid, and veterans benefits, to name the principal ones. Others have failed and have been discarded, although they have left behind valuable lessons for the nation's policymakers: two examples are the Model Cities Program and general revenue sharing.

Along the way political leaders and fiscal experts have learned how to use governmental policy to make timely adjustments in the economy so that recessions are less severe and boom periods less volatile. During the 1990s, the national economy experienced the longest period of sustained and noninflationary expansion in history, an expansion that ended in 2001. This expansion resulted in a temporary reprieve from deficit spending and unprecedented federal revenue surpluses. A brief recession followed the end of the 1990s boom, during which millions of jobs were transferred overseas. The recovery was marked with further job losses and slow economic growth. In 2001, a Republican administration and a Republican-dominated Congress passed major tax cuts to hasten economic recovery. The economy responded and job growth picked up, although it was far short of the numbers of jobs lost. The federal surpluses of the 1990s disappeared and record deficits took their place

No matter how promising the prospect of national and global prosperity appears to be, there remains the danger that shortsighted policies could undermine the future prospects of continued prosperity. As the 1990s drew to a close, the nation and its leaders rode a wave of optimism fueled by the unprecedented growth. Indeed, the economic successes of the decade had brought increased prosperity to cities that were once thought to be "beyond the point of no return." Throughout the 1990s, the economy was able to support more and more workers (Figure 10.1). And as unemployment reached its lowest levels in decades, poor urban areas also felt the effect. In Figure 10.2, we show the unemployment rates in two sets of MSAs: those identified by David Rusk as the "point of no return" cities, and all others. As expected, in the early part of the 1990s when unemployment was on the rise, the Rusk cities had relatively high unemployment figures. But as the boom progressed, these cities actually enjoyed higher employment rates than other cities. Thus, even cities experiencing the worst economic conditions can begin recovery when sustained by a strong national economy. The specific city conditions and policy strategies that allow "point of no return" cities to recover is the topic of our next book, which carefully examines poverty and prosperity from 1990 to 2000 in the 34

Percent

Figure 10.1 U.S. Unemployment Rate, 1990–2004

cities identified by Rusk as being in the worst condition at the beginning of the last decade of the twentieth century.

The boom period of the 1990s ended in a brief downturn in 2001 through part of 2002. A major worldwide economic slowdown began in 2000 related in part to the "dot-com bust"—failures of Internet startup companies—and the terrorist attacks of September 11, 2001. Within weeks of the attacks, estimates of the cost to the U.S. economy were in the trillions of dollars. The eventual impact of these economic downturns on relatively weak urban centers is discussed in our forthcoming book, *The Future of Poverty in American Cities*, in which we show that the gains made by the "point of no return" cities can be lost as quickly as they were made in a "last hired, first fired" reaction to economic difficulty.

The principal criterion of economic success in our view is its inclusiveness of all the people. Even at the height of the 1990s prosperity, one out of seven Americans still lived in poverty.[2] Two or three decades into the future, if the economy continues to expand, no one should be living in poverty. Those who are living in poverty should be buoyed up by effective public assistance. That should be the aim of the nation's political leaders and policymakers, and that is our aim in framing this chapter. What, though, of America's political leadership as it bears upon the question of long-term prosperity?

Our view of the past half-century is that the Democratic Party and its adherents have focused priorities on programs and fiscal policies that have chipped away at the number of citizens who live in poverty. The Republican Party and its adherents have been reluctant to give priority to programs that would enhance economic opportunity for people born into poverty. They have focused on tax reductions and/or subsidies that enhance investments and profits. In Barry Carroll's words, "As one party concentrates on seeing to it that everyone gets a fair share of the golden egg, the other is more concerned with the health of the goose."[3]

As both parties have followed the nation toward the political center, social policy has hung in the balance, and it has been unclear that either party is yet positioned, short of bipartisan coalitions, to move decisively on programs that could finally reduce poverty to a minimum. The key to social policy aimed at ending poverty is to reverse the course of deficit spending toward a balanced federal budget while maintaining a sound pace in expanding the gross domestic product.

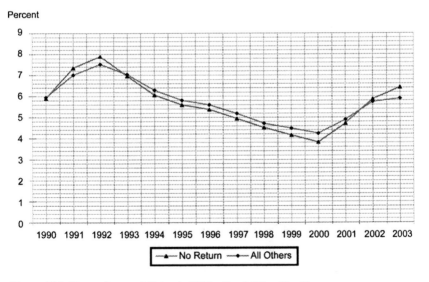

Percent

Figure 10.2 Unemployment Rates in MSAs Containing Rusk's "Point of No Return" Cities

All things considered, we are better off today than we were fifty or sixty years ago. An improved national economy and better employment opportunities have reduced poverty everywhere, even in the acutely distressed neighborhoods of the thirty or forty cities identified by Waste and Rusk. The "hardcore" poor and others whose income is below the poverty line are forced by economic circumstances to live in acutely distressed neighborhoods. Inadequate public services and high crime rates characterize their neighborhoods. Housing is old, run-down, and expensive. Their public schools are among the worst in the nation. Unemployment rates are high, especially for young males. In the 1990s, the populations of distressed neighborhoods were largely made up of minorities—predominantly Black and Hispanic.

As the twenty-first century gets under way, we must prepare succeeding generations for the ongoing challenges of technological and scientific revolution, for the evolution of economic regionalism, and for our part in developing policies that assure the future of humanity. This is a tall order for a nation still absorbing new citizens from every part of the globe and still resolving its own internal dilemmas. We spent much of the twentieth century consolidating our economic base; inventing and reinventing programs to help the poor and the elderly; putting behind us racial, gender, and age discrimination; improving education, healthcare, welfare, and more.

We have emerged from the years of trial and error better off than we were but not yet in command of our own moral and political aspirations. We have achieved great wealth, but we have not yet established the priorities to match our aspirations. We have achieved great political power, but we are uncertain about how to use it to promote our democratic and humanitarian ideals at home and abroad. We have preserved our Constitution and form of government from destructive forces at home and abroad. We have, therefore, established the foundations upon which to build a truly great and lasting society—a society that could lead the world toward the prosperity and freedom from which so many Americans benefit.

Thus, the next pages of this chapter address the condition of millions of Americans who do *not* benefit from the prosperity and freedom of which the rest of us are justly proud. The "Other America" of which Michael Harrington wrote four decades ago is still with us, as Jonathan Kozol has so poignantly shown in many of his writings.[4] The "Other America" is largely in our cities, where unemployment remains high in a time when overall unemployment is low. Joblessness is, after all, the principal reason for bad or nonexistent housing, for widespread and rising homelessness. Joblessness is also a reason for high rates of crime in cities. Conditions in inner-city neighborhoods create negative environments for the children of poor families, many of whom cannot benefit from the educational programs offered by the public schools that they attend. Many of these children rebel against the best efforts of their teachers, and disciplinary measures crowd out teaching and learning. A vicious cycle sets in and education is compromised.

The result is a waste of talent and educational opportunity. We must find ways to educate children in our inner-city poverty neighborhoods. (As Norman Elkin observes, "When it comes to education, you can't necessarily tell *in advance* who will or will not benefit!")[5] Most Americans know from personal experience that there are many talented youth among the poor—the "rough diamonds" among the hard-core poor—who must be the object of special educational efforts.[6] Talent among the children of the poor is as prevalent as talent among the affluent, and the motivation of the child of poverty can often be greater. The rough diamonds are there in poverty neighborhoods, and for the good of the country they must be raised up. We address this crucial issue later in the chapter.

What Is Poverty?

Edward C. Banfield has defined poverty by distinguishing several *degrees* of poverty in order of severity: destitution, want, hardship, and relative deprivation. He explains these terms:

> [D]estitution, which is a lack of income sufficient to assure physical survival and to prevent suffering from hunger, exposure, or remediable or preventable illness; want, which is a lack of enough income to support "essential welfare" (as distinguished from comfort and convenience); hardship, which is lack of enough to prevent acute, persistent discomfort or inconvenience; and relative deprivation, which is lack of enough to prevent one from feeling poor by comparison with others.[7]

These definitions or comparable ones permit the policy planner to determine what kinds of programs are appropriate to apply in efforts (public or private) to reduce or eliminate poverty.

In our discussion of remedies for poverty, we apply Banfield's four degrees of poverty to government programs that aim at its reduction. Poverty can never be entirely eliminated, but its effects can be mitigated for the hard-core poor and eased for the rest. The mitigation requires well-designed and carefully managed government-aid programs. Such programs should be established for the different categories of the poor and, where individuals fit into more than one category, adjustments can be made to accommodate overlaps.

Permanent government programs should continue to be available to support the dependent poor: the cognitively incapacitated (including cognitively unemployables), the chronically ill, the aged (although not the well-off aged), and the situationally (the temporary) poor. The objective should be to head off destitution and want and to mitigate hardship. Those who merely suffer from a sense of relative deprivation (absent *absolute* deprivation) should not receive government assistance.

Government programs should be redesigned to meet the criteria suggested here. Some of the programs should be expanded. Other programs require restaffing to assure competence in the difficult task of placing individuals in appropriate poverty categories. The official poverty line should be restudied to make sure it includes the destitute, those in want, and those in hardship. Once the poverty line is adjusted, policy regarding income redistribution should be reexamined.

Direct payments to the poor have been the principal form of income redistribution ever since the 1930s. The federal Social Security system makes direct payments to participants who reach age sixty-two to sixty-five. The Medicare health insurance program supplements these payments for participants when they reach age sixty-five. The state-operated Medicaid program supports healthcare for qualified poor. The Social Security system also makes direct payments to qualified persons who are incapacitated.

As we pointed out in Chapter 3, a simple method of transferring income to the poor is the so-called negative-income-tax idea, originally proposed by Milton Friedman in 1962.[8] Prominent economists across the political spectrum—

conservatives and liberals—agreed that the negative income tax would be the most efficient method to supplement the income of the poor. The version of the negative income tax enacted in 1975 as the Earned Income Tax Credit (EITC) program, subsequently amended and expanded in 1986 and indexed for inflation, expanded again in 1990 and 1993, when a credit was added for families with no children. EITC was addressed in President George W. Bush's 2001 tax-cut legislation: the program was expanded for married families, and provisions were included to simplify it and to reduce errors and fraud.

EITC allows millions of families (a "family" refers to a single individual, a single head of household with children, or a married couple) to eliminate their income-tax liability and, because it is a refundable credit, gives families a cash payment to offset the high (15.3%) payroll tax burden. Since 1993 families with or without children may claim the EITC. A primary rationale of the EITC "is to prevent the government from taxing families into poverty."[9] The shortcoming of the EITC is that it is available only to families who have earnings from employment. Those who are unemployed must seek aid from the welfare system or fend for themselves.

Like Social Security, the negative income tax has the advantage of benefiting recipients directly. A negative income tax applied across the board (that is, to families *without* earnings from employment) would have the additional advantage of eliminating the tedious business of sorting out the poor by degrees of poverty, which would be necessary in an income-supplement plan modeled on traditional welfare programs like AFDC. The only professionals involved in a negative-income-tax plan are the staff at the Internal Revenue Service. A negative-income-tax plan would work as follows: all families file their income tax returns and those reporting incomes below the official poverty line would receive a check from the government for the difference between their reported income and that of the poverty line.

When the negative-income-tax plan was first proposed in the early 1960s, some policymakers and social scientists worried that the plan would discourage employable persons from working for their living. When President Nixon proposed the plan during his first term in the early 1970s, opponents in Congress used this point to ridicule the proposal. Explaining the plan in the 1970 edition of *The Unheavenly City*, Banfield wrote, "To discourage able-bodied persons from taking advantage of the plan, the government might pay only a part of the income deficiency."[10]

This concern faded toward the end of the last century, especially in the context of large-scale restructuring and automation of big corporations and many small ones as well. Even in a period of low unemployment, hundreds of thousands of jobs were disappearing permanently. Jeremy Rifkin documented the trend in his 1995 book *The End of Work*, in which he concluded that "a near-workerless economy is within sight."[11] We think the outcome of the trends Rifkin cites is decades away, but they lend credence to the type of public-policy initiative the negative-income-tax plan offers. Milton Friedman and President Nixon were decades ahead of their time, but economic conditions seemed ripe at the beginning of the twenty-first century for the negative income tax plan to be expanded as a way to continue the reduction of poverty in America.

Government policies and programs that increase earning power can also achieve income redistribution for the benefit of the jobless and underemployed. Government programs designed to counteract recessions and/or to create jobs should be enhanced and made to work. Educational subsidies and job training programs could be especially productive in a period when the nation is undergoing a sea change from an industrial/manufacturing economy to a service and high-tech/information economy. As jobs both skilled and unskilled in industry are on the decline, new ones in the high-tech and information industries are being created at a rapid rate. Training of unskilled workers and retraining of skilled workers were well under way in the early years of the twenty-first century and should be accelerated and fine-tuned in the years ahead.

The government side of this strategic effort underwent serious reform in the Personal Responsibility and Work Opportunity Reconciliation Act of 1996 (popularly known as the Welfare Act of 1996). The act replaced Aid to Families with Dependent Children (AFDC) with Temporary Assistance to Needy Families (TANF), which imposed a five-year lifetime cap on benefits able-bodied welfare recipients could receive.

TANF originated in local programs of "mothers' aid" or "mothers' pensions" and more formally in Aid to Families with Children (AFC), which was part of the 1935 Social Security Act. These original federal aid programs were designed to help mothers faced with supporting children in circumstances of death, divorce, or desertion of the father, or because disabled fathers could not provide support. AFC was intended as a temporary bridge until families could qualify under permanent Social Security programs. "The sentiment behind the program was to support families on behalf of their children because the mothers did not work outside the home because their absence would be harmful to their children. With the social evolution of women in the workplace and the diversity with which a 'family' was subsequently defined, AFC also evolved into AFDC and then into TANF."[12]

The 1996 act authorized federal subsidies for state and local training and retraining programs and also contained incentives for private-sector employers to hire and train people from the welfare rolls. The act came along at a time when the nation's economy was in the midst of a period of expansion—as it turned out, the longest in history. The Welfare Act of 1996 placed the welfare system largely in the hands of state governments, with block grants from the federal government. A time limit on individual welfare dependency was thought to be a sound policy because it gradually shifted employables from welfare dependency to wage-earning status. Of course, success of the policy depended on the availability of jobs that matched the capabilities of the former welfare recipients. Success of the policy also depended on the ability of former welfare recipients to adapt to the available jobs and to the world of work. Where jobs for the able-bodied are not available or are scarce, the welfare system must adapt to accommodate them. Also, childcare programs must be in place to accommodate parents who must take jobs and lack the means to pay for private childcare.

As the welfare reform programs deriving from the 1996 Welfare Reform Act move able-bodied recipients into the workforce, they must also continue to accommodate recipients who are temporarily or permanently incapacitated. The permanently incapacitated recipients should receive income supplements from the Social Security system rather than from a welfare program. The temporarily incapacitated should receive income supplements from the welfare system, where the recipients can be monitored and removed from the rolls when they are no longer incapacitated.

With several years' experience under the 1996 act, welfare reform in 2001 was just getting under way. A series of follow-up studies to the Welfare Reform Act of 1996 by professors from the University of Chicago and Northwestern University provides important insights into some early results of state welfare programs.[13]

The act required state governments to cut their welfare rolls in half by 2002 without specifying how. The act did give state governments broad discretion in how they use federal block grants to pay for and administer welfare benefits. In effect each state was free to design its own TANF management program with its own incentives. The U.S. Department of Health and Human Services (HHS), which oversees the federal block-grant program ($16 billion in 1999), by the terms of the act requires that welfare recipients work thirty hours a week in a subsidized or unsubsidized job, or be seeking a job, enrolled in a job-training program, performing community service, or providing childcare to community-service participants.

In 1994, before passage of the 1996 Welfare Reform Act, 14.3 million people were on welfare. That number had been reduced to 8 million by September 1998, down 44%. By December of that year, 28% of adult welfare recipients in thirty-six states had found a job or were preparing to work. Despite a weaker economy, this trend continues to the present. According to the Department of Health and Human Services, less than 5 million people were receiving welfare benefits at the end of 2003.

Susan Mayer, director of the Northwestern University/University of Chicago Joint Center for Poverty Research, remarked in an interview with *The University of Chicago Magazine* that welfare reform might help "a third or half of the people who were on AFDC," but that "another two-thirds or half might need different programs."[14] The typical welfare recipient, according to HHS, is a thirty-year-old, single African American or Hispanic woman living in a city with two or more children born out of wedlock, with no college degree, and a greater-than-average chance to be a victim of domestic violence. Such a person could have difficulty forcing the father of her children to pay child support, to take a job without reliable childcare or transportation, or to acquire marketable job skills. The point is that when the welfare-reform programs begun after 1996 move former recipients into the job market (or its equivalent), there are likely to be people still left on the welfare rolls whose complicated situations may require more help than the post-1996 programs have the funds to offer. In these hard-core cases—there are likely to be millions of them—the federal and state governments will be faced with providing the funds for the additional childcare, healthcare, and job-training support needed to get them into the job market or relaxing the time limit to allow them to remain on the rolls. In 2001, the early beneficiaries who were not yet employed were approaching the five-year limit on benefits, a fact that promises to test the workability of the program's parameters.

President Clinton addressed some of these concerns in his 2000 budget, in which he sought additional funds for job training for *fathers*, for housing vouchers, and for transportation to job interviews. Clinton also sought childcare credits and restored health and disability benefits and food stamps for *legal* immigrants who had lost coverage in the 1996 welfare legislation.

Julia Henley, a professor at the University of Chicago Graduate School of Social Service Administration, focused on this issue in a study of stability among welfare families in Los Angeles County. She interviewed mothers receiving welfare, other low-income mothers, and employers and found that these women faced numerous barriers to steady work and sufficient income. Two-thirds earned $9 or less an hour; two-thirds had jobs that did not provide health insurance; one-fourth worked thirty hours a week or less; 19% did not have regular childcare, while most of those who did relied on relatives or friends. In addition, employers often had to lay off their low-wage, part-time workers when business slowed.[15]

Waldo Johnson, also on the faculty of the U.C. School of Social Service Administration, has emphasized the importance of recognizing the father's role in the lives of welfare women and children. If fathers are ignored, he cautions, "we're not getting the full picture."[16] James Heckman adds that estranged fathers complicate the future welfare reform because they may be worse off in the low-wage workforce than on welfare.[17] Steps must be taken to adjust income supplement policy to account for their predicament. We discuss welfare reform using updated research on the results of the 1996 Welfare Reform Act at greater length in our forthcoming book *The Future of Poverty in American Cities* (Chandler & Sharp, 2006).

A review of the complexities of the existing welfare system and the variations it requires to accommodate people with differing needs recalls the simplicity inherent in the negative-income-tax plan. No wonder it received the endorsement of economists and social scientists! We think a negative-income-come-tax plan will surface again on the national agenda in the first decade of the twenty-first century and some version adopted and become the central feature of federal government programs to reduce poverty.

By 2025, "welfare" *as we have known it* will have disappeared from the political landscape in America. As our national wealth increases and finds a secure base, the standard definition of poverty is likely to be raised by Congress to a point where it is a *floor* below which no one in our society falls. In the process, the gap between the "haves" and the "have-nots" will be narrowed through redistributive measures such as an enhanced earned income tax credit program. We are also likely to see significant administrative improvements in the delivery of welfare programs for those people who require professional personal care.

One of the imponderables in forecasting the future course of welfare is the impact on public policy and public opinion of the "new immigration." By "new immigration," we mean the large numbers of people who have come to the United States in the past twenty-five years or so from Asia, the Pacific Islands, Latin America, the Caribbean, and the Middle East—all from cultures very different from that of the traditional European immigrants. We do not know how their cultural traditions and faith-based beliefs regarding the status and treatment of the poor, the afflicted, and the unfortunate comport with prevailing American attitudes. Nor do we know the extent to which these new immigrants bring with them communal institutions that practice group programs of mutual aid and support (for example, the Korean communities in America). To what extent and in what ways will such practices (or absence thereof) affect their own attitudes toward public provision versus private charity? How will that play out in the political dialogue of the twenty-first century and how will mainstream, faith-based, and eleemosynary institutions respond?

Racial Discrimination and Housing

If poverty were the only cause of urban blight in America, federal antipoverty programs set in motion in the 1930s and added to in the 1960s would probably already have succeeded in reducing poverty to manageable proportions. What has made urban poverty in America intractable is racial discrimination. By 1980, the race factor still held median incomes of Black families to about 60% of those of white families. The gap was higher in previous decades and it has not narrowed much since 1980.

Numerous studies since the 1950s have identified discriminatory practices in the labor market as the major cause of relatively lower earnings of minority workers and incomes of households. The discriminatory factors in the labor market can be traced to *prior* discrimination in the schools, to *past* market discrimination affecting work skills and experience, to *current* labor market discrimination, and to *continuing* discrimination in the housing market. Discrimination in the housing market has for generations put serious limitations on Black residential choice. In spite of federal, state, and local laws prohibiting housing discrimination, Blacks have been effectively excluded from some white neighborhoods in central cities and many suburban locations where employment is available and public schools are better than those in poverty neighborhoods.

Forcing people into poverty by cutting off employment opportunities and the training required for qualification was at one time a deliberate (often de jure) form of racial discrimination. Yet an even more effective strategy for cutting people off from economic opportunity has been housing discrimination, especially in metropolitan areas, where commuting can be a problem for everyone. Impose a policy of housing segregation on an entire urban area, and everyone is inconvenienced; some are deprived of work.

That is what happened in American cities as they grew in population throughout the twentieth century. Housing segregation was established early in the history of the country when free Blacks established themselves in towns and cities. Once the Great Migration was under way in the twentieth century, the tradition held; it was relaxed somewhat only when the Fair Housing Act of 1968 prohibited discrimination in housing. In spite of this legislation and similar actions of state legislatures, de facto housing discrimination has persisted and, as a consequence, by the end of the century Blacks and other minorities continued to settle in central cities and older suburbs. A few middle- and upper-class minorities increasingly found housing in white suburbs, but only a few. Affluent minorities who remained in the older neighborhoods either had their businesses there or commuted to jobs elsewhere in the metropolitan area. Whites established themselves in the newer suburbs, and most became commuters.

A 1999 study by University of Michigan researchers looking at residential segregation in the 107 largest U.S. cities found that Blacks were extremely isolated in one-third of them. David Williams, a co-author, told the *Christian Science Monitor* that racism was largely to blame for segregated housing patterns. For historical reasons, Williams said, many African Americans are afraid to live in mixed residential neighborhoods. He noted that segregation levels in major cities have declined only slightly since the Fair Housing Act of 1968.[18]

John Kain's words, written in 1979, still have currency:

> If racial discrimination had not existed in urban housing markets, private location decisions would have produced a far different geographic distribution of the low-income Black population. Blacks employed in the suburbs would have selected housing near their places of employment, just as similar White workers do. The relative and often absolute dispersal of employment, rising incomes, and declining real transport costs would have reduced the demand for central city dwelling units, which centrally employed middle- and high-income households would have been encouraged by low prices to buy and renovate. In neighborhoods where units were unsuitable for renovation, still lower prices would have encouraged private developers, perhaps assisted by government programs, to carry out more comprehensive urban renewal schemes.[19]

To underscore the point about racial discrimination as a barrier to social mobility in America, take the case of the Roma (popularly called "Gypsies") in Eastern Europe. The discrimination against them is as well known and well documented as that against African Americans in the U.S. Of the Roma, Aviezer Tucker writes, "The plight of East Europe's Roma is real and acute.

They cannot get equal education and suffer severe discrimination in housing and employment. High unemployment leads to poverty, petty criminality, welfare dependence, high birth rates, high infant mortality, and resentment by ethnic majorities." The Roma are, he says, "the new Jews" of Eastern Europe.[20]

Americans would also recognize in the plight of East Europe's Roma that of African Americans. The point is underscored in this country by the abundance of wealth and employment opportunities. In Eastern Europe the discrimination was partly justified by competition for jobs in a struggling economy in the process of recovery from a long period of domination and exploitation by a powerful neighbor. No such justification can apply in this country.

The lesson of the Roma is that where racial discrimination cuts off opportunities for education and job training as well as employment, the victims are likely to be poor—even in a wealthy society. The consequences of discrimination provide the foundation for a permanent culture of poverty that is hard to eradicate. That is what we are dealing with in this country.

John Kain's point was that racial discrimination in housing has made urban areas inconvenient and inefficient—in practical ways that affect the quality of everyone's life. Yet those inconveniences and inefficiencies are of small consequence compared to the moral issues raised by the impoverishment of the most vulnerable among us. Racial discrimination in housing markets requires aggressive enforcement of antidiscrimination law, reeducation of those who practice or "go along with" discrimination, and adoption of new attitudes by other citizens. Also, minorities should act individually and through organizations to end discrimination. The enforcement could be made metropolitan- or region-wide by assigning that function to an administrative unit of the proposed substate districts.

Racial discrimination as Americans have experienced it will gradually fade from our national culture. By the middle of the twenty-first century, possibly by 2025, *class* rather than race will largely determine where people live, attend school, work, and shop. Even now, sociologists question whether the concept of class as we have interpreted it is still applicable in American society. Norman Elkin asks, "Is it 'class' or behaviors and life styles?" He suggests that historically "class" translated to certain behaviors and life styles, but, he asks, is that true anymore? "People want to live next door to others whose behavior is *predictable, nonaggressive,* and *acceptable,* regardless of income, education, occupation, etc.; that is the current 'civility' crisis in society."[21]

Who can say when that process took hold? Perhaps in the aftermath of the inner-city riots of the 1960s that set off a period of national soul-searching. That collective national soul-searching was reflected in the McCone Report,[22] which examined the causes of one of the early inner-city riots of the period (Watts in Los Angeles, 1965). The Kerner Commission Report,[23] published in 1968 in response to the growing crescendo of inner-city riots, asserted the existence of two societies in America, one Black and one white. The decline of prejudice and discrimination could not have begun *before* the riots, and the decline has been gradual. But the momentum was increasingly noticeable as the twentieth century drew to a close. Gunnar Myrdal, in his classic analysis of race relations in America, published in 1944, called the process "the principle of cumulation."

> White prejudice and discrimination keep the Negro low in standards of living, health, education, manners and morale. This, in turn, gives support to White prejudice. White prejudice and Negro standards thus mutually "cause" each other. . . . Such a static "accommodation" is, however, entirely accidental. If either of the factors changes, this will cause a change in the other factor, too, and start a process of interaction where the change in one factor will continuously be supported by the reaction of the other factor.[24]

Troubled Schools in Inner Cities

The fact of extreme housing segregation by race in most American metropolitan areas guarantees segregated public schools in those areas. For two or three decades after *Brown v. Board of Education* in 1954, the courts tried to force integration of public schools by imposing intercommunity busing. The busing solution gradually lost ground as the numbers of students who had to be bused increased and parents, both Black and white, raised objections. After *Milliken v. Bradley* in 1974 ruled that segregation in schools had to result from deliberate public policy to require a court-enforced busing remedy, the busing movement lost momentum. At the end of the century, there was more public-school segregation than ever.

The trouble with segregated schools, as the Supreme Court concluded in *Brown v. Board of Education,* is that the ones with a majority of minority students almost always have inferior educational programs, especially the ones that serve impoverished neighborhoods. Therefore, as long as discriminatory practices in housing persist in urban areas, priority must be given to improving public schools in minority neighborhoods. Federal and state educational funds must be allocated disproportionately to the schools with substandard programs, as measured by standard student achievement tests. Teachers in these schools who do not test to appropriate levels on *teacher* achievement tests should be replaced with teachers with *better than average* records. Higher-than-average salaries and bonuses must be offered to the replacements as inducements to work in difficult schools.

To ease the job of teachers, public schools should end the policy of requiring children to continue their education until they are sixteen or seventeen. Children in their teens who do not want to go to school should not be forced to do so by public authorities. Of course, parental authority is another matter. But parents who insist that reluctant children attend school should take *full responsibility* for keeping them there—and for ensuring their behavior in the classroom. Teachers and principals should have the authority to expel disruptive students and their parents should have the responsibility of negotiating reentry.

We think that such improvements in substandard inner-city public schools would help to ensure that the rough diamonds among the hard-core poor emerge from negative social environments and have a chance to reach their full potential as productive people. Therefore, we must reverse the starvation-diet policies of national, state, and local support for public education. We must begin without delay to provide adequate and equalized funds for all of our public schools. To achieve that goal, a new federal revenue-sharing program should be designed to equalize per pupil expenditures among all school districts in the nation. Once expenditures per pupil are equalized to support core educational programs, local communities should be allowed to spend as they choose in their school systems. No federal or state revenue-sharing program should lessen local control of public schools or parent involvement in decisions about core or extracurricular programs.

There must be a special emphasis in federal education policy on elementary and secondary education. The Great Society program Head Start should be funded to cover all children who meet eligibility requirements, and it should be extended through high school. The states should refocus on educational standards with special emphasis on teacher qualification and teacher education. Local school districts should focus on the performance of teachers and students in the classroom and on parent participation.

Jonathan Barnett, in "National Agenda for Action," the closing chapter of his book *The Fractured Metropolis*, is specific: "The failure of schools in inner-city areas perpetuates their tragedies," he asserts. "Establishing national educational standards, and overcoming entrenched funding inequalities, will help give everyone access to a good education."[25] The establishment of national educational standards was precisely the objective of the No Child Left Behind Act of 2001, sponsored by the George W. Bush administration, who declared education to be his highest domestic priority.

Barnett, a professor of architecture and urban design, emphasizes that schools are a critical factor in economic development and, without good ones in all parts of urban regions, businesses with jobs to offer will not locate in the community. But good schools anywhere will attract businesses that need a ready supply of well-trained and well-educated people. Barnett's point is an obvious one for the suburbs, but less so for inner-city communities populated by the poor where such investment is needed most. The planning and research functions of the proposed substate districts could help public school systems make the connection in their curricula to regional economic development.

It would be hard to think of a more powerful strategy for identifying and nurturing the rough diamonds of distressed neighborhoods in our central cities than providing public schools of excellence linked to nearby knowledge-based industries eager to have them on the payroll once they complete their schooling. Such programs exist in some parts of the country. In Beaumont, Texas, a group of shopping-center partners sponsors the "I have a dream" program, which guarantees youngsters support for college and a job if they stay in school and achieve reasonable goals.

The first quarter of the twenty-first century should see positive, and sometimes imaginative, developments in improving public-school education in our central cities. Pressure of competition from charter schools and vouchers supported by special state and federal programs will impel big-city public school systems to follow the lead of Chicago, Dallas, and other education-minded cities in curriculum and classroom improvements that will give talented students what they seek and pull most of the rest along behind them. Programs like the federally sponsored school-based twenty-first-century Community Learning Centers for after-school programs could set the pace for parallel nonprofit and private corporation projects. By the fall of 1999, there were 468 Learning Centers in forty-nine states.

The charter schools movement, which originated in the early years of the 1990s, was still in the experimental stage in 2001 and not much further along in 2005. A federal report "The Schools and Staffing Survey," released in August 2004, showed that students in charter schools largely trailed comparable students in traditional public schools on math and reading tests. The New American Schools Development Corporation, created in 1991 in response to the first President Bush's challenge to private businesses to develop "break the mold" schools that would offer excellence in public education, was followed by Theodore Sizer's "essential schools," Henry Levin's "accelerated schools," and Christopher Whittle's "Edison schools." In the ensuing years, thirty-seven states have passed legislation to charter such alternative schools. By 2000, more than 1,700 charter schools had been established, along with a Center for Educational Reform to promote them, to advise prospective founders, and to offer guidance in the formulation and adjustment of authorizing state legislation.

The first decade of the new century should provide the evidence needed to assess the contribution of charter schools to American public education.[26] The beneficial challenge they present to public education was already apparent in 2000, but the data were not yet available to answer the question, "Do students achieve more in charter schools than they would in traditional public schools?" The jury was still out on the question in 2001. In this regard, critics Thomas Good and Jennifer Braden, authors of *The Great Debate: Choice, Vouchers, and Charters*, found that "charter schools spend less on classroom instruction than traditional schools and have not engineered new approaches to teaching."[27]

A cause for optimism for public education in the decades ahead is the fact that education emerged in the mid-1990s as a high national priority. President Clinton continued the Reagan administration's initiative in emphasizing education early in his eight-year tenure of office and never let up pressure on Congress to increase federal support for reducing classroom size and adding teachers, and for funding numerous programs targeting urban and inner-city schools. A Republican administration elected in 2000 underscored education as a national priority and backed legislation in Congress to increase federal funding and establish annual national student performance testing in the "No child left behind" legislation. However, public educators were largely critical of the administration's failure to recommend full funding for the program.

Another cause for optimism is that with the nation's growing wealth support for improvement of public education was growing in 2001. People were also recognizing the need for a public education system that can produce graduates who are competent to move into the workaday world of knowledge-based industry. By the time the first decade of the new century is over, most Americans will have accepted the fact of the global economy and its implications for the education of their children.

The Future of Regional Health Planning

The comprehensive regional health planning that got its start in the Partnership for Health Act of 1966 (P.L. 89-749) seemed at the time to be a promising and much-needed initiative, although the program was resisted and then co-opted by the medical and health professions. Up to the 1960s and 1970s, the medical establishment and related health professionals always opposed any government-sponsored medical or health programs. The profession opposed Medicare and Medicaid in the mid-1960s until negotiations produced a bill that satisfied the leaders of the profession.

In the 1960s and 1970s, the medical profession generally regarded "community medicine" as offbeat or radical.[28] The predominant view of health planning among physicians and many health professionals was that planning might lead to "socialized medicine," in which the government would operate hospitals and health clinics and reimburse physicians for most medical services. Hospital administrators have always regarded government-sponsored planning as a threat to their independence.

The medical establishment continued to resist health facilities planning in the 1960s and 1970s. Even group practice was frowned upon for many years after Medicare and Medicaid were implemented—until practitioners and their patients began to appreciate the benefits of direct federal payments to physicians.

Today, we have a plethora of government-sponsored facilities and services—Medicare and Medicaid, Veterans Administration hospitals, military hospitals and clinics, health clinics in rural communities and in poor inner-city neighborhoods, all of which employ physicians and other health professionals. We also have private and nonprofit hospitals and clinics, which also employ physicians and health professionals. Group practice has become the norm and solo practice the exception. What we do not yet have is a medical and healthcare system to which everyone in the nation has access. Forty-five million people (and counting) do not have any form of healthcare insurance. There is no reliable network of "first echelon" community diagnostic centers. Existing community clinics are uneven in professional staff, both qualitatively and in numbers. Some are well staffed but lack a full range of diagnostic capabilities and/or referral services. Others are hard-pressed to provide the services demanded of them. Many of the nonprofit clinics must spend scarce resources to raise private funds as well as foundation and government grants.

The track record of comprehensive health planning during the past quarter-century does not bode well for the first quarter of the new century. There is no vitality left in the Partnership for Health program of the 1960s and 1970s, and there is no sign of a revival any time soon. Should the states adopt the substate district model we propose, the need for closing gaps in regional healthcare systems will probably emerge as a priority target for study. Such studies are most likely to be initiated once we achieve a national healthcare insurance program that places the uninsured in the ranks of the insured. The new demand for health and medical services will then spur action in improved and expanded facilities.

The Future Impact of
New Technologies on Urban Regions

The difficulty in foreseeing the impact of new or emerging technologies on urban areas is that we can only guess at what technologies may appear on the scene in the future. It is even hard to see what applications emerging technologies may be put to as new demands arise and inventive minds focus on them. Moreover, as Aaron Fleisher observed in 1961, "The flows of urban and technological time are not commensurate and therefore fifty years of urban history is at most equivalent to thirty years of technology."[29] Probably Fleisher would revise his estimate of the technological time to a much smaller number if he were writing that article today. At the time he wrote his article, Fleisher was on the MIT faculty and an expert user of MIT's then state-of-the-art IBM research computers, which filled a large room and operated with tapes and punch cards.

Nobody in 1961 foresaw the development of the PC and the laptop, the rapid evolution of the computer chip, the rapid deployment of the fiber-optic cable, satellite-assisted telecommunications, the Internet, e-mail, and the rest. Yet the impact of these technologies on the physical shape and form of cities was by the end of the twentieth century a fair approximation of Fleisher's projections. Norman Elkin argues that "the impact of communications technologies up to the present has been on the pace (sense of time) of urban life rather than on its physical shape or form ... it is the transportation technologies—the automobile and highways, ships and ports, trucks and tollways, air travel and airports—that have had the greatest impact on the physical shape of the metropolitan area and is one of the real dynamics in the evolution of *regional consciousness* and political interaction."[30]

Yet some spectacular technological developments were in the making at the turn of the third millennium, and their impact on society is as yet hardly discernible. Consider the predictions of another MIT professor, Ray Kurzweil, in his 1999 book *The Age of Spiritual Machines: When Computers Exceed Human Intelligence.* Within a decade the translating telephone will allow one to speak in English with, say, a Chinese colleague who hears the words in Chinese. By the 2020s, neural implants will be available to improve one's sensory experiences, memory, cognitive faculties, and creativity. By 2025 or sooner, we will have the resolution, speed, and bandwidth to scan the entire human brain—about 20 billion calculations per second. A mind-boggling prediction: by the 2030s, people will be able to download their brains into a computer and create a self-replica! In a previous book, *The Age of Intelligent Machines* (1990), Kurzweil predicted the World Wide Web, defeat by a computer of a world-class chess champion, and near-total reliance on digital image pattern recognition and other software-based technologies in warfare. All of these predictions had come to pass by the turn of the new century.

The computer and its related technologies have displaced people in offices in every sector of the economy, have encouraged the concentration of business controls and of people, and have freed up business-location decisions of all kinds. The decreasing cost of computers and the increasing mobility and convenience of PCs and laptops have only made location decisions easier.

Fleisher's hint at the concentration of business controls in cities due to computers is borne out by the flocking of telecommunication companies to locations where fiber-optic cable networks are available. Downtown Los Angeles is a case in point. James Blair has described the ambivalence of Los Angeles officials toward the rapid influx of telecommunications companies aiming to locate switching equipment as close as possible to the network of downtown fiber-optic cables. The companies have moved into old buildings long emptied of previous tenants, who moved to industrial and office facilities around the regional airports or to suburbs outside the city. The concern of Los Angeles officials and some real estate people was that the telecom industry would fill the abandoned office spaces with a mass of humming wires but very few people. They feared "peopleless" factories in the center of downtown that would leave the city with fewer people than would be healthy for its people-oriented service businesses—restaurants, flower shops, boutiques, and the like. One real estate broker remarked to the writer of the *Christian Science Monitor* story, "With moderation, I think we'll be fine."[31] The reality is that telecom-oriented downtowns will not be peopleless. Just as the interstate highway system attracts automobiles, fiber-optic networks will attract telecom companies. But the telecom companies attract people to operate and service them. They are the kinds of people who want to live near their job, even if they are in the center of a city. The boutiques, restaurants, and service providers will have their customers and downtown Los Angeles and other telecom-oriented downtowns will be better places in which to live ten years and twenty-five years hence.

Of all the various technologies that find application in and around cities, transportation is especially relevant to the physical shape and form of cities because in its various modes it spans distance and time. It is the application and organization of transportation and communications technologies rather than the invention of new types that will change the shape and size of cities and urban regions. To be sure, better automobiles, trains, buses and communications devices—especially wireless ones—are being developed, but it will be *how* these technologies are used that will impact cities and the regions around them. Pollution-free automobiles and buses—some in use in 2005—are beginning to reduce the contamination of the air urban dwellers breathe and that contribute to improved personal health. (The city of Chattanooga is operating a federally funded experimental downtown "free" bus shuttle system with a fleet of battery-operated buses. Chattanooga was once one of the more air-polluted cities in the nation.)

Pollution-free automobiles already in use are smaller, better engineered for maintenance, and better adapted to city driving conditions than vehicles typical of twentieth-century models. Quantum advances in the technology of trains and the construction and design of mass transportation systems in and around cities are contributing to the efficiency of moving goods and people. The redesign and reconstruction of the Berlin railroad system, moving toward completion in 2001, is an impressive example of how a well-planned urban mass-transportation system can free a great metropolitan area to achieve its economic and cultural potential. With the reconversion of the city into the nation's capital, Berlin has become a delightful new city. Other large cities that have not yet undertaken such major development or redevelopment of their mass-transportation systems would of course face planning and construction time horizons that might take several decades. The costs involved in such projects are always a hindrance because they are hard to project with any reasonable accuracy, much less control.

Boston's hemmed-in central area, with water on three sides, is undergoing a transformation as a major elevated-highway arterial has opened below ground level, with new tunnels under the harbor. The project was thought to be the largest engineering undertaking in history and was known as "the big dig." The Boston metropolitan area has a rail system that crisscrosses the city and reaches down the Northeast Corridor to New York and Washington, D.C.; a high-speed train on that corridor promises further efficiencies for business and recreational travel. These improvements are likely to be completed by 2010.

As these physical improvements in transportation are made in city after city around the globe in the twenty-first century, the cities will be the recipients of communications systems that enhance everyday living and make them convenient, comfortable, and profitable places in which to do business. No more rushing across the city or even next door to meetings; these can now take place without anyone being required to traverse space or to experience any of the discomforts we associate with traversing space against the clock.

The downside is that, while people may not need to travel for work in future years, private vehicle ownership and usage will continue to grow because people have to commute for more and more *other* daily needs—medical services, entertainment, leisure activities, education, shopping, and even visiting relatives and friends. The result for the foreseeable future will be more rather than less traffic.

However, we can confidently say that solutions for transportation and communications problems affecting cities are at hand or are likely to be achieved as needs arise. We can confidently say that we know how to do these things or that we know how to discover how to do them. What remains to be invented is a zero emissions technology for disposing of industrial and residential wastes, and a foolproof technology for disposal of nuclear wastes. Of course, once they do come to pass these inventions will have no effect on the size or form of urban regions. Only the shortage of water can limit the size of cities.

Growth Control—from the Bottom Up

Local zoning was the original form of growth control in the United States. In 1926, the U.S. Supreme Court upheld the concept as a valid exercise of local police power in *Village of Euclid v. Ambler Realty Co.*, 272 U.S. 365 (1926).[32] By that year, more than two hundred localities had zoning ordinances, some guided by the U.S. Department of Commerce's Model Standard Zoning Enabling Act, issued in 1924 and subsequently adopted by most of the states. The movement came to be known as Euclidean zoning and was an early influence in spreading the idea of the general plan as a guide to city growth.

In succeeding decades, the courts gradually sorted out the constitutional validity of state, regional, and municipal zoning and other growth-control measures, generally approving those that did not violate the Equal Protection clause of the Fourteenth Amendment (especially as it applied to racial discrimination), the Fifth Amendment clause prohibiting taking private property without just compensation (substantive due process), or the constitutionally protected right to travel (not explicitly mentioned in the Constitution but treated by the Supreme Court as a fundamental right). The courts also tended to approve zoning and growth-control measures that were shown to be a valid exercise of the police power in promoting the general welfare.

In the past several decades, deliberate growth control by governments in urban areas has usually been aimed at limiting the quantity and quality of physical development and at controlling population influx. As in the earlier zoning cases, the courts have generally supported local and state governments in growth-control actions as long as they do not violate any of the constitutional principles summarized above. For example, the Ramapo Plan adopted by the Planning Board of the Town of Ramapo, New York, and the Petaluma Plan adopted by the City Council of Petaluma, California, were enacted by local authorities to protect the character of the communities and to slow growth while public services maintained or stayed ahead of the pace of development. In Ramapo plaintiffs charged that the plan was exclusionary and that it took property without compensation. In Petaluma plaintiffs charged infringement of the right to travel. Both plans were upheld over plaintiffs' objections of unconstitutionality.[33] Likewise at the regional level, the courts have upheld land-use-control programs in the face of charges of the taking of private property without compensation.[34]

In cases where zoning was blatantly exclusionary, the courts have not hesitated to rule for plaintiffs. Several such cases have originated in Pennsylvania and New Jersey courts. In *National Land Investment Co. v. Kohn*, a four-acre minimum lot requirement in Easttown Township, Pennsylvania, was found exclusionary and therefore unconstitutional because the policy did not bear a substantial relationship to proper police-power purposes. Zoning is, after all, an exercise of the police power of local government, but where four-acre zoning may exclude lower-class buyers, the argument can be made that such large-lot zoning, which was intended to reduce pressure on the limited capacity of local services, went too far and resulted in the unfair exclusion of a class of buyers. In a similar case the same court declared that Concord Township's two- and three-acre minimum lot requirements in certain residential neighborhoods were "thinly veiled justifications for exclusionary zoning." In the oft-cited case *Southern Burlington County NAACP v. Township of Mt. Laurel*, the New Jersey Supreme Court ruled that the township acted to control development to attract a selective type of growth, "and that through its zoning ordinances has exhibited economic discrimination in that the poor have been deprived of adequate housing and the opportunity to secure the construction of subsidized housing."[35]

We described in Chapter 9 the efforts of thirteen states which, starting with Hawaii in 1971, have tried to control the form and location of new development. These efforts at the state level were instigated primarily by the environmental movement, which, like the feminist movement of the day, has had a long tradition of activism. The environmental movement, again like the feminist movement, gained fresh vitality and momentum from the antiwar (Vietnam) and Black protest movements of the 1960s.[36] The states, as we saw in Chapter 9, were by the early 1970s already deeply involved in federally mandated local and regional comprehensive planning and planning review. Some of the states were moved more aggressively toward comprehensive land-use measures than others, notably the thirteen whose growth control programs we summarized in Chapter 9. But the thirteen have set the stage for increasing state leadership in growth control in the decades ahead. In this area, the states were in effect running experiments and comparing notes. Some state growth-control efforts were working well, while others faltered. Tests of legality and constitutionality have been moving through the court system. Tests of political feasibility were moving through legislatures and running gauntlets assembled by the private interests. Tests of public interest are constantly put before the citizenry.

A New Cycle in the Urbanization of American Society: Reinvestment and Civic Enhancement of Cities

Patterns of urban development that have characterized American cities and their environs throughout the twentieth century—central-city deterioration and suburban sprawl—are increasingly the subject of critical scrutiny by professional planners and some of the public officials with whom they work. The phrase "smart growth" came into currency in the 1990s to describe in a sound-bite phrase the concept of controlling urban growth by deliberate public policies—most originating at the state level—to coordinate infrastructure and transportation planning with public and private urban development. The essence of the concept was to encourage development around or in conjunction with train and bus facilities and to discourage the further spread of automobile-dependent "bedroom" communities. Paul Pezzotta has cautioned that suburban development during the last half of the twentieth century devoured land, roadway networks, land-fill disposal sites, and other public resources around cities until, toward the end of the century, the costs of further development exceeded the returns in most urban areas. In Pezzotta's words, "The free ride is over."[37] There has been no effective governmental mechanism at the regional level with the authority to manage and implement solutions.

As matters stand, much more automobile-dependent development will continue to go on in the early decades of the twenty-first century because of the momentum of know-how and because of habit. But the new thinking encapsulated in the phrase "smart growth" has taken hold in the states that initiated the early legislative experiments and has spread to most of the others, as benefits are shown to outweigh costs of change. The smart-growth movement can be expedited and made practical by the new system of substate districts described in Chapter 9 and summarized later in this chapter.

The principal features of "smart growth" begin with the "greening" of the automobile itself in more efficient fuel systems and perhaps eventually in a hydrogen-based fuel cell. In 2000, Honda and Toyota had begun successful marketing of gas-electric hybrids in the U.S. A partnership was developed between America's "Big Three" automakers and the U.S. government aimed at putting ultraefficient cars on the road by 2004. Also, automobile use for commuting may be greatly reduced in new communities in which transit modes, shopping, service, and recreation facilities are within walking distance (see Chapter 8). These new communities, once they gain greater currency, will provide a balance between automobile access and pedestrian/bicycle paths. The heart of smart growth is transit-oriented development, Peter Calthorpe's concept of new urban development designed to make it more convenient for people to walk and to ride public transit than to use the automobile, and simultaneously minimize congestion on surrounding roads.[38]

A second feature of the smart-growth concept is the establishment or revival of transit networks that connect development nodes in metropolitan regions. Some of this has been and continues to be done in cities around the globe, but it will be more deliberately done in the United States in the next two or three decades as new, mixed-use communities are developed in central cities and on their fringes. Much of this kind of development will have replaced suburban sprawl by 2025, and sprawl development may by then be seen as an anachronism.

A third feature of the smart-growth concept is several related policies that may be used to direct regional development into compact urban centers and nodes, some of which will be planned new communities. These policies include urban-growth boundaries, transfers of development rights, "clustering," and "concurrency."

Urban-growth boundaries, taken for granted in some European countries, were beginning to be incorporated in the smart-growth policies of some states and municipalities in the 1990s. An urban-growth boundary is a mapped line that separates potential urban land from rural land within which urban growth is contained for a specified period of time. Because urban-growth boundaries require large areas in order effectively to contain regional growth, they are often designated on a regional basis or by intergovernmental agreement.

State law in Washington and Oregon requires urban-growth boundaries. The smart-growth concept promulgated by state government is based on the premise that the state is entitled to make investments that are most likely to make efficient use of resources over the long run. "If the state builds schools, libraries, roads, and sewage treatment plants, it should be able to limit those investments to the 'smartest' locations, or areas most capable of supporting that growth."[39]

In Portland, Oregon, the urban-growth boundary is administered by Metro, the only elected *regional* government in the United States. The urban boundary is used in the Portland region to ensure that an appropriate mixture of new development and in-fill development occurs. For its part in the regional smart-growth strategy, the city of Portland has placed an emphasis on redeveloping the central city, especially downtown.

Transfer of development rights (TDR) is a useful tool when landowners are faced with zoning restrictions that would prevent a proposed development plan. State law or local ordinances permitting purchase of development rights give landowners the option of acquiring the appropriate development rights from a landowner elsewhere. Thus, a TDR policy provides flexibility in areawide planning by allowing landowners in restricted areas ("sending" areas) to transfer densities and development rights to landowners in areas appropriate for higher densities ("receiving" areas). Robert Freilich offers the following example: "A TDR system can be used to support transit-oriented development by designating areas around transit stops as receiving areas for TDRs."[40] Freilich observes that the TDR system may also have the secondary effect of channeling development into transit-oriented development areas by restricting development *outside* transit centers.

"Clustering" is simply the application of zoning in areas that require densities in order to encourage utilization of public transit. Cluster development is a feature of new communities and the key to transit-oriented development. Thus, new communities and transit-oriented development go hand in hand.

The principle of concurrency in urban planning is the use of construction permits to tie new development to availability of public services and facilities. In transit-oriented development, the establishment of transit-concurrency-management areas is a strategic administrative framework for utilizing concurrency management to assure coordination of mass transit, economic development, and desirable urban form in the planning of new communities.

It will take most of the first quarter of the twenty-first century for the smart-growth concept to become the accepted mode of urban growth in America, and perhaps in Europe as well, where signs of the sprawl mode have appeared. By the early 1990s, several states—including Florida, California, Oregon, and Washington—had incorporated transit-oriented development and neotraditional planning principles into their zoning and planning statutes. Neotraditional planning uses traditional town or village design features such as narrow streets, front porches, detached rear parking, and a central green area.

The California legislature in 1963 created local agency formation commissions (LAFCOs) for each county in the state. These seven-member commissions have two representatives from cities, two from the county supervisors, two from the special districts, and one public member chosen by the other six. The LAFCOs regulate the growth of cities and special districts, setting "spheres of influence" and boundaries beyond which cities and special districts (but not school districts) are not allowed to grow without LAFCO approval. LAFCOs are also the bodies to which would-be cities apply to incorporate. If LAFCO deems the prospective city capable of funding and delivering city services, LAFCO will instruct the county supervisor to call for an incorporation election in which the citizens of the planned new city vote on incorporation. LAFCOs have no land-use planning authority beyond setting spheres of influence, but LAFCOs were mentioned in a statewide commission studying local government as potential candidates to serve within each county as a regional or quasi-regional land-use and regional planning body. Yet, in the first four decades of their existence, LAFCOs lacked the resources and political clout to be more than reactive agencies with minimal impact on land-use patterns.[41]

The basic factors driving sprawl are strong everywhere: demand for housing choice, flight from central cities where crime and school quality are issues, and on-again, off-again efforts by public officials to implement smart-growth policies. Also, shifting land-use demands can frustrate efforts by public officials to provide transportation services.[42] The consequences of sprawl include disappearing agricultural acreage and open space, longer commutes, and the constant increase in exhaust-driven smog. The cross-boundary constituency for a comprehensive-planning approach to the regional problems includes work-ers trapped in long commutes who want to live closer to their jobs, employers located in exurban areas whose workers need affordable housing, and local residents of areas of the city and inner-ring suburbs who seek redevelopment for revitalizing deteriorating tax bases.[43]

In Chapter 8 we sketched the American experience in the twentieth cen-tury with new communities. We noted the new-communities legislation on the books at the federal level and some of the projects that resulted from the legislation. We concluded that new communities could be a means of coun-tering urban conditions now pejoratively termed "sprawl." We see in a revived federal commitment to the new-communities concept the possibility of re-newing major tracts in some of our central cities, perhaps in all of our largest ones. In the new century, the new-town concept could be used as the leading edge of an effort to harness urban growth so that it can work in the public interest. After all, the quality of life in America in the century ahead depends on the quality of life in cities.

Substate Districts: Improving Planning and Delivery of Urban Services in the Twenty-first Century

We think that by 2025, the time horizon of this book, the planning process at the state level will have sorted itself out and that most of the states will by then have enacted politically sound and legally defensible programs of growth con-trol. By 2025 the states will have developed the planning and administrative structures at the regional and local levels for implementing those programs. The substate planning and administrative districts proposed in Chapter 9 are ideal for the job. Each state should tailor the model to its specific political and administrative needs.

Here we address some of the broader issues bearing upon the quality of life in our cities and their environs. A good quality of life cannot be achieved in isolated suburban enclaves in which people pursue the illusion of social homogeneity and the good life and eschew responsible participation in the broader regional community. We should feel free to live where we please, among people like ourselves or not like ourselves, in open communities or gated ones, in the "madding crowd" or away from the madding crowd. Regardless of the personal life style we choose, however, we should create and support governmental institutions that provide the public services we require, equally available to all of the people of the community, the region, the state, and the nation. The general proposition is that all public services should be equally distributed in the jurisdiction that provides them. Economies of scale and efficiency should determine what level of government provides which services. Since most public services require some participation by each of the levels of government in our federal system, it is important that governmental agencies at all levels be organized to carry out their responsibilities and be coordinated with the agencies at all levels that share responsibilities for the services.

Ours is a complex system of service delivery, and because it is complex, optimal coordination among the levels of government and among the various agencies of government has been hard to achieve. As a result, we have struggled with limited success to achieve equitable—and effective—service delivery, especially of those services that are intended to improve the quality of life in our cities and environs and those for the hard-core poor. What is needed is a legally and politically competent regional polity that can make and implement plans to improve the lives of its people.[44] Such a regional polity in the form of the substate districts we propose has the potential to overcome the dysfunctional fragmentation of local governments and the far more serious fragmentation of the urban society (Chapter 4). We review here how the proposed substate districts would be structured and how they would function.

The proposed substate planning and administrative districts are organizational tools to improve the planning and delivery of public services in urban areas throughout the nation. At the end of the twentieth century, the missing link in public-service delivery in most states was the no-man's-land between state government and local government and between the federal government and municipalities.

In Chapter 9, we described three different models that characterized the substate districts established in the years following federal efforts to promote the concept. The three models reflected the increasing fragmentation of substate and regional planning and service organizations. The first assumed that federal agencies at the local level and in the substate district organization were separate, with minimal interagency communication and coordination. In a second model, local agencies administering federal programs (as well as regional single-purpose, nonfederal agencies) were separate from the substate district organization but the latter assumed a dominant position and reviewed the budget and planning actions of the federal-program agencies. There could also be unofficial ties between the two bodies through overlapping board membership and shared staff. In a third model, the substate district assumed total responsibility for the organization, financing, staffing, and operation of the agencies charged with administering federal programs.

The three models are reflected in existing regional planning commissions and councils of governments based in substate districts. They concentrate on physical and economic planning, are rarely involved in service delivery operations, and do little or no *social* planning. Regional social planning is the job of special-purpose planning agencies—health, manpower, and community action—and is not usually incorporated in any regional comprehensive plan.

In a reformulation of the substate district concept, we consider how to restructure regional planning so that it comprehends physical *and* social planning and links the planning function to the delivery and implementation of public services and programs. A revised substate district system should be wall-to-wall in all the states. To avoid boundary and jurisdictional barriers, the new districts should be based on *county* boundaries or *groups of counties.*

The new districts would absorb existing councils of governments, regional planning commissions, economic development districts, comprehensive health-planning agencies and other special-purpose regional planning agencies and assume their functions.

They would be authorized to combine regional planning as well as administrative functions of state agencies whose services and operations impact urban and economic development and populations.

A single new state planning and administrative department should be established in the office of the governor to combine state-level planning and administrative functions. The new substate districts should be authorized by the state legislature to review the plans of all federal and state projects and programs that impact urban and economic development and populations.

The new substate districts would have an administrator and a governing council with the authority to make comprehensive regional plans and to implement them. This structure would overcome the principal weakness of existing regional planning commissions and councils of governments—their inability to attract and support political leadership. The administrator could be directly elected (as with some mayors and county executives) or appointed by the governor.

To overcome the age-old problem of getting single-purpose agencies to work together in planning and implementing local and regional projects, the state would assign to the substate districts regional administrators representing the state departments with responsibilities for regional services and infrastructure. These regional administrators would then continue to report to their respective state commissioners, who in turn would report to the governor. In states where the substate district administrator is appointed by the governor, the governor would in effect be the chief executive in metropolitan-area business, as Martin Meyerson and Edward Banfield suggested more than forty years ago.[45] The role of the governor and legislature in the administration of the substate districts would be through the administrator of the regional offices of the state departments assigned to the substate districts. A legislature's authority is, of course, in the allocation of state funds.

The federal government should assign a "metropolitan expediter" to each substate district office. It should reaffirm federal support for the substate planning and administrative system in a new Office of Management and Budget (OMB) directive to resurrect and reaffirm policies described in Bureau of the Budget (BOB) Circular A-80 and OMB Circular A-95. Also, as we suggested in Chapter 9, the operational authority of the substate districts should have the backing of a congressionally established federal requirement that the states coordinate all federal grants and funds for regional and local programs through the substate districts.

The district administrator would have a planning and administrative staff and district budget, but not direct control over project budgets of state departments residing in the district office. The district administrator would work with the state's regional directors to prepare a district budget related to a regional plan. The district administrator's primary role would be that of political administrator, whose job would be to mediate among the regionalized state departments, as well as between state interests and local concerns.

The district administrator, the heads of the regional state departments and the federal representative would serve as the regional planning committee based in the substate district headquarters. This committee would resolve differences among local governments in the district. The emphasis of the regional-planning function would be on setting priorities among state and federal programs. The planning function of the substate districts would thus be fulfilled. Their other major function would be coordination and implementation of projects sponsored by the federal and state governments—a giant step beyond that of existing regional planning agencies and councils of governments.

Notes

1. *Schechter Poultry Corporation v. United States*, 295 U.S. 495 (1935).
2. U.S. Bureau of the Census.
3. Personal correspondence to Conant commenting on Chapter 10.
4. See especially Jonathan Kozol, *Ordinary Resurrections: Children in the Years of Hope*, (New York: Crown, 2000).
5. Personal correspondence to Conant commenting on Chapter 10.
6. Ralph W. Conant, "Rough Diamonds among the Hard-Core Poor," *Dialogue: An Essay of Opinion and Policy* 8 (April 1999). New York: The Phelps Stokes Fund.
7. Edward C. Banfield, *The Unheavenly City* (Boston: Little, Brown, 1968, 1970), p. 116.
8. Milton Friedman, *Capitalism and Freedom* (Chicago: University of Chicago Press, 1962), Chapt. 12.
9. U.S. Senate Joint Economic Committee, "The EITC and the Taxation of Lower-Income Working Families," Joint Economic Committee Staff Report, March 2000.
10. Banfield, *Unheavenly City*, p. 121.
11. Jeremy Rifkin, *The End of Work: The Decline of the Global Labor Force and the Dawn of the Post-Market Era* (New York: G.P. Putnam's Sons, 1995), p. 292.
12. Diana M. DiNitto, *Social Welfare Politics and Public Policy*, 4th edn. (Boston: Allyn & Bacon, 1995), pp. 167–168. Quoted in "Federalism at the Millennium," *Urban Lawyer* 31 (4): 740n357.
13. Reported in the article by Charlotte Snow, "Is Welfare Working?" *University of Chicago Magazine* 91, no. 4 (April 1999).
14. Interview with Susan Mayer, quoted in Snow, "Is Welfare Working?" p. 24.
15. Julia Henley, her chapter in *Women and Work in the Post-Welfare Era*, ed. J. F. Handler and L. White (White Plains, N.Y.: M. E. Sharpe, 1999). See also Susan Mayer, *What Money Can't Buy: How Parental Income Influences Children's Outcomes* (Cambridge, Mass.: Harvard University Press, 1998); and James Heckman, "Education and Job Training Myths," *Public Interest* (Spring 1999).

16. Waldo E. Johnson, quoted in Snow, "Is Welfare Working?" p. 28.

17. James Heckman, quoted in Snow, "Is Welfare Working?" p. 28.

18. Chiquita Collins and David R. Williams, "Segregation and Mortality: The Deadly Effects of Racism," *Social Forum* 14, no. 3 (1999): 493–521. The quote from David Williams appeared in the *Christian Science Monitor*, November 12, 1999, p. 24. The *Monitor* listed from the study the ten most segregated U.S. cities in the following order: Atlanta (the most segregated); Cleveland; Detroit; Chicago; Gary, Ind.; Jackson, Miss.; Baltimore; Washington; St. Louis; and Birmingham, Ala.

19. John F. Kain, "Failure in Diagnosis: A Critique of the National Urban Policy," *Urban Lawyer* 11, no. 2 (1979): 256.

20. Aviezer Tucker, *Christian Science Monitor*, November 5, 1999, p. 11.

21. Personal correspondence to Conant commenting on Chapter 10.

22. Governor's Commission on the Los Angeles Riots, *Violence in the City—an End or a Beginning?* Los Angeles, December 2, 1965.

23. *Report of the National Advisory Commission on Civil Disorders* (New York: Bantam Books, 1968).

24. Gunnar Myrdal, *An American Dilemma* (New York: Harper, 1944), pp. 75–76.

25. Jonathan Barnett, *The Fractured Metropolis, Improving the New City, Restoring the Old City, Reshaping the Region* (New York: HarperCollins, 1995), p. 234.

26. Chester E. Finn Jr., Bruno V. Manno, Gregg Vanourek, *Charter Schools in Action: Renewing Public Education* (Princeton, N.J.: Princeton University Press, 2000).

27. Thomas Good and Jennifer Braden, *The Great School Debate: Choice, Vouchers, and Charters* (Mahwah, N.J.: L. Erlbaum & Associates, 2000).

28. Alan Shank and Ralph W. Conant, "Politics and Policies of Community Health Planning," in *Urban Perspectives: Politics and Policies* (Boston: Holbrook Press, Inc., 1975).

29. Aaron Fleisher, "The Influence of Technology on Urban Forms," in "The Future Metropolis," special issue, *Daedalus* 90, no. 48 (Winter 1961): 48–60.

30. Personal correspondence to Conant commenting on Chapter 10.

31. *Christian Science Monitor*, November 22, 1999, p. 2.

32. *Village of Euclid v. Ambler Realty Co.*, 272 U.S. 365 (1926).

33. Ramapo: *Golden v. Planning Board of the Town of Ramapo*, 30 N.Y. 2d 359, 285 N.E. 2d 291, 334 N.Y.S.2d 138, appeal dismissed, 309 U.S. 1003 (1972). Petaluma: *Constr. Indus. Ass'n. v. City of Petaluma*, 375 F. Supp. 574, rev'd, 522 F.2d 897 (9th Cir. 1975), cert. denied, 96 S. Ct. 1148, 47 L. Ed. 2d 342 (1976).

34. Ronald A. Zumbrun and Thomas A. Hookano, "No-Growth and Related Land-Use Legal Problems: An Overview," *Urban Lawyer* 9, no. 1 (1977): 35–136.

35. Ibid., pp. 132–133.

36. Ralph W. Conant, *The Prospects for Revolution* (New York: Harper's Magazine Press, 1971).

37. Paul J. Pezzotta II, "Emerging Evidence of the Erosion of Economic Competitiveness Caused by Development Patterns Based on the Single-Occupant Auto," *Urban Lawyer* 30, no. 3, p. 509. A paper delivered at the United States-German Workshop on Sustainable Transportation in Metropolitan Areas, Berlin, Germany, October 29–30, 1997.

38. Peter Calthorpe, *The Next American Metropolis: Ecology, Community, and the American Dream* (Princeton, N.J.: Princeton Architectural Press, 1993).

39. David L. Winstead, "Smart Growth, Smart Transportation: A New Program to Manage

Growth in Maryland," *Urban Lawyer* 30, no. 3: 540; and Barnett, *Fractured Metropolis*; See also, David Rusk, *Inside Game, Outside Game: Winning Strategies for Saving Urban America* (Washington, D.C.: Brookings Institution Press, 1999), especially Chapt. 8.

40. Robert H. Freilich, "The Land-Use Implications of Transit-Oriented Development: Controlling the Demand Side of Transportation Congestion and Urban Sprawl," *Urban Lawyer* 30, no. 3 (Summer 1998): 566.

41. Margaret Weir, "Coalition Building for Regionalism," in Bruce Katz, ed., *Reflections on Regionalism* (Washington, D.C.: Brookings Institution, 2000).

42. Winstead, "Smart Growth, Smart Transportation," p. 541n26.

43. Merrill Goozner, "Smart Growth: The Lesson We Can't Seem to Learn," *Chicago Tribune*, May 21, 2000.

44. Norton E. Long, "Regionalism in the Year 2000," unpublished, undated ms., ca. 1974, University of Missouri-St. Louis. See also Melvin B. Mogulof, *Governing Metropolitan Areas* (Washington, D.C.: Urban Institute, 1971).

45. Martin Meyerson and Edward C. Banfield, "Boston: The Job Ahead, the Power to Govern," first in a series of ten articles commissioned by New England Merchants National Bank, 1962 and 1963.

Bibliography

Abrams, Charles. *The City Is the Frontier.* New York: Harper and Row, Colophon edition, 1967.

Adrian, Charles R. *Governing Urban America.* New York: McGraw-Hill, 1955, 1961.

Advisory Commission on Intergovernmental Relations. *Governmental Structure, Organization, and Planning in Metropolitan Areas: Suggested Action by Local, State, and National Governments.* Washington, D.C.: ACIR, 1961.

———. Alternative Approaches to Intergovernmental Reorganization in Metropolitan Areas. Washington, D.C.: ACIR, 1962.

———. *Urban and Rural America: Policies for Future Growth.* Washington, D.C.: ACIR, 1968.

———. *Urban America and the Federal System.* Washington, D.C.: ACIR, 1969.

———. *Federalism in 1970.* 12th Annual Report. Washington, D.C.: ACIR, 1970.

———. *Revenue Sharing: An Idea Whose Time Has Come.* Information report. Washington, D.C.: ACIR, December 1970.

———. *Measuring the Fiscal Capacity and Effort of State and Local Areas.* Washington, D.C.: ACIR, March 1971.

———. *Substate Districting Systems in Twelve States.* Washington, D.C.: ACIR, 1972.

———. *Regional Decisionmaking: New Strategies for Substate Districts.* Washington, D.C.: ACIR, 1973.

———. *Substate Regionalism and the Federal System: The Challenge of Local Government Reorganization.* Washington, D.C.: ACIR, 1974.

———. *Improving Urban America: A Challenge to Federalism.* Washington, D.C.: ACIR, 1976.

——. *Citizen Participation in the American Federal System.* Washington, D.C.: ACIR, 1979.

——. *State and Local Roles in the Federal System.* Washington, D.C.: ACIR, 1981.

——. *Intergovernmental Service Arrangements for Delivering Local Public Services: Update 1983.* Washington, D.C.: ACIR, 1985.

——. *The Question of State Government Capability.* Washington, D.C.: ACIR, 1985.

——. *Federal Regulation of State and Local Governments.* Washington, D.C.: ACIR, 1993.

——. *State Laws Governing Local Government Structure and Administration.* Washington, D.C.: ACIR, 1993.

Altschuler, Alan A. *Community Control: The Black Demand for Participation in Large American Cities.* Indianapolis, Ind.: Pegasus, 1970.

Anderson, Martin. *The Federal Bulldozer: A Critical Analysis of Urban Renewal, 1949–1962.* Cambridge, Mass.: MIT Press, 1964.

Ardrey, Robert. *The Territorial Imperative.* New York: Dell, 1966.

Aristotle. *Politics*, Book III, Chapters 6–13.

Axelrod, Donald. *Shadow Government: The Hidden World of Public Authorities and How They Control over $1 Trillion of Your Money.* New York: Wiley & Sons, 1992.

Bain, Henry. *The Development District.* Washington, D.C.: Washington Center for Metropolitan Studies.

——. *The Reston Express.* Washington, D.C.: Washington Center for Metropolitan Studies, 1969.

Banfield, Edward C. *Political Influence.* New York: Free Press of Glencoe, 1961.

——. *The Unheavenly City: The Nature and Future of Our Urban Crisis.* Boston: Little, Brown & Co., 1968.

——. *The Unheavenly City Revisited.* Boston: Little, Brown & Co., 1970.

——. *Urban Government.* New York: Free Press, 1971.

Banfield, Edward C., and Morton Grodzins. *Government and Housing in Metropolitan Areas.* New York: McGraw-Hill, 1958.

Barnett, Jonathan. *The Fractured Metropolis, Improving the New City, Restoring the Old City, Reshaping the Region.* New York: HarperCollins, 1995.

Bartholomew, Harland. *Land Uses in American Cities.* Cambridge, Mass.: Harvard University Press, 1955.

Beckinsale, R. P., and J. K. Houston, eds. *Urbanization and Its Problems.* Oxford: Blackwell, 1968.

Berry, Jeffrey, Kent Portney, and Ken Thomson. *The Rebirth of Urban Democracy.* Washington, D.C.: Brookings Institution, 1993.

Bish, Robert L. *The Economy of Metropolitan Areas.* Chicago: Markham, 1971.

Bish, Robert L., and Vincent Ostrom. *Understanding Urban Government: Metropolitan Reform Reconsidered.* Washington, D.C.: American Enterprise Institute, 1973.

Blau, Joel. *The Visible Poor: Homelessness in the United States.* New York: Oxford University Press, 1992.

Bogue, Donald J. *The Structure of the Metropolitan Community.* Ann Arbor, Mich.: Horace Rocham Graduate School, University of Michigan, 1949.

———. *The Population of the United States.* Glencoe, Ill.: Free Press, 1959.

Bollens, John C. *Special District Governments in the United States.* Berkeley: University of California Press, 1957.

———, ed. *Exploring the Metropolitan Community.* Berkeley: University of California Press, 1961.

Bowman, Ann O'M., and Richard Kearney. *The Resurgence of the States.* Englewood Cliffs, N.J.: Prentice-Hall, 1986.

Bradbury, Katharine L., Anthony Downs, and Kenneth A. Small. *Urban Decline and the Future of American Cities.* Washington, D.C.: Brookings Institution, 1982.

Braeman, et al. *Change and Continuity in Twentieth-Century America: The 1920s.* Columbus: Ohio State University Press, 1968.

Bratt, Rachel G. *Rebuilding a Low-Income Housing Policy.* Philadelphia: Temple University Press, 1989.

Bratt, Rachel G., Chester Hartman, and Ann Myerson, eds. *Critical Perspectives on Housing.* Philadelphia: Temple University Press, 1986.

Break, George F. *Intergovernmental Fiscal Relations in the United States.* Washington, D.C.: Brookings Institution, 1967.

Browning, Rufus, Dale Rogers Marshall, and David H. Tabb, eds. *Protest Is Not Enough: The Struggle of Blacks and Hispanics for Equality in Urban Politics.* Berkeley: University of California Press, 1984.

———. *Racial Politics in America's Cities.* White Plains, N.Y.: Longman, 1990.

Burgess, Ernest W. *The Urban Community.* Chicago: University of Chicago Press, 1926.

Burgess, Ernest W., and Donald J. Bogue, eds. *Contributions to Urban Sociology.* Chicago: University of Chicago Press, 1964.

Burkhead, Jesse, and Jerry Miner. *Public Expenditure.* Chicago: Aldine-Atherton, 1972.

Burns, James MacGregor. *Dead Center.* New York: Scribner, 1999.

Burrows, Edwin G., and Mike Wallace. *Gotham: A History of New York City to 1898.* Oxford: Oxford University Press, 1999.

Burt, Martha R. *Over the Edge: The Growth of Homelessness in the 1980s.* New York: Twentieth Century Fund, 1989.

Calthorpe, Peter. *The Next American Metropolis: Ecology, Community, and the American Dream.* Princeton, N.J.: Princeton Architectural Press, 1993.

Campbell, Alan K., and Seymour Sacks. *Metropolitan America: Fiscal Patterns and Governmental Assistance.* New York: Free Press of Glencoe, 1967.

Canty, Donald, ed. *The New City.* New York: Praeger, 1969

Carnegie Foundation for the Advancement of Teaching. *School Choice: A Special Report.* Princeton, N.J.: Princeton University Press, 1994.

Carson, Rachel. *Silent Spring.* Boston: Houghton Mifflin, 1962.

Chapin, F. Stewart, Jr., *Urban Land-Use Planning.* New York: Harper, 1957.

Chapin, F. Stewart, Jr., and Shirley D. Weiss. *Urban Growth Dynamics.* New York: John Wiley, 1962.

Cheah, Pheng, and Bruce Robbins. *Cosmopolitics: Thinking and Feeling beyond the Nation.* Minneapolis: University of Minnesota Press, 1998.

Childs, Richard S. *Civic Victories.* New York: Harper and Row, 1952.

Chinitz, Benjamin, ed. *City and Suburb: The Economics of Metropolitan Growth.* Englewood Cliffs, N.J.: Prentice-Hall, 1964.

Cisneros, Henry G., ed. *Interwoven Destinies, Cities and the Nation.* New York: W. W. Norton, 1993.

———. *Regionalism: The New Geography of Opportunity.* Washington, D.C.: U.S. Department of Housing and Urban Development, 1995.

Clapp, Gordon R. *An Approach to the Development of a Region.* Chicago: University of Chicago Press, 1954.

Cole, Richard. *Citizen Participation and the Urban Policy Process.* Lexington, Mass.: D. C. Heath, 1974.

Colean, Miles L. *American Housing: Problems and Prospects.* New York: Twentieth Century Fund, 1944.

Columbia Commission. *Columbia Commission Report.* Ellicott City, Md.: Office of the County Executive, 1971.

Commission on Population Growth and the American Future. *Population and the American Future.* New York: New American Library, 1972.

Conant, James Bryant. *Slums and Suburbs: A Commentary on Schools in Metropolitan Areas.* New York: McGraw-Hill, 1961.

Conant, Ralph W. "The Politics of Metropolitan Reorganization in a Michigan Area." Doctoral dissertation, University of Chicago, 1960.

———. *The Public Library and the City.* Cambridge, Mass.: MIT Press, 1965.

———. *The Politics of Community Health.* Washington, D.C.: Public Affairs Press, 1968.

———. *The Prospects for Revolution: A Study of Riots, Civil Disobedience, and Insurrection in Contemporary America.* New York: Harper's Magazine Press, 1970.

Conant, Ralph W., and Daniel J. Myers. *The Future of Poverty in American Cities.* Novato, Calif.: Chandler & Sharp, 2006.

Conlan, Timothy. *New Federalism: Intergovernmental Reform from Nixon to Reagan.* Washington, D.C.: Brookings Institution, 1988.

Connery, Robert, and Richard Leach. *The Federal Government and Metropolitan Areas.* Cambridge, Mass.: Harvard University Press, 1960.

Cooley, Charles H. *Theory of Transportation. Sociological Theory and Social Research.* New York: Henry Holt, 1930.

Coons, J., W. Clune, and S. Sugarman. *Private Wealth and Public Education.* Cambridge: Harvard University Press, 1970.

Council of State Governments. *The States and the Metropolitan Problem: A Report to the Governors' Conference.* Chicago: Council of State Governments, 1956.

Cozzetto, Don, Mary Kweit, and Robert Kweit. *Public Budgeting: Politics, Institutions and Processes.* White Plains, N.Y.: Longman, 1995.

Crecine, John P., ed. *Financing the Metropolis.* Beverly Hills, Calif.: Sage, 1970.

Cullingworth, J. Barry. *The Political Culture of Planning: American Land-Use Planning in Comparative Perspective.* New York: Routledge, 1993.

Dalaker, Joseph, and Mary Naifeh, U.S. Census Bureau. *Current Population Reports*, Series P60-201, Poverty in the United States: 1997. Washington, D.C.: U.S. Government Printing Office, 1998.

Danielson, Michael N. *Metropolitan Politics: A Reader.* Boston: Little, Brown, 1971.

———. *The Politics of Exclusion.* New York: Columbia University Press, 1976.

Delafons, John. *Land-Use Controls in the United States.* Cambridge: Joint Center for Urban Studies of MIT and Harvard University, 1962.

Derthick, Martha. *The Influence of Federal Grants: Public Assistance 3 in Massachusetts.* Cambridge, Mass.: Harvard University Press, 1970.

Dillon, John F. *Commentaries on the Law of Municipal Corporations*, 5th edn. Boston: Little, Brown, 1911.

DiNitto, Diana M. *Social Welfare Politics and Public Policy*, 4th edn. Boston: Allyn & Bacon, 1995.

DiPasquale, Denise, and Keyes Langley, eds. *Building Foundations: Housing and Federal Policy.* Philadelphia: University of Pennsylvania Press, 1990.

Dobinger, William, ed. *The Suburban Community.* New York: Putnam, 1958.

———. *Class in Suburbia.* Englewood Cliffs, N.J.: Prentice-Hall, 1963.

Donovan, John C. *The Politics of Poverty.* New York: Pegasus, 1967.

Douglass, H. P. *The Suburban Trend.* New York: Century, 1925.

Downs, Anthony. *An Economic Theory of Democracy.* New York: Harper and Row, 1957.

———. *Opening Up the Suburbs: An Urban Strategy for America.* New Haven, Conn.: Yale University Press, 1973.

———. *New Visions for Metropolitan America.* Washington, D.C.: Brookings Institution, 1994.

Drucker, Peter. *Post-Capitalist Society.* New York: HarperCollins, 1993.

Duhl, Leonard, ed. *The Urban Condition.* New York: Basic Books, 1963.

Duncan, Otis D., et al. *Metropolis and Region.* Baltimore: Johns Hopkins University Press, 1960.

Duncan, Otis D., and Albert Reiss. *Social Characteristics of Urban and Rural Communities, 1950.* New York: John Wiley, 1962.

Editors of Fortune. *The Exploding Metropolis.* Garden City, N.Y.: Doubleday Anchor Books, 1958.

Ehrenreich, Barbara. *Nickel and Dimed: On (Not) Getting by in America.* New York: Henry Holt and Company, LLC, 2001

Eichler, Edward P., and Marshall Kaplan. *The Community Builders.* Berkeley: University of California Press, 1967.

Ellwood, D. T., and M. J. Bane. *Rhetoric to Reform.* Cambridge, Mass.: Harvard University Press, 1994.

Feagin, Joe R., and Robert Parker. *Building American Cities: The Urban Real Estate Game*, 2nd edn. Englewood Cliffs, N.J.: Prentice-Hall, 1990.

Finn, Chester E., Bruno V. Manno, and Gregg Vanourek. *Charter Schools in Action: Renewing Public Education.* Princeton, N.J.: Princeton University Press, 2000.

Fishman, Robert. *Bourgeois Utopias: The Rise and Fall of Suburbia.* New York: Basic Books, 1987.

Fitch, Lyle C., et al. *Urban Transportation and Public Policy.* San Francisco: Chandler Publishing Co., 1964.

Fitch, Lyle C., and Annamarie Hauck Walsh, eds. *Agenda for a City: Issues Confronting New York.* Beverly Hills, Calif.: Sage, 1970.

Foley, Donald L. *Governing the London Region: Reorganization and Planning in the 1960s.* Berkeley: Institute of Governmental Studies and University of California Press, 1972.

Freedman, Leonard. *Public Housing: The Politics of Poverty.* New York: Holt, Rinehart and Winston, 1969.

Frieden, Bernard J. *The Environmental Protection Hustle.* Cambridge, Mass.: MIT Press, 1979.

Frieden, Bernard J., and Marshall Kaplan. *The Politics of Neglect: Urban Aid from Model Cities to Revenue Sharing.* Cambridge, Mass.: MIT Press, 1975.

Frieden, Bernard J., and Lynne B. Sagalyn. *Downtown, Inc.: How America Builds Cities.* Cambridge, Mass.: MIT Press, 1989.

Friedman, Milton. *Capitalism and Freedom.* Chicago: University of Chicago Press, 1962.

Galbraith, John Kenneth. *The Affluent Society.* New York: New American Library, 1958.

Gans, Herbert. *The Urban Villagers: Group and Class in the Life of Italian-Americans.* New York: Free Press of Glencoe, 1962.

Garreau, Joel. *Edge City: Life on the New Frontier.* New York: Doubleday, 1991.

Geddes, Patrick. *Cities in Evolution.* New York: Oxford University Press, 1950.

Gist, Noel P., and L. A. Halbert. *Urban Society,* 4th edn. New York: Thomas Y. Crowell, 1956.

Glaab, Charles N., and A. Theodore Brown. *A History of Urban America.* New York: Macmillan, 1967.

Glazer, Nathan, and Davis McEntire, eds. *Studies in Housing and Minority Groups.* Berkeley: University of California Press, 1960.

Glendening, Parris N., and Mavis Mann Reeves. *Pragmatic Federalism: An Intergovernmental View of American Government,* 2nd edn. Pacific Palisades, Calif.: Palisades Publishers, 1984.

Goldwin, Robert A., ed. *A Nation of States: Essays on the American Federal System.* Chicago: Rand McNally, 1961.

Good, Thomas, and Jennifer Braden. *The Great School Debate: Choice, Vouchers, and Charters.* Mahwah, N.J.: L. Erlbaum, 2000.

Gottman, Jean. *Megalopolis.* New York: Twentieth Century Fund, 1961.

Gottschalk, P., S. McLanahan, and G. Sandefur. "The Dynamic and Intergenerational Transmission of Poverty and Welfare Participation." In *Confronting Poverty: Prescriptions for Change,* ed. Sheldon H. Danziger, Gary D. Sandefur, and Daniel H. Weinberg. Cambridge, Mass.: Harvard University Press, 1994.

Governor's Commission on the Los Angeles Riots. *Violence in the City—an End or a Beginning?* Los Angeles, December 2, 1965.

Green, Christopher. *Negative Taxes and the Poverty Problem.* Washington, D.C.: Brookings Institution, 1967.

Green, Constance McLaughlin. *American Cities in the Growth of the Nation.* New York: DeGraff, 1957.

———. *The Rise of Urban America.* New York: Harper and Row, 1965.

Greenstone, David, and Paul E. Peterson. *Race and Authority in Urban Politics: Community Participation in the War on Poverty.* Chicago: University of Chicago Press, 1976.

Greer, Scott. *The Emerging City.* New York: Free Press of Glencoe, 1961.

———. *Metropolitics: A Study of Political Culture.* New York: John Wiley & Sons, 1963.

———. *Urban Renewal and American Cities: The Dilemma of Democratic Intervention.* Indianapolis: Bobbs-Merrill, 1965.

Grier, George S. *The Baby Bust.* Washington, D.C.: Washington Center for Metropolitan Studies, 1972.

Grodzins, Morton. *The Metropolitan Areas as a Racial Problem.* Pittsburgh: University of Pittsburgh Press, 1958.

Grogan, Paul, and Tony Proscio. *Comeback Cities: A Blueprint for Neighborhood Revival.* Boulder, Colo.: Westview, 2001.

Gulick, Luther. *The Metropolitan and American Ideals.* New York: Knopf, 1962.

Gurr, Ted Robert, and Desmond S. King. *The State and the City.* Chicago: University of Chicago Press, 1987.

Haar, Charles M. *Between the Idea and the Reality: A Study in the Origin, Fate, and Legacy of the Model Cities Program.* Boston: Little, Brown, 1975.

Haar, Charles M., et al. *The Effectiveness of Metropolitan Planning,* prepared in cooperation with the Subcommittee on Intergovernmental Relations of the Committee on Government Operations, United States Senate, by the Joint Center for Urban Studies of the Massachusetts Institute of Technology and Harvard University. Washington, D.C.: U.S. Government Printing Office, 1964.

Haar, Charles M., and Jerold S. Kayden, eds. *Zoning and the American Dream: Promises Still to Keep.* Chicago: APA Planners Press, 1989.

Hacker, Andrew. *Two Nations: Black and White, Separate, Hostile, Unequal.* New York: Ballantine, 1992.

Hahn, Harlan, and Charles H. Levine, eds. *Urban Politics: Past, Present and Future.* White Plains, N.Y.: Longman, 1984.

Hall, Peter. *Cities in Civilization.* New York: Pantheon Books, 1998.

Hallenbeck, W. C. *American Urban Communities.* New York: Harper & Brothers, 1951.

Handler, J. F., and L. White, eds. *Hard Labor: Women and Work in the Post-Welfare Era.* Armonk, N.Y.: M. E. Sharpe, 1999.

Hansen, Nils. *Rural Poverty and the Urban Crisis.* Bloomington: Indiana University Press, 1970.

Harrigan, John J. *Political Change in the Metropolis*, 4th edn. Glenview, Ill.: Scott, Foresman, 1989.

Harrington, Michael. *The Other America.* New York: Macmillan, 1962.

Harris, Fred R. and Lynn A. Curtis, eds. *Locked in the Poorhouse: Cities, Race, and Poverty in the United States.* Lanham, Md.: Rowman & Littlefield, 1998.

Harvey, David. *Consciousness and the Urban Experience: Studies in the History and Theory of Capitalist Urbanization.* Baltimore: Johns Hopkins University Press, 1985.

———. *The Urbanization of Capital: Studies in the History and Theory of Capitalist Urbanization.* Baltimore: Johns Hopkins University Press, 1985.

Hatt, Paul, and Albert Reiss, eds. *Cities and Society.* Glencoe, Ill.: Free Press, 1957.

Hauser, Philip M. *Population Perspectives.* New Brunswick, N.J.: Rutgers University Press, 1960.

Hawley, Amos. *Human Ecology: A Theory of Community Structure.* New York: Ronald Press, 1950.

———. *The Changing Shape of Metropolitan America.* Glencoe, Ill.: Free Press, 1956.

Hawley, Willis, et al. *Theoretical Perspectives on Urban Politics.* Englewood Cliffs, N.J.: Prentice-Hall, 1976.

Heller, Walter W. *New Dimensions of Political Economy.* Cambridge: Harvard University Press, 1967.

Henig, Jeffery R. *Rethinking School Choice: Limits of the Market Metaphor.* Princeton, N.J.: Princeton University Press, 1994.

Hirsch, Arnold R., and Raymond A. Mohl. *Urban Policy in Twentieth-Century America.* New Brunswick, N.J.: Rutgers University Press, 1993.

Hirsch, Werner Z., ed. *Urban Life and Form.* New York: Holt, Rinehart & Winston, 1963.

Hofstadter, Richard. *Social Darwinism in American Thought.* Boston: Beacon Press, 1992.

Hoover, Edgar M., and Raymond Vernon. *Anatomy of a Metropolis.* Cambridge, Mass.: Harvard University Press, 1959.

Howard, Ebenezer. *Garden Cities of Tomorrow.* Cambridge, Mass.: MIT Press, 1965; first issued in 1898 under the title *To-morrow: A Peaceful Path to Real Reform.*

Hoyt, Homer. *One Hundred Years of Land Values in Chicago.* Chicago: University of Chicago Press, 1933.

Huttman, Elizabeth D., ed. *Urban Housing Segregation of Minorities in Western Europe and the United States.* Durham, N.C.: Duke University Press, 1991.

Imbroscio, David L. *Restructuring City Politics: Alternative Economic Development and Urban Regimes.* Thousand Oaks, Calif.: Sage, 1997.

Isard, Walter. *Methods of Regional Analysis: An Introduction to Regional Science.* New York: Technology Press of MIT and John Wiley & Sons, 1960.

Jackson, Kenneth T. *Crabgrass Frontier: The Suburbanization of the United States.* New York: Oxford University Press, 1985.

Jacobs, Jane. *The Death and Life of Great American Cities.* New York: Random House, 1961.

——. *The Economy of Cities.* London: Jonathan Cape, 1970.

Jencks, Christopher, and Paul E. Peterson. *The Urban Underclass.* Washington, D.C.: Brookings Institution, 1991.

Johnson, Tobe. *Metropolitan Government: A Black Analytical Perspective.* Washington, D.C.: Joint Center for Political Studies, 1972.

Joint Center for Political and Economic Studies. *Black Elected Officials: A National Roster.* New York: UNIPUB, 1984.

Jones, Victor. *Metropolitan Government.* Chicago: University of Chicago Press, 1942.

Judd, Dennis R. *The Politics of American Cities.* Glenview, Ill.: Scott, Foresman, 1988.

Judd, Dennis R., and Susan S. Fainstein. *The Tourist City.* New Haven, Conn.: Yale University Press, 2001.

Juster, F. Thomas, Jr. *The Economic and Political Impact of General Revenue Sharing.* Washington, D.C.: Government Printing Office, 1976.

Kaplan, Marshall, and Franklin James, eds. *The Future of National Urban Policy.* Durham, N.C.: Duke University Press, 1990.

Katz, Bruce. *Reflections on Regionalism.* Washington, D.C.: Brookings Institution, 2000.

Katz, Michael B. *In the Shadow of the Poorhouse: A Social History of Welfare in America.* New York: Basic Books, 1986, 1996.

Keating, W. Dennis. *The Suburban Racial Dilemma: Housing and Neighborhoods.* Philadelphia: Temple University Press, 1994.

Kelly, Barbara M., ed. *Suburbia Re-examined.* New York: Greenwood Press, 1989.

Kennedy, Paul. *Preparing for the Twenty-first Century.* New York: Random House, 1993.

Kozol, Jonathan. *Illiterate America.* New York: Anchor Press/Doubleday, 1985.

——. *Savage Inequalities.* New York: Crown, 1991.

——. *Ordinary Resurrections: Children in the Years of Hope.* New York: Crown, 2000.

Kuehn, Robert H., Jr. *The Home Building Industry: What Will It Take to Produce More Affordable Housing?* Cambridge, Mass.: Center for Real Estate Development, MIT, 1988.

Laska, Shirley Bradway, and Daphne Spain. *Back to the City.* New York: Pergamon Press, 1980.

Laurenti, Luigi. *Property Values and Race.* Berkeley: University of California Press, 1960.

Lazare, Daniel. *America's Undeclared War: What's Killing Our Cities and How We Can Stop It.* New York: Harcourt, 2001.

Leacock, E. *The Culture of Poverty: A Critique.* New York: Simon and Schuster, 1971.

LeMann, Nicholas. *The Promised Land: The Great Black Migration and How It Changed America.* New York: Vintage, 1991.

Levy, John M. *Contemporary Urban Planning.* Englewood Cliffs, N.J.: Prentice-Hall, 1988.

Lineberry, Robert H., Jr. *Equality and Urban Policy: The Distribution of Municipal Services.* Beverly Hills, Calif.: Sage Publications, 1977.

Lineberry, Robert H., Jr., and Ira Sharkansky. *Urban Politics and Public Policy.* New York: Harper and Row, 1971.

Long, Norton E. *The Polity.* Chicago: Rand McNally and Co., 1962.

————. *The Unwalled City, Reconstituting the Urban Community.* New York: Basic Books, 1972.

Lowi, Theodore. *The End of Liberalism.* New York: W. W. Norton, 1969.

Lowry, Ritchie P. *Who's Running This Town? Community Leadership and Social Change.* New York: Harper and Row, 1965.

Lynch, Kevin. *The Image of the City.* Cambridge: MIT Press and Harvard University Press, 1960.

Maass, Arthur, ed. *Area and Power.* New York: Free Press, 1959.

MacIver, Robert M. *The Web of Government.* New York: Macmillan, 1947.

Marcou, O'Leary and Associates, Inc. *New Community Development: Location Analysis of Potential Sites/Economic and Legal Settings.* Washington, D.C.: Marcou, O'Leary and Associates, 1972.

Marshall, Dale Rogers, Bernard Frieden, and D. W. Fessler. *The Governance of Metropolitan Regions: Minority Perspectives.* Washington, D.C.: Resources for the Future, 1972.

Martin, Roscoe C. *Metropolis in Transition: Local Government Adaptation to Changing Urban Needs.* Washington, D.C.: Housing and Home Finance Agency, September 1963.

————. *The Cities and the Federal System.* New York: Atherton Press, 1965.

Martinson, Tom. *American Dreamscape: The Pursuit of Happiness in Postwar Suburbia.* New York: Carroll & Graf, 2000.

Massey, Douglas S., and Nancy A. Denton, eds. *American Apartheid.* Cambridge, Mass.: Harvard University Press, 1993.

Mayer, Harold M., and Richard C. Wade. *Chicago: Growth of a Metropolis.* Chicago: University of Chicago Press, 1969.

McCandless, Carl A. *Urban Government and Politics.* New York: McGraw-Hill, 1970.

McEnery, Tom. *The New City-State, Change and Renewal in America's Cities.* Niwot, Colo.: Roberts Rinehart, 1994.

McEntire, Davis. *Residence and Race.* Berkeley: University of California Press, 1960.

McFarland, M. Carter. *Federal Government and Urban Problems.* Boulder, Colo.: Westview Press, 1978.

McGeary, Michael, and Laurence E. Lynn, Jr., eds. *Urban Change and Poverty.* Washington, D.C.: National Academy Press, 1988.

McKelvey, Blake. *The Emergence of Metropolitan America, 1915–1966.* New Brunswick, N.J.: Rutgers University Press, 1968.

Meier, Richard L. *A Communications Theory of Urban Growth.* Cambridge: Joint Center for Urban Studies of MIT and Harvard University; MIT Press, 1962.

Merton, Robert K. *Social Theory and Social Structure.* New York: Free Press, 1957.

Merton, Robert K., and Robert A. Nisbet, eds. *Contemporary Social Problems.* New York: Harcourt, Brace and World, 1961.

Metropolitan Fund. *Regional New-Town Design: A Paired Community for Southeast Michigan.* Detroit: Metropolitan Fund, Inc., 1971.

Meyerson, Martin, and Edward C. Banfield. *Politics, Planning, and the Public Interest: The Case of Public Housing in Chicago.* Glencoe, Ill.: Free Press, 1955.

Meyerson, Martin, Barbara Terrett, and William L. C. Wheaton. *Housing, People and Cities.* New York: McGraw-Hill, 1962.

Mickelman, Frank R., and Terrence Sandalow. *Government in Urban Areas.* New York: West Publishing Co., 1970.

Mitchell, Robert B., ed. *Building the Future City.* Philadelphia: Annals of the American Academy of Political and Social Science, 1945.

Mitchell, Robert B., and Chester Rapkin. *Urban Traffic: A Function of Land Use.* New York: Columbia University Press, 1954.

Mitchell, William J. *City of Bits: Space, Place and the Infobahn.* Cambridge, Mass.: MIT Press, 1995.

Mogulof, Melvin B. *Governing Metropolitan Areas.* Washington, D.C.: Urban Institute, 1971.

Mosher, Frederick. *Democracy and Public Service.* New York: Oxford University Press, 1968.

Mowry, George E. *The Urban Nation: 1920–1960.* New York: Hill and Wang, 1965.

Moynihan, Daniel Patrick. *The Negro Family: The Case for National Action.* Washington, D.C.: U.S. Department of Labor, 1965.

———. *Maximum Feasible Misunderstanding: Community Action and the War on Poverty.* New York: Free Press, 1970.

———. *Toward a National Growth Policy.* New York: Basic Books, 1970.

———. *The Politics of a Guaranteed Income, the Nixon Administration and the Family Assistance Plan.* New York: Random House, 1973.

Mumford, Lewis. *The Culture of Cities.* New York: Harcourt, Brace & Co., 1938.

———. *The City in History: Its Origins, Its Transformations, and Its Prospects.* New York: Harcourt, Brace & World, 1961.

Murray, Charles. *American Social Policy: 1950–1980.* New York: Basic Books, 1984.

Mushkin, Selma J., ed. *Public Prices for Public Products.* Washington, D.C.: Urban Institute, 1972.

Mushkin, Selma J., and John F. Cotton. *Sharing Federal Funds for State and Local Needs: Grants-in-Aid and PPB Systems.* New York: Praeger, 1969.

Myrdal, Gunnar. *An American Dilemma.* New York: Harper, 1944.

Nathan, Richard P., and Charles F. Adams. *Revenue Sharing: The Second Round.* Washington, D.C.: Brookings Institution, 1977.

National Advisory Commission on Civil Disorders. *Report of the National Advisory Commission on Civil Disorders.* New York: Bantam Books, 1967.

National Association of Latino Elected and Appointed Officials. *National Roster of Hispanic Elected Officials.* Los Angeles: UCLA, Chicano Studies Research Center, 1983.

National Bureau of Economic Research. *Public Finance: Needs, Resources, and Utilization.* Princeton, N.J.: Princeton University Press, 1961.

National Commission on Excellence in Education. *A Nation at Risk: The Imperative for Educational Reform.* A Report to the Nation and the Secretary of Education, April 1983.

National Resources Committee. *Our Cities: Their Role in the National Economy.* Report of the Urbanism Committee to the National Resources Committee. Washington, D.C.: U.S. Government Printing Office, 1937.

Nice, David C. *Federalism: The Politics of Intergovernmental Relations.* New York: St. Martin's, 1987.

Nisbet, Robert. *The Quest for Community: A Study in the Ethics of Order and Freedom.* New York: Oxford University Press, 1953.

O'Connor, Alice. *Poverty Knowledge: Social Science, Social Policy, and the Poor in Twentieth-Century U.S. History.* Princeton, N.J.: Princeton University Press, 2001.

Osborne, Sir Frederick J. *The New Towns: Answer to Megalopolis.* London: McGraw-Hill, 1963.

Owen, Wilfred. *The Metropolitan Transportation Problem.* Washington, D.C.: Brookings Institution, 1956.

Palen, J. John, and Bruce London. *Gentrification, Displacement and Neighborhood Revitalization.* Albany: State University of New York Press, 1984.

Park, Robert E., et al. *The City.* Chicago: University of Chicago Press, 1925.

Peachey, Paul. *New Town, Old Habits.* Washington, D.C.: Washington Center for Metropolitan Studies, 1970.

Pechman, Joseph. *Federal Tax Policy.* Washington, D.C.: Brookings Institution, 1966.

Pecorella, Robert F. *Community Power in a Post-Reform City.* Armonk, N.Y.: M. E. Sharpe, 1994.

Perloff, Harvey S. *Regions, Resources, and Economic Growth.* Baltimore: Johns Hopkins University Press, 1960.

———. *Planning and the Urban Community.* Pittsburgh: University of Pittsburgh Press, 1961.

———. *The Quality of the Urban Environment.* Baltimore: Johns Hopkins University Press, 1969.

Perloff, Harvey S., and R. Nathan, eds. *Revenue Sharing and the City.* Baltimore: Johns Hopkins University Press, 1968.

Peterson, Paul E. *City Limits.* Chicago: University of Chicago Press, 1981.

———, ed. *The New Urban Reality.* Washington, D.C.: Brookings Institution, 1985.

Peterson, Paul E., Barry G. Rabe, and Kenneth K. Wong. *When Federalism Works.* Washington, D.C.: Brookings Institution, 1986.

Pettingill, Robert B., Kuan T. Chen, and J. S. Uppal. *Cities and Suburbs, the Case for Equity.* Albany: New York Conference of Mayors and Municipal Officials, 1970.

Piven, F. F., and R. A. Cloward. *Poor Peoples' Movements.* New York: Pantheon, 1981.

Popenoe, David. *The Suburban Environment: Sweden and the United States.* Chicago: University of Chicago Press, 1977.

Pressman, Jeffery. *Federal Programs and City Politics.* Berkeley: University of California Press, 1975.

Queen, Stuart A., and David B. Carpenter. *The American City.* New York: McGraw-Hill Book Co., 1953.

Rabinovitz, Francine F. *City Politics and Planning.* New York: Atherton Press, 1969.

Rainwater, Lee, and William L. Yancey. *The Moynihan Report and Politics of Controversy*. Cambridge, Mass.: MIT Press, 1967.

Rapkin, Chester, and William Grigsby. *Residential Renewal in the Urban Core*. Philadelphia: University of Pennsylvania Press, 1960.

Ratcliff, Richard U. *Urban Land Economics*. New York: McGraw-Hill, 1949.

Rauch, Basil. *The History of the New Deal: 1933–1938*. New York: Creative Age Press, 1944.

Reagan, Michael D., and John G. Sanzone. *The New Federalism*, 2nd ed. New York: Oxford University Press, 1981.

Reich, Robert. *The Work of Nations: Preparing Ourselves for 21st-Century Capitalism*. New York: Random House, 1992.

Reps, John W. *The Making of Urban America: A History of City Planning in the United States*. Princeton, N.J.: Princeton University Press, 1965.

Reuss, Henry S. *Revenue Sharing*. New York: Praeger, 1970.

Riesman, David. *The Lonely Crowd*. Garden City, N.Y.: Doubleday, 1957.

Rifkin, Jeremy. *The End of Work: The Decline of the Global Labor Force and the Dawn of the Post-Market Era*. New York: G. P. Putnam's Sons, 1995.

Riles, Wilson C. *Urban Education Task Force Report to the Department of Health, Education and Welfare*. New York: Praeger, 1970.

Rodwin, Lloyd. *The British New Towns Policy: Problems and Implications*. Cambridge, Mass.: Harvard University Press, 1956.

———. *The Future Metropolis*. New York: George Braziller, 1961.

Ross, Bernard H., and Myron A. Levine. *Urban Politics: Power in Metropolitan America*, 7th edn. Belmont, Calif.: Wadsworth Publishing, 2005.

Rossi, Peter, and Dentler, Robert A. *The Politics of Urban Renewal*. New York: Free Press of Glencoe, 1961.

———. *Without Shelter: Homelessness in the 1980s*. New York: Twentieth Century Fund, 1989.

Rousseau, Jean-Jacques. *The Social Contract*. Translated by Maurice Cranston. Hammersmith, U.K.: Penguin, 1968 (1762).

Rubin, Herbert J. *Renewing Hope within Neighborhoods of Despair*. Albany: State University of New York Press, 2000.

Rubin, Irene. *The Politics of Public Budgeting*, 2nd edn. Chatham, N.J.: Chatham House, 1993.

Rusk, David. *Cities without Suburbs*. Baltimore: Johns Hopkins University Press, 1995.

———. *Inside Game, Outside Game: Winning Strategies for Saving Urban America*. Washington, D.C.: Brookings Institution Press, 1999.

Ryan, W. *Equality*. New York: Pantheon, 1981.

Sack, Robert. *Homo Geographicus: A Framework for Action, Awareness, and Moral Concern*. Baltimore: Johns Hopkins University Press, 1997.

Savich, H. V., and John Clayton Thomas. *Big City Politics*. Newbury Park, Calif.: Sage, 1991.

Sayre, Wallace S., Herbert Kaufman, et al. *Governing New York.* New York: Russell Sage Foundation, 1960.

Schlesinger, Arthur M. *The Rise of the City.* New York: Macmillan, 1933.

Schneider, Mark. *Suburban Growth: Policy and Process.* Brunswick, Ohio: Kings Court Communications, 1980.

Schoor, Lisbeth R., and Daniel Schoor. *Within Our Reach: Breaking the Cycle of Disadvantaged.* New York: Doubleday, 1988.

Schultze, Charles L., Edward R. Fried, Alice M. Rivlin, and Nancy H. Teeters. *Setting National Priorities: The 1972 Budget.* Washington, D.C.: Brookings Institution, 1971.

Schwartz, John E. *America's Hidden Success: A Reassessment of Twenty Years of Public Policy.* New York: W. W. Norton, 1983.

Schwartz, Thomas R., and Frank J. Bonello, eds. *Urban Finance under Siege.* Armonk, N.Y.: M. E. Sharpe, 1993.

Scott, Mel. *American City Planning.* Berkeley: University of California Press, 1969.

Shank, Alan, and Ralph W. Conant. *Urban Perspectives: Politics and Policies.* Boston: Holbrook, 1975.

Shannon, David A. *The Great Depression.* Englewood Cliffs, N.J.: Prentice-Hall, 1960.

Sharp, Elaine B. *Urban Politics and Administration: From Service Delivery to Economic Development.* New York: Longman, 1990.

Shea, M. "Dynamics of Economic Well-Being: Poverty, 1991–1993." *Current Population Reports.* Washington D.C.: U.S. Department of Commerce, 1995.

Sitton, Tom, and William Deverell. *Metropolis in the Making: Los Angeles in the 1920s.* Berkeley: University of California Press, 2001.

Smallwood, Frank. *Greater London: The Politics of Metropolitan Reform.* New York: Bobbs-Merrill Co., 1965.

Smith, Bruce L. R., and D. C. Hague. *The Dilemma of Accountability in Modern Government.* New York: St. Martin's, 1970.

Smith, Michael Peter. *The City and Social Theory.* New York: St. Martin's, 1979.

———. *City, State, and Market: The Political Economy of Urban Society.* New York: Blackwell, 1988.

Smith, Neil, and Peter Williams, eds. *Gentrification of the City.* Boston: Allen and Unwin, 1986.

Spectorsky, A. C. *The Exurbanites.* Philadelphia: J. B. Lippincott, 1955.

Spiegel, Hans B., ed. *Citizen Participation in Urban Development.* Washington, D.C.: NTL and National Education Association, 1968.

Squires, Gregory D., ed. *Unequal Partnerships: The Political Economy of Urban Redevelopment in Postwar America.* New Brunswick, N.J.: Rutgers University Press, 1989.

Stedman, Murray S. *Urban Politics.* Cambridge, Mass.: Winthrop, 1972.

Stegman, Michael A. *More Housing, More Fairly.* New York: Twentieth Century Fund, 1991.

Stein, Clarence. *Toward New Towns for America.* Liverpool: Liverpool University Press, 1951; Cambridge, Mass.: MIT Press, 1966.

Stein, Maurice. *The Eclipse of Community.* Princeton, N.J.: Princeton University Press, 1960.

Stone, Clarence, and Heyward T. Sanders, eds. *The Politics of Urban Development.* Lawrence: University of Kansas Press, 1987.

Stone, Kathryn. "Reston: A Study in Beginnings." Washington, D.C.: Washington Center for Metropolitan Studies, unpublished MS., 1966.

Studenski, Paul. *The Government of Metropolitan Areas in the United States.* New York: National Municipal League, 1930.

Sundquist, James L. *Making Federalism Work.* Washington, D.C.: Brookings Institution, 1969.

Sussman, Marvin, ed. *Community Structure and Analysis.* New York: Crowell, 1951.

Sweeney, Stephen B., ed. *Metropolitan Analysis.* Philadelphia: University of Pennsylvania Press, 1958.

Tableman, Betty. *Governmental Organization in Metropolitan Areas.* Ann Arbor: University of Michigan Press, 1951.

Temporary State Commission to Study Governmental Operations of the City of New York. *Report of the Task Force on Jurisdiction and Structure: Restructuring the Government of New York City,* March 15, 1972.

Theobald, Robert. *The Guaranteed Income.* New York: Anchor, 1967.

Thoreau, Henry David. *Walden and Civil Disobedience.* Harmondsworth, U.K.: Penguin, 1983.

Tocqueville, Alexis de. *Democracy in America.* Edited by Harvey C. Mansfield. Translated by Delba Winthrop. Chicago: University of Chicago Press, 2000.

Truman, David B. *The Governmental Process.* New York: Knopf, 1951.

Twentieth Century Fund. *New Towns: Laboratories for Democracy.* New York: Twentieth Century Fund, 1971.

UK Department of the Environment, Transport and the Regions. *Toward an Urban Renaissance.* Report of the Urban Task Force, Chaired by Lord Rogers of Riverside, British Labor Government, 1999.

Urban Development Corporation. *New Communities for New York.* New York: Urban Development Corporation, 1970.

Vernon, Raymond. *The Changing Economic Function of the Central City.* New York: Committee for Economic Development, 1959.

————. *The Myth and Reality of Our Urban Problems.* Cambridge, Mass.: Joint Center for Urban Studies of MIT and Harvard University, 1962.

Von Hertzen, Heikke, and Paul Spreiregen. *Building a New Town.* Cambridge, Mass.: MIT Press, 1971.

Richard E. Wagner. *The Fiscal Organization of American Federalism.* Chicago: Markham, 1971.

Walker, David B. *Toward a Functioning Federalism.* Boston: Little, Brown, 1981.

————. *The Rebirth of Federalism: Slouching toward Washington.* Chatham, N.J.: Chatham House, 1995.

Walker, Robert A. *The Planning Function of Urban Government*. Chicago: University of Chicago Press, 1950.

Warner, Sam Bass, Jr. *Streetcar Suburbs: The Process of Growth in Boston, 1870–1890*. Cambridge, Mass.: Harvard University Press, 1962.

——, ed. *Planning for a Nation of Cities*. Cambridge, Mass.: Harvard University Press, 1966.

——. *The Private City*. Philadelphia: University of Pennsylvania Press, 1968.

Waste, Robert J. *Independent Cities*. New York: Oxford University Press, 1998.

Weber, Max. *The City*. New York: Free Press of Glencoe, 1958.

Webster, Donald. *Urban Planning and Municipal Public Policy*. New York: Harper and Bros., 1958.

White, Leonard D. *The States and the Nation*. Baton Rouge: Louisiana State University Press, 1953.

White, Morton, and White, Lucia. *The Intellectual versus the City: From Thomas Jefferson to Frank Lloyd Wright*. Cambridge, Mass.: Harvard University Press and MIT Press, 1962.

White, William H. *Organization Man*. New York: Simon & Schuster, 1956.

Wikstrom, Nelson. *Councils of Governments: A Study of Political Incrementalism*. Chicago: Nelson Hall, 1977.

Willhelm, Sidney. *Urban Zoning and Land-Use Theory*. New York: Free Press of Glencoe, 1962.

Williams, Oliver P., et al. *Suburban Differences and Metropolitan Policies*. Philadelphia: University of Pennsylvania Press, 1965.

Wilner, Daniel, et al. *The Housing Environment and Family Life*. Baltimore: Johns Hopkins University Press, 1962.

Wilson, James Q. *Urban Renewal: The Record and the Controversy*. Cambridge, Mass.: MIT Press, 1966.

——. *Varieties of Police Behavior*. New York: Atheneum, 1968.

Wilson, William Julius. *The Declining Significance of Race: Blacks and Changing American Institutions*. Chicago: University of Chicago Press, 1987.

——. *The Truly Disadvantaged: The Underclass and Public Policy*. Chicago: University of Chicago Press, 1987.

——. *When Work Disappears: The World of the New Urban Poor*. New York: Knopf, 1996.

——. *The Bridge over the Racial Divide: Rising Inequality and Coalition Politics*. Berkeley: University of California Press, 1999.

Wingo, Lowdon, Jr. *Transportation and Urban Land*. Washington, D.C.: Resources for the Future, Inc., 1961.

——, ed. *Reform of Metropolitan Governments*. Washington, D.C.: Resources for the Future, Inc., 1972.

Wirt, Frederick M. *On the City's Rim: Politics and Policy in Suburbia*. Lexington, Mass.: D. C. Heath, 1972.

Wolfgang, Marvin E., ed. *The Future Society: Aspects of America in the Year 2000.* Philadelphia: Annals of the American Academy of Political and Social Science, 1973.

Wood, Robert C. *Suburbia, Its People and Their Politics.* Boston: Houghton Mifflin Co., 1958.

———. *1400 Governments.* Cambridge, Mass.: Harvard University Press, 1961.

Woodbury, Coleman. *The Future of Cities and Urban Redevelopment.* Chicago: University of Chicago Press, 1953.

———, ed. *Urban Redevelopment Problems and Practices.* Chicago: University of Chicago Press, 1953.

Wright, Deil S. *Understanding Intergovernmental Relations*, 3rd edn. Monterey, Calif.: Brooks/Cole Publishing, 1988.

Wright, Gwendolyn. *Building the Dream: A Social History of Housing in America.* Cambridge, Mass.: MIT Press, 1981.

Yates, Douglas. *The Ungovernable City: The Politics of Urban Renewal and Policy Making.* Cambridge, Mass.: MIT Press, 1977.

Zimmerman, Joseph. *Contemporary American Federalism: The Growth of National Power.* New York: Praeger, 1992.

Index

Boulder, Colo., 169
Braden, Jennifer, 289
Brook Farm community (Mass.), 203
Brown v. Board of Education, 5, 62, 286–87
building codes, and housing provision,
    246–47
*Building Foundations: Housing and Federal
    Policy* (DiPasquale and Keyes, eds.), 2
Bureau of the Budget (BOB), 177
bureaucracy, 149
Burnham, Daniel, 168
Bush, George H. W. (Bush
    administration), 9:
    housing policy, 58
Bush, George W. (Bush administration), 9:
    education policy, 11, 288, 290
    tax cuts by, 271, 277
    urban program, 13
busing, 5, 153

California, 51–52, 240
    land-use planning in, 301
    school financing in, 62, 63
Calthorpe, Peter, 215, 299
Carroll, Barry, 77
Carson, Rachel, 70
Carter, Jimmy (Carter administration), 59
    poverty programs and, 12
    urban renewal and, 54
Cedar Riverside, Minn., 210
Census Bureau, 5
    definition of urban areas, 17–19
Census
    1950, 1, 18
    1960, 18
    1970, 21, 29, 68
    1990, 33, 34
    2000, 34, 42
Charleston, S.C., 204
Chattanooga, Tenn., 293
Chevy Chase, D.C., 26
Chevy Chase, Md., 26
Chicago, Ill., 52, 53, 54, 204, 229, 239
    Marina City in, 75
    planning in, 169
    urban renewal in, 52, 75

Chinese Americans, 28
Circular A-80, 251
Circular A-95, 177
Cities Without Suburbs (Rusk), 2
cities
    consolidation of, 10, 41–42, 46, 124
    downtowns, 25, 74–75
    effect of suburbs on, 106
    ethnic diversity of, 29–30
    functions of, 73–75
    migration to, 96, 214
    minorities in, 27–28, 96–97, 102, 274
    neighborhoods, 220
    optimum size of, 215–16
    "point of no return," 13, 271–72, 274
    political influence of, 40–41
    poverty in, 31–32, 97, 273–74
    revitalizing central cities, 75–76, 299
    social problems of, 45–46, 77, 104,
        274–75
    transportation and, 299
    and upward mobility, 96
"City Beautiful, The," 168
"City Functional, The," 168
civil rights movement, 40, 104
class, economic, 285–86
Clinton, Bill (Clinton administration), 9
    education policy, 290
    healthcare proposals, 65–66
    housing program, 58
    urban program, 12–13
Cloward, Richard A., 3
Columbia, Md., 75, 207–8, 211, 225
Columbus, Ohio, 153
Committee on Juvenile Delinquency, 178
communications infrastructure, 37, 67
communities of interest, 7
community action agencies, 156, 251
Community Block Development Grants,
    9, 192
community land trusts, 58
community
    governments, 119–21, 140–41
    importance of, 154–55
Comprehensive Planning Assistance
    Program, Section 701, 176

Printed in the United States
130072LV00001B/1-24/A